Return to Mexico

To Temudjinn, Hamish, Aram, Arash
To Jordan

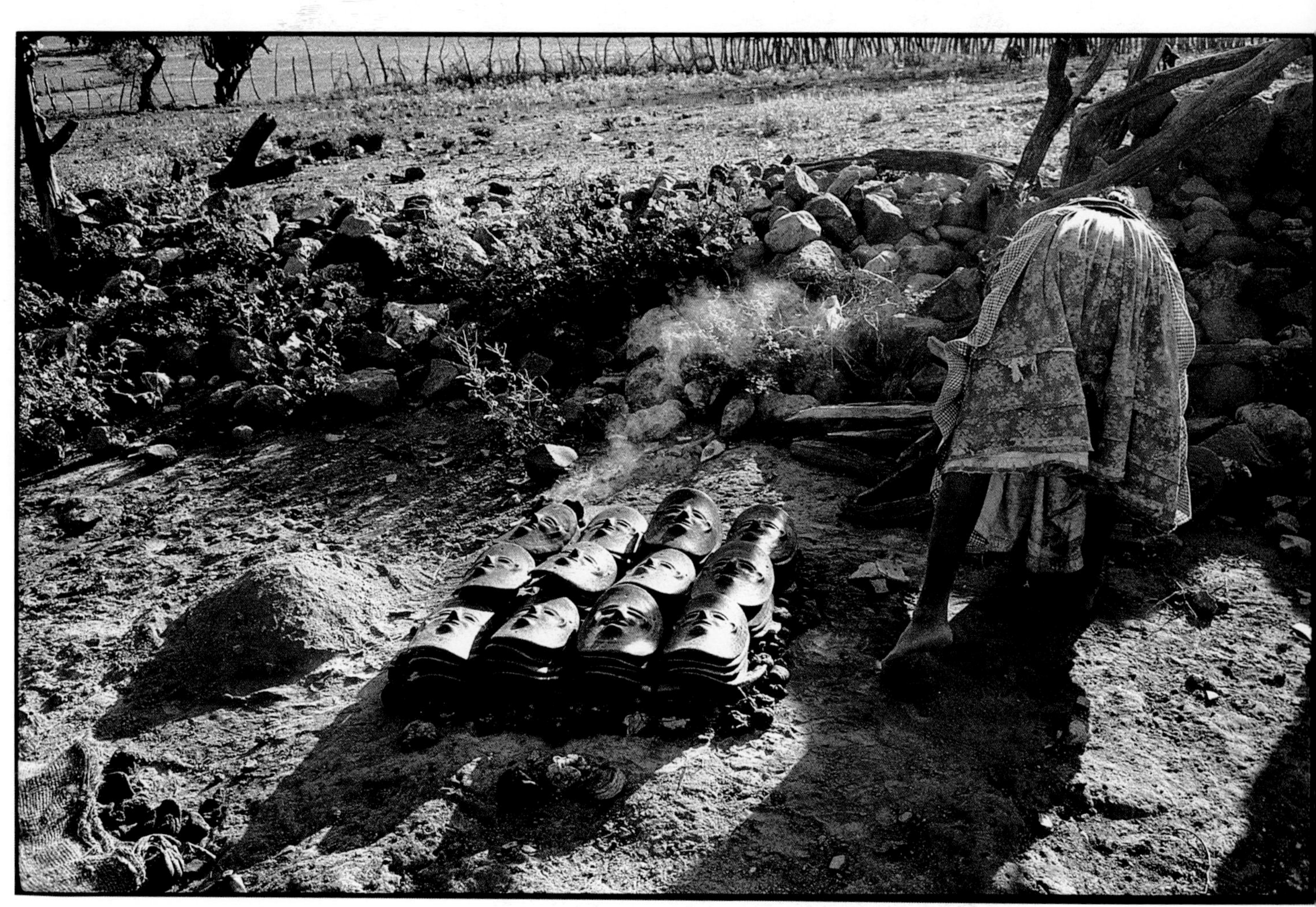

Return to Mexico

MEXICO

Journeys Beyond the Mask

Photographs by Abbas

Introduction by Carlos Fuentes

W. W. Norton & Company ■ New York • London

Printed in Italy.

This book is composed in Joanna.
Composition by Trufont Typographers, Inc.
Manufacturing by Amilcare Pizzi S.P.A., Italy.
Book design by Katy Homans.

First Edition

ISBN 0-393-03435-6
ISBN 0-393-30983-5 (pbk)

W. W. Norton & Company, Inc., 500 Fifth Avenue, New York, N.Y. 10110
W. W. Norton & Company, Inc., 10 Coptic Street, London WC1A 1PU

1 2 3 4 5 6 7 8 9 0

Introduction

Carlos Fuentes

There are many people in Abbas's photos of Mexico. Many young people. If his portrait of Mexico were a treatise on population, it would reflect reality: a nation of eighty-five million people half of whom are children and adolescents under fifteen years of age. A portrait of Mexico has to be a portrait of young people, children, and adolescents.

Here they are: a dreamy girl, distant, and self-absorbed who accompanies her father. He's painting masks; what the father does ceases to be a daily job and becomes a ceremony, part of a ritual, thanks to the dreamy presence of the girl. The girl forces us to imagine that she herself is imagining: what is my father doing? For whom is he painting those masks? What is a mask? What's it for?

The answer is not slow in coming. A mask is an ideal face—even in the sense of being *another* possible face. Every child in Abbas's photos has at least two faces. The one the photographer captured—but that's merely an appearance. There is already another face within the child's eyes—the face the child imagines. Around him, the world offers him its version of the other face. Another girl anticipates it. Smiling, dressed in white, reclining on a bed like a modest Venus (or an untouched Lolita), she covers her eyes with tiny skulls made of sugar. The commonplace of Mexican death—sweet, playful, present but imperceptible—is transformed by Abbas and his accomplice (the girl: Venus in poplin, Lolita Morena) into an almost unbearable erotic dream. All this purity will only be preserved if death saves it from corruption. In the simple figure of a girl dressed in white and lying on a doubtlessly noisy bed covered by a clean but hardly elegant blanket, the artist manages to inscribe the mysteries of sex and death.

In every mythology, Venus is an ambiguous star: first light of day and first light of night as well. Dawn and dusk. Abbas's girl really inhabits Venus's two houses, the House of Dawn and the House of Dusk. Her double, mortal gaze, the eyes of her dual death, are also those of a double life, which opens and closes only to open again.

Abbas's Mexican children bear this duality, which is only one form of the dramatized continuity, presented as a paradox only to capture our attention and to force us to reflect. There is a Mexican song which has always disquieted me. Its words are: "What a pretty little dolly; it would be better if she died." Abbas's girl, with her mortal little eyes, is most certainly that "dolly" to whom nothing better than death can happen. Thus she would avoid life's disasters, its tears, disillusion, humiliations, and give herself, prepubescent and nubile, to death.

*Translated from the Spanish by Alfred J. Mac Adam.

Abbas prolongs the life of the child Venus in a pair of photographs, one lyrical, the other comic, of small-town girls on the day of their First Communion. In the lyric photo, the group of girls dressed in white enters a deep tropical forest, following a shadowy path. It's as if they were on their way to a wedding with nature. But perhaps this downhill path is taking them to the land of Mictlan, the Indian paradise which was also hell. Both places were one, although the attributes of paradise were superimposed on those of Christian hell. The land of Mictlan, hell and paradise, is both things only to allow the opposition between life and death to disappear and what we call "death" to be seen as part of life: continuity, phase, renewal, all together. "We shall all have to go to the place of mystery," says an Indian poem. If death is inevitable, it cannot be bad. But is it necessary to hasten it, is it better to die, is "life not worth anything" as another popular song says?

That isn't the meaning of death, neither in Mexico nor in Abbas's photographs. I was saying about those girls entering a tropical forest like souls entering the land of Mictlan (described as hot, humid, flower covered, and moistened by perpetual dew) that two of them leave the others and stop to play at the side of the road, rocking back and forth, about to fall, making funny faces (more masks). The accident, the stumble, the comic incident, interrupts the solemnity of the rite, the road to the ceremony of communion, and instead celebrates life in its thousand unforeseen incidents. . . .

Between these Mexican extremes, fighting, alongside its protagonists, in order to dissolve them in a kind of shared light, of charitable fear, of vital continuity and resistance, Abbas opens a fan of roads, of possibilities. The reclining girl looks at the world through her eyes of sugared death; another girl looks at the world while her father paints masks. Other groups of young people don't look: they act, energetically, joyfully. We see them playing on soccer fields, running through streets, tearing through the night with the uproar of their races and lights: playing at bullfighting, fireworks. . . .

But looking at this proof of the life of our young people, we always come back to the two observing girls: one with the distant look while her father paints masks; the other, improvising her own mask through the eyes of smiling death. It's perfectly possible, in my opinion, that those two girls see the other young people running and playing. They see the same thing we see: the volleyball court set up in a poor neighborhood of tin roofs, walls made of planks and rusty iron; the boy who runs by is marvelously moistened by an oral dew spewed out by a street triton, doubtless his friend, to help him keep going and win the race: a street Ulysses helped by youthful gods, poor gods, but gods gifted by the air of Aeolus and Ehecatl, the lungs of the city . . . And the boys who play at fiery bullfighting are about to be burned by their own game.

Life and death, and between them: accidents—sometimes comic, sometimes tragic, but always full of the ability to go beyond mere resistance to a new beginning. Abbas's art impresses me for that very reason: his photos are memorable, even symbolic instants of life and death. But everything in them, beginning with life and death, is always recommencing. Nothing is finished. Let's see now: that girl seated at the feet of her father, the artisan making the masks; that girl lying down so she can get a better view of life through the pupils of death; those other two girls see a dead child in his coffin, surrounded by family and friends. No one's weeping. The other children try to find a guide for their own emotions in the attitude of the mother; she looks at her dead child with a serious sadness, a rejection of all sentimentality that is much more deeply committed to the sad fact than a scene of torn clothing, wailing, and Mediterranean melodrama.

The mother of the dead child forces us to reflect on the almost aristocratic, distant and contained seriousness of the world of Mexican poverty. The other children search for their reaction in the mother's reaction. One of the girls has already found it: she smiles at her dead brother with a living tenderness and sweetness, as if the boy had come back to life or if she herself had died. Another girl, nearer the head of the dead boy, possesses an absent look, as if she remembered (she's the youngest) that on another occasion she too was dead before returning to life.

And the dead boy, every hair in place, dressed, with his hands crossed over his chest, resting on a bed of flowers, illuminated by a solitary candle stuck in an empty Coca-Cola bottle, sleeps covered by a primary mask of cotton. His nose and mouth no longer belong to him, the cotton fills the orifices of life: we don't know if the cotton was placed there to keep *more* death from entering him or so that the life he *still* needs for the journey to Mictlan doesn't escape. The traditional offerings are there: jars of preserves, possibly sloe fruits (*tejocotes*) in syrup.

But there is an intrusive eye at the funerary scene: the television set. It's as if that audiovisual device were to remain there, once the child is brought to the cemetery, forever holding the living memory, the image, of the departed. Curiously, three geese fly on top of the machine: migratory birds in a perpetual flight of farewell.

I want to emphasize the richness of observation and composition in Abbas's photographs in order to repeat my belief that the camera never gives us a product that is static or subordinate to captured reality. The truth is that perhaps we could see this scene without Abbas's camera. What we could never do is stop its movement in order carefully to study the details gathered in it just that one time: immortal gestures saved from the riptide of history that surrounds and drags down all of us. But there is something more, and it's that, inevitably, a collection of photos like this one convokes its own continuity, its montage.

I've already pointed out that a photo by Abbas gives us an instant in a perpetual recommencement. That capacity to begin again seems to me fundamental in a world where all the powers that be insinuate how convenient it would be for us to think everything's finished—history, questioning, creation—because they have resolved everything for us, and everything is infinitely renewable, but only if we repeat ad infinitum the reproductive, profitable, comforting model.

Abbas is an artist because, among other things, he imagines. And to imagine, as Baudelaire said, is to see relationships between things. Dynamic photography, Abbas photographs analogies, relationships among things. I am free to order this pile of photos by the great artist, but it's impossible for me not to associate the two observing girls with the object of their stare, which may be the dead boy, but which may also be the next scene: another boy, this one in a museum standing next to a pre-Conquest figure which is not only identical to the child but which precedes and certainly prolongs him.

This simple scene of the boy and the sculpture catches an essential movement: the work of art outlives those who created and contemplated it only because each time someone contemplates it and re-creates it by looking at it over the course of time it becomes contemporary.

Beginning with that photo in the museum, I can stand the pain of that colossal expenditure of energy in tasks of pure survival. Mexico has a handsome, intelligent, energetic youth wasting its strength on useless things. The economic crisis has thrown boys and girls out of homes and schools, when before they went through primary and secondary school and, with luck, university as well. Now the economic crisis has forced them to give up their studies at the age of ten or eleven and go out onto the streets to clean windshields, perform acrobatic tricks, be fire-eaters, join criminal gangs, and that way to survive, help their families, and justify everything by means of that Mexican clannishness, family solidarity, the nexus of blood and emotion.

Abbas does not show the worst sides of this drama. But discreetly, all he has to do is show us a young seller of green corn or ask a boy to turn his back to us and walk, weighed down by shovels and a U.S. Air Force bag, into an almost Chaplinesque horizon—infinite, hopeless, but also filled with irregularities, and, therefore, renewable and hopeful. When the boy stops and turns to face us, he's also facing the world and two more girls. One of them is terrible, a sad, self-involved Medusa, her gaze lost in an unbearable melancholy without horizons. In her hand, she holds a machete. She could be a figure of terrible revenge against political lies and social oppression. Her passivity is deceptive. The machete is about to rise. The terrible goddess is going to be reborn.

As if he knew the humor of life well, Abbas flips the card over and shows us instead a small, coquettish goddess in a pose that is natural, inviting, seductive, and charming: this odalisque of Mexican rooftops is perfect in every detail: the position of her feet, hips, arms, shoulders, head, all of it is as perfect as a painting by Delacroix or a fashion show by Ungaro. The towel around her head provides the final coquettish touch. We really are in a neoclassical harem by Ingres, except that this time the floors are dirt instead of Oriental rugs, the walls made of brick instead of marble, and the columns are not made of jasper but of iron, aluminum, and smoke. The girl-goddess of the roof is staring at the industrial landscape of an oil refinery.

Is she about to throw herself off, transforming coquettishness into despair? But wouldn't there be a friendly wing which, when it saw her jump from the roof, would bear her up so she'd fall among her friends in a tropical river, peering out like naiads, dark-skinned Botticellis, in a renewed, pure, breathable world?

Abbas's girls are going to be born again. The river is going to carry them away and deliver them to a great maternal breast. Renewal presides over everything, a power of resistance that leads to change which is not imposed but found in freedom by a graceful people which has lived with itself, with its gods, with its art, with its catastrophes, with its joys, with its parents and its children since time immemorial. All of Abbas's girls have been reborn in the arms of the beautiful mestiza Madonna crowned with flowers, surrounded by candles, covered with incense, who wraps the reborn girl in her rebozo.

The marvelous masks made by the Toltecs and Aztecs had a practical purpose, which was to disguise the dead, giving them an ideal face for the journey to Mictlan. Proust said that after forty we all have the face we deserve. Modern plastic surgery has attempted the opposite: we can have the face we want at any age. It isn't true. Plastic surgery usually erases the beauty a face acquires and only gives in exchange an old age without character. The ancient Mexicans, much wiser, allowed each human to obtain a new face, but only for eternity.

But what is the eternity of Abbas's Mexican characters? Again, the answer comes to us under a mask. A small child covers his face with a cardboard box. We see that the box once held soap. He's seen fit to adapt it to his eyes and ears. This, next to the jade and obsidian masks of ancient Mexico, is the saddest, most fragile, and, perhaps, the most laughable of all masks: the face of garbage instead of the face of ruin.

Between garbage and ruin, today's Mexico tries to forge a modernity. Abbas, like all observers of our country, immediately sees the contrasts between an ancient, on many occasions, primitive country, and the objects, the things that proclaim the "modernity" of those who possess them. We already saw that in the wake of the poor boy: the television set presides over the scene like the eye of God, and the candle is jammed into the vitreous anus of the Coca-Cola bottle.

There are, nevertheless, other more secret contrasts that show us how profoundly Abbas has looked, from his Asiatic and European perspective, into the newness of the American New World. He contrasts death with Coca-Cola, the solitude and abandonment of one of the thousands of Mexico's street dogs with three modern men (jogging suits, running shoes) carrying a huge television set with a naked old wall behind them. And in another picture, a serious, ugly, old man crosses his arms next to a classical statue: a female nude inspired by the Renaissance; again the reclining Venus, the dis-Oriented, Occidental odalisque. The closed eyes of the man allow us to suppose he's indifferent to what's next to him—or, just the opposite, that he dreams about her and desires her.

Another of Abbas's visual contrasts is one in which a woman turns her back on a Christ praying during the Agony in the Garden. A young, drunken Indian who's passed out at the foot of the cross that came to bring him redemption and alcohol. That same cross, abandoned, without other figures, cracks in another photograph, like those old Indian trees, the *ahuehuetes*, that withstood everything—storms, earthquakes, and time—until industrial pollution split and broke them right down the middle. The hem of the suffering Christ has been put on his abandoned cross; a humble gathering of corn husks tries to make it sacred and keep it standing. Where is its Jesus? Abbas's Christ lies elsewhere, also alone and surrounded by wood shavings, planks, and hammers, as if Saint

Joseph had just caressed Him. We realize that Abbas has surprised this Mexican Christ in the act of being made, of being born, or reborn or re-vived. I repeat this vision of Abbas's in his photos: the world is making and remaking itself with each step, with each click of the shutter, with each squint or wink of our eyes.

This constant renovation of the world, amid poverty, humility, dust, skinny coyotes and ownerless dogs, dead children and drunken Indians, proposes a radical fact of today's time. Over the past few years, we've all learned what many poets, artists, and ordinary human beings who happen to be close to the sounds of the earth and the movements of soul have always known. Nothing dies completely. The trick played by progress has been to tell us we can leave behind what we were. In Abbas's photographs there is no "what we were." There is a "we are being, going to be" because we go on being everything we've been. The surprise of this fin-de-siècle Abbas and I are living through together, is that what seemed dead—religion, regionalism, memories, languages, dreams—was alive, coinciding with everything that characterizes modernity, from a fax to fiber optics, from an industrial design to a jet or a cellular telephone.

How is this technological modernity going to live with the cultural presence that holds, by definition, past and future in the present?

Abbas gives us a possible answer in his photographs of Mexico. What we see here is the coexistence of many levels of time in every mind. None of these photos is gratuitous; in each one, in one way or another, we are made to see and understand that in the head of each one of these men, women, and children there is room for many times, many realities, different cultures, each coloring the others, commingling with one another but not killing one another. And this in a country that was brutally conquered, but which learned to disguise its culture, to mask it and save it in the arms of the culture of the Other, in a warm copulation like the dew in the land of the dead, Mictlan.

The faces and masks, ultimately, the dreams of these Mexicans he surprised one day in their living and dying tell Abbas's eye that nothing has to be sacrificed. Many levels of time in every mind. Many histories in each face. This is the only possible modernity.

When Abbas asked me to write something for his album on Mexico I accepted with pleasure. But I asked him for time to do it. How much? the artist asked, understandably alarmed. Until I dream your photos, I answered; I have to see your photos and then dream them before writing about them.

Well, I've dreamed them.

The Soul

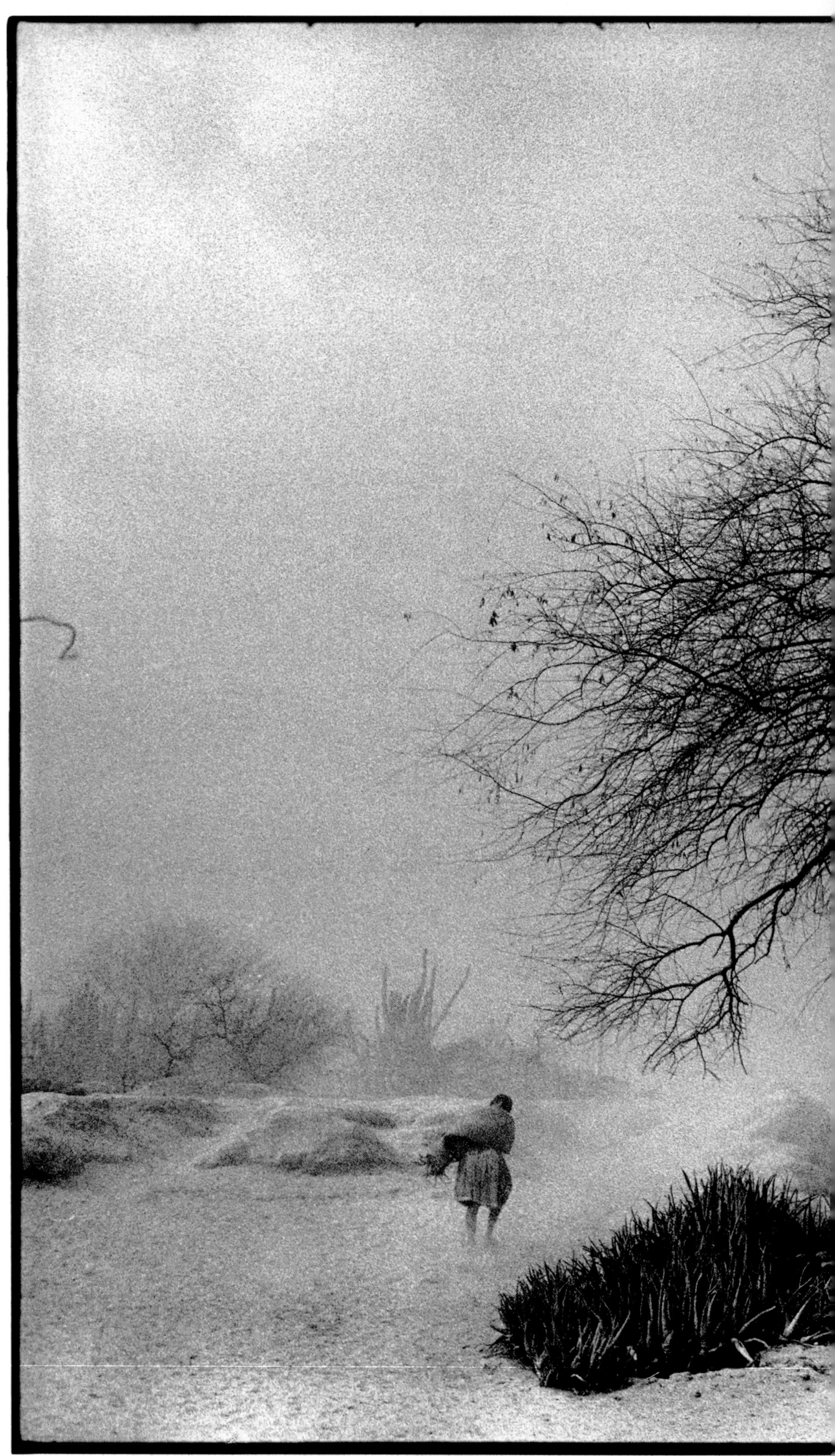

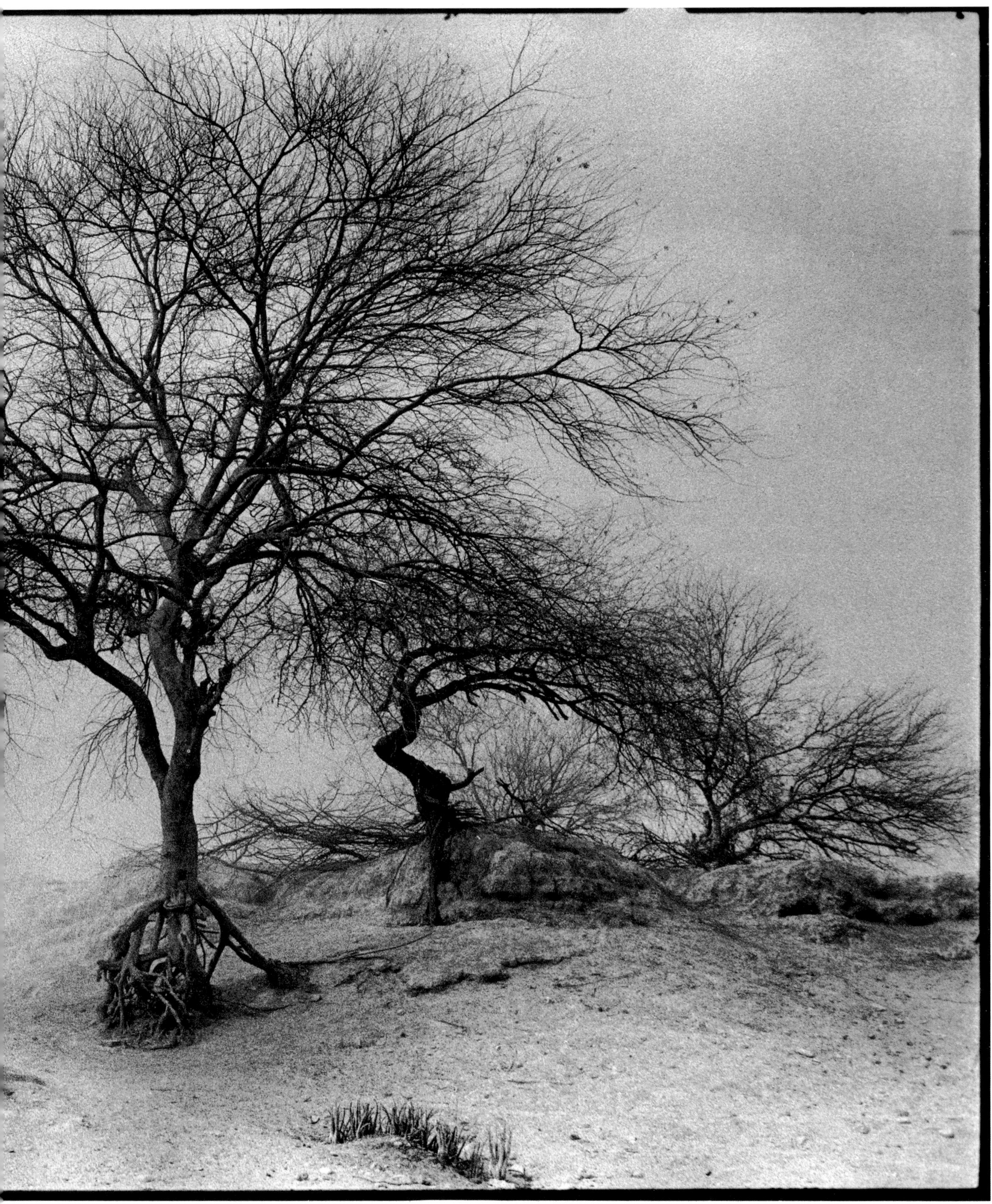

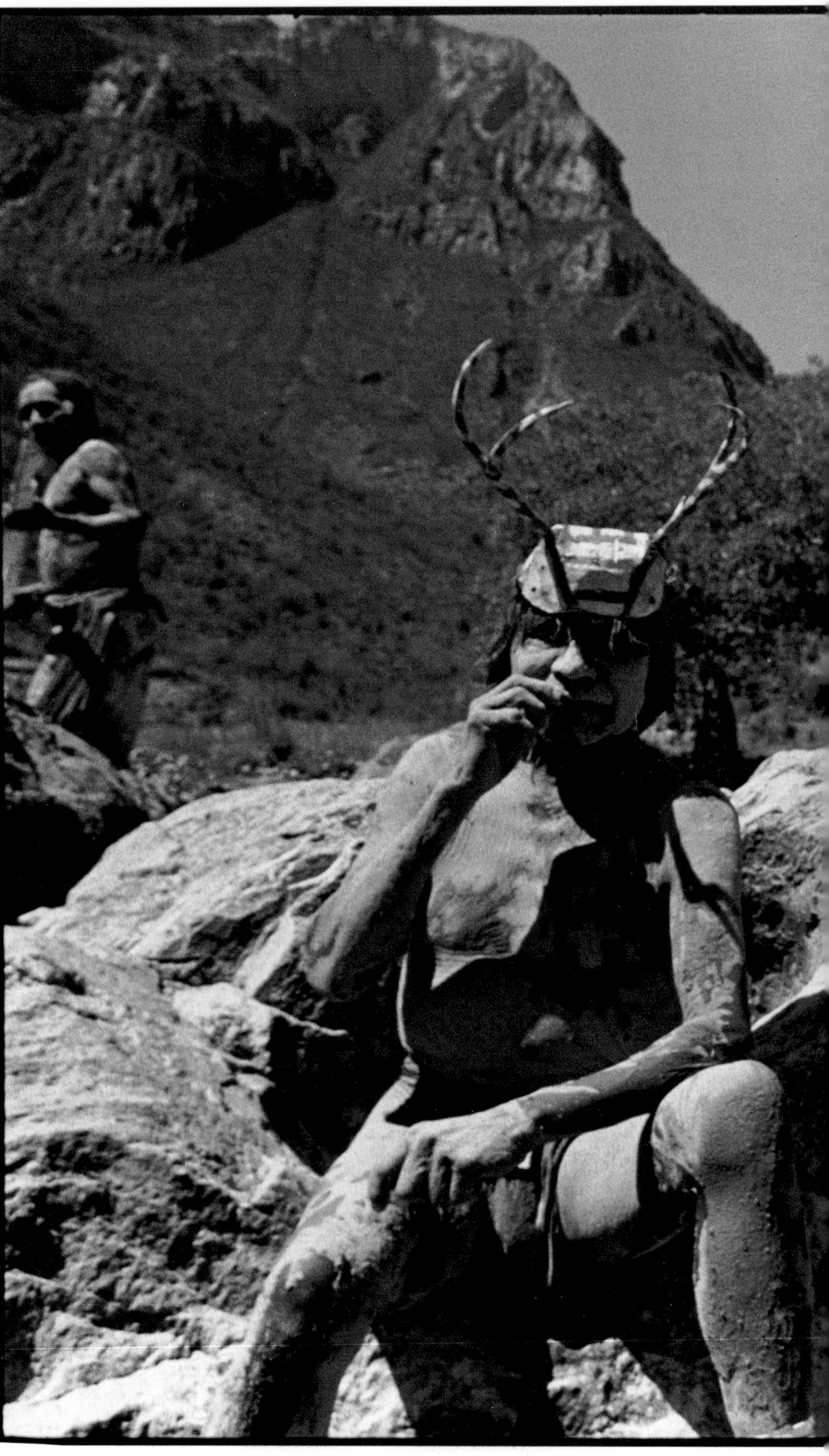

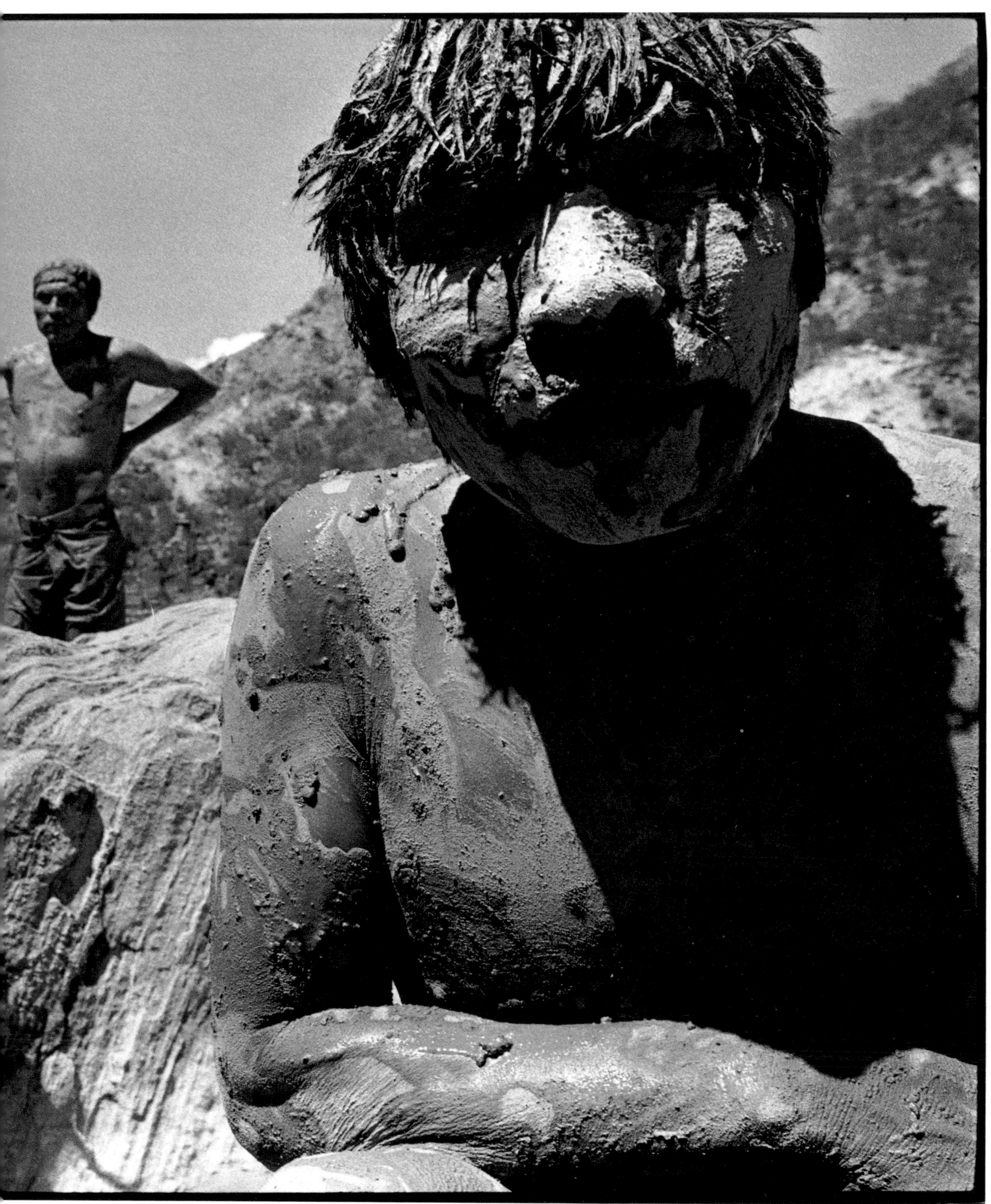

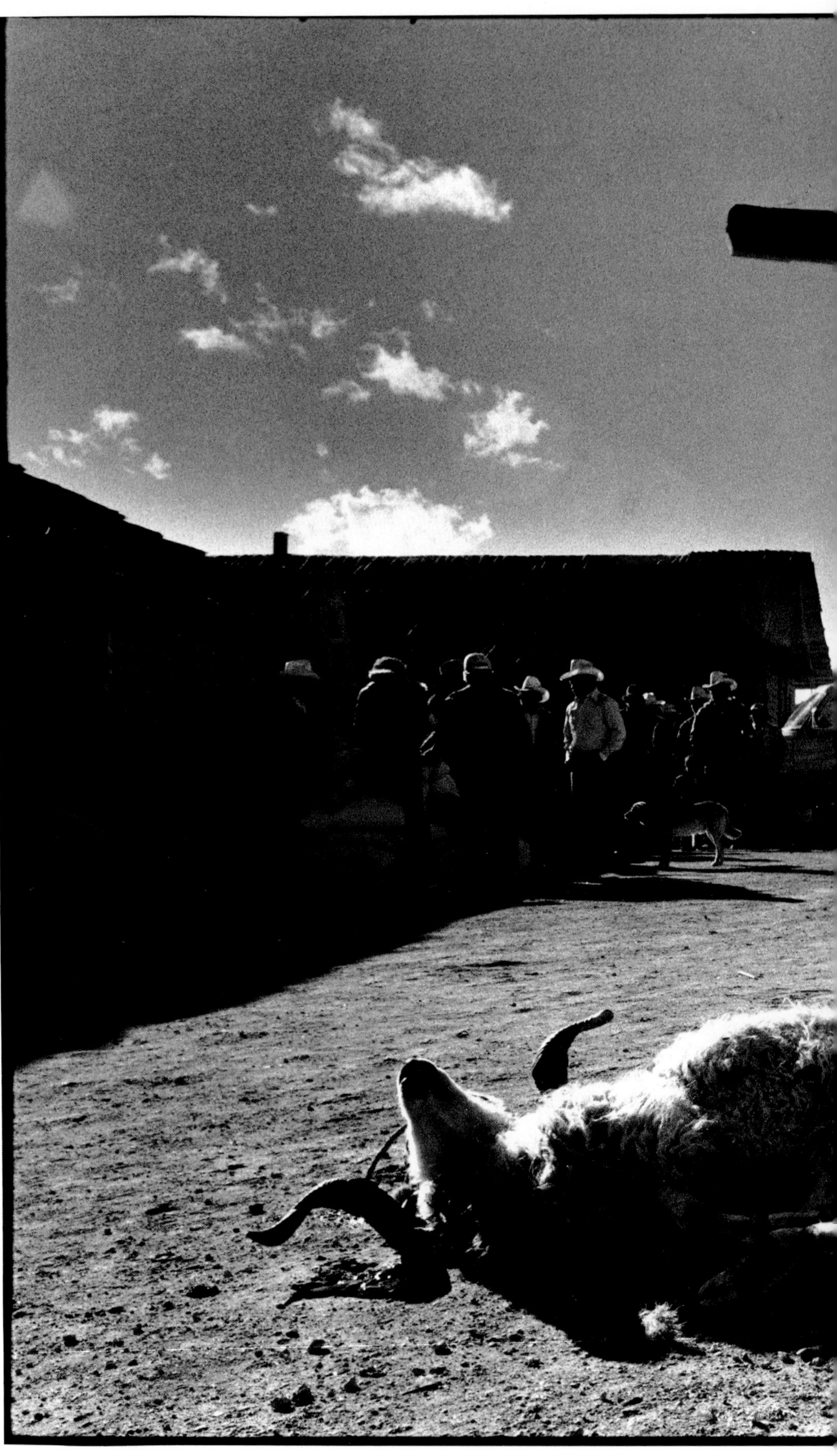

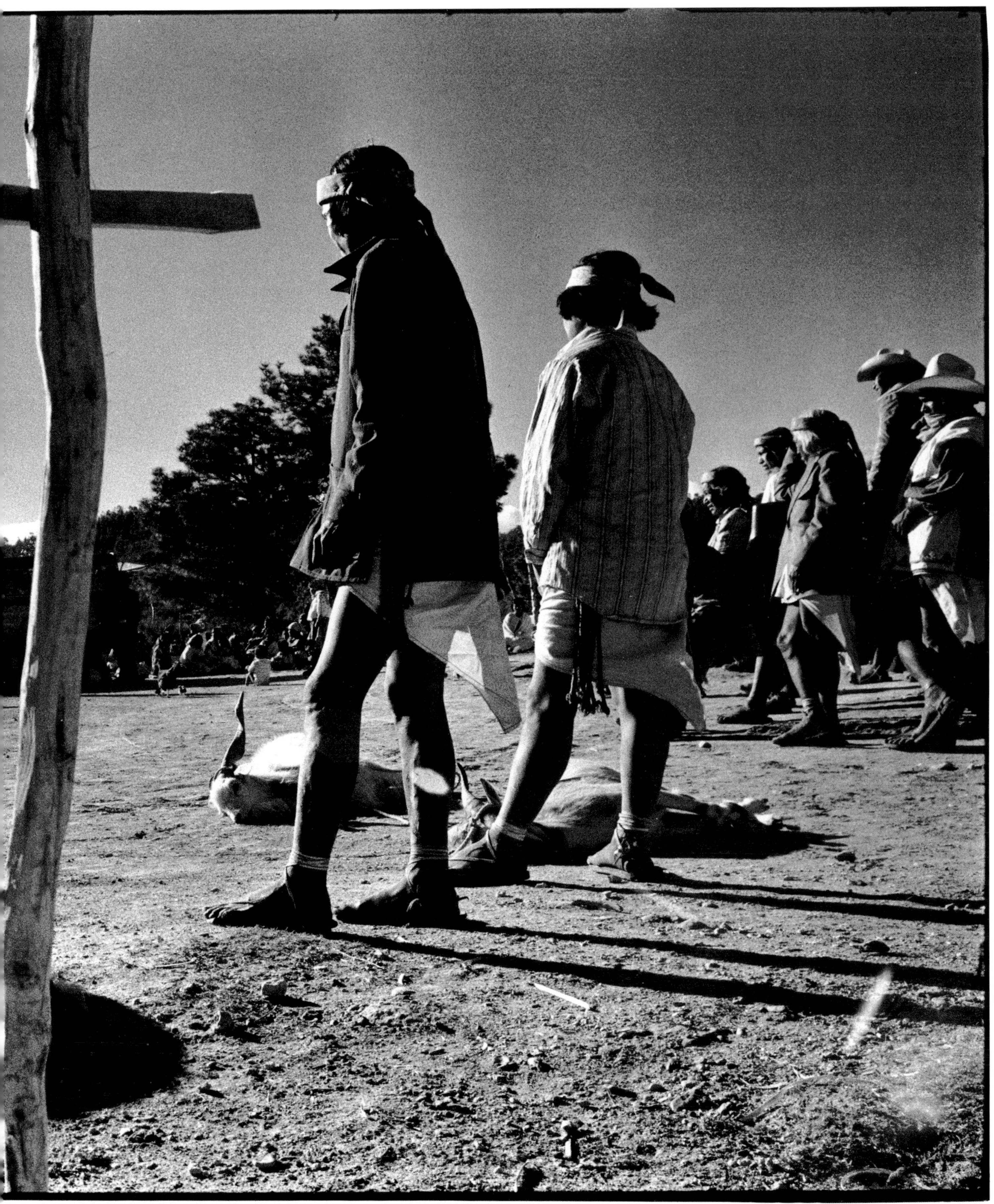

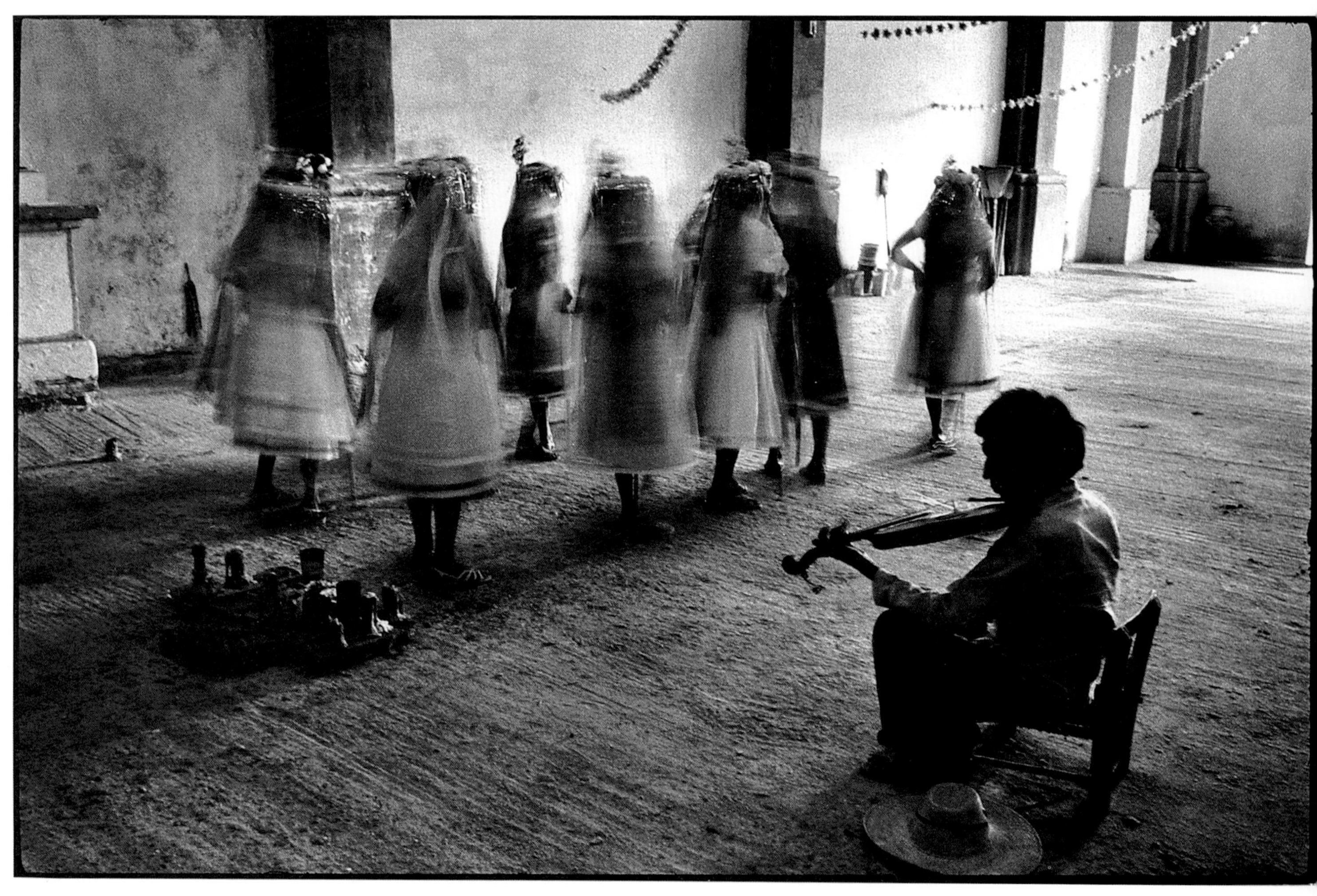

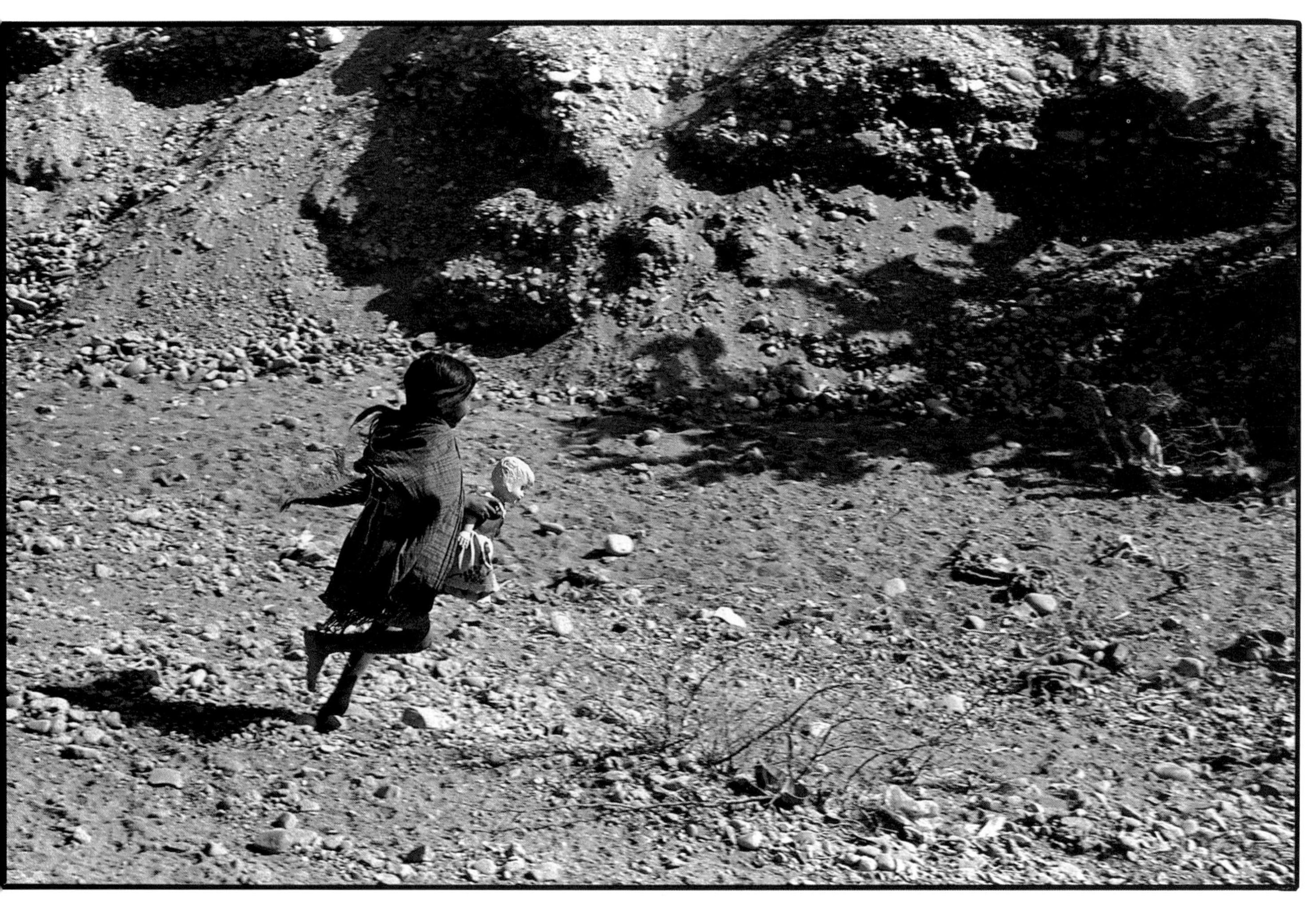

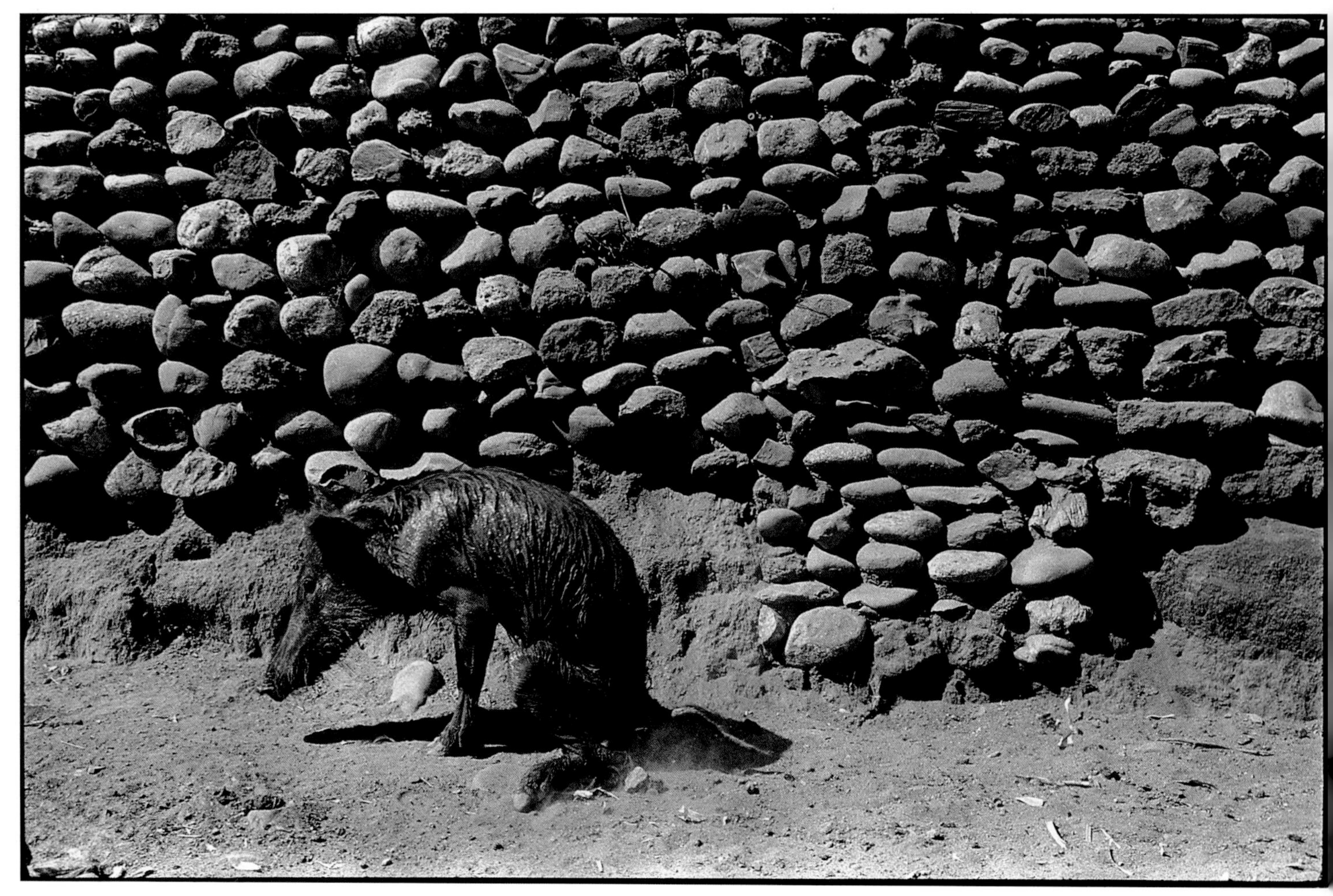

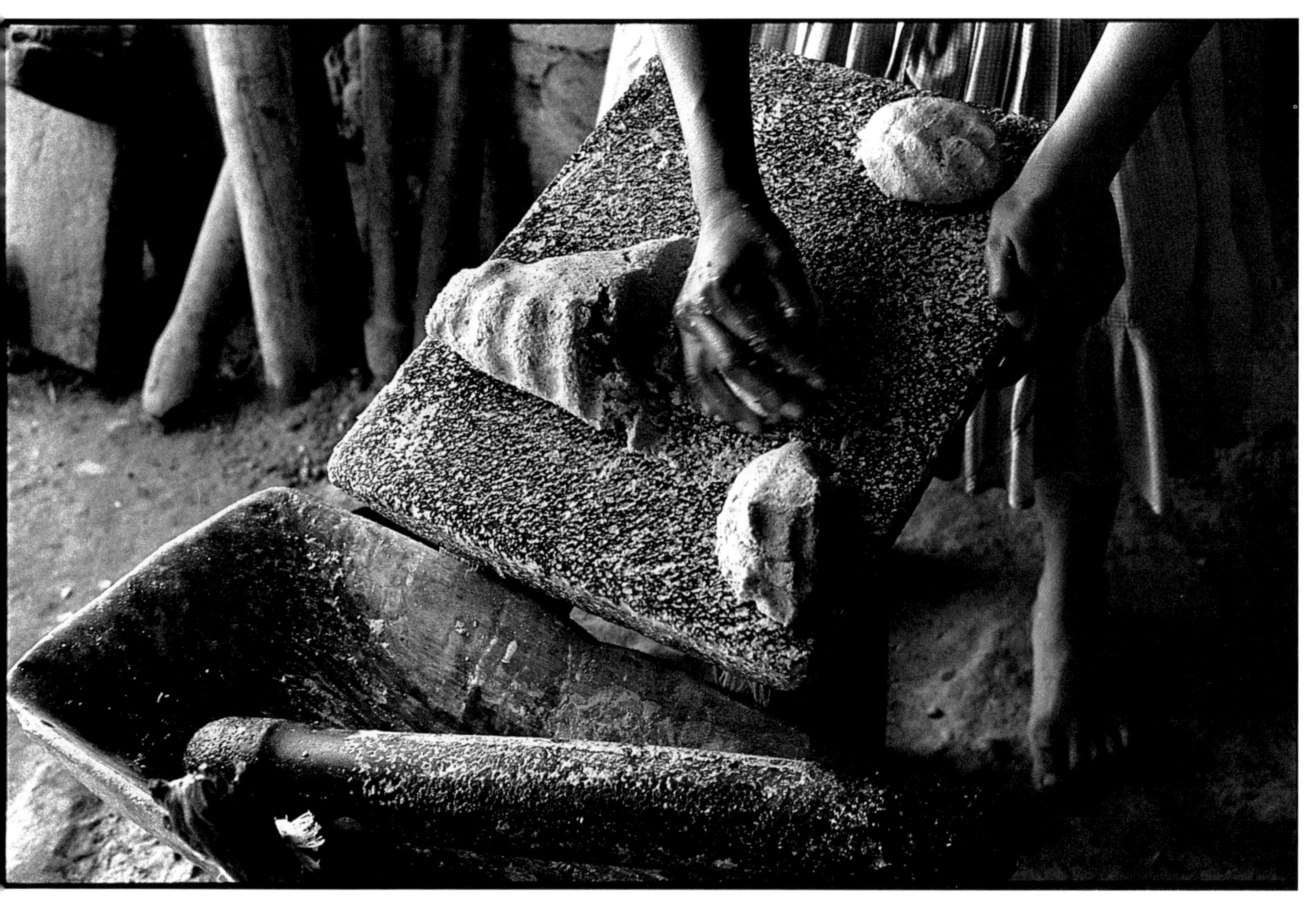

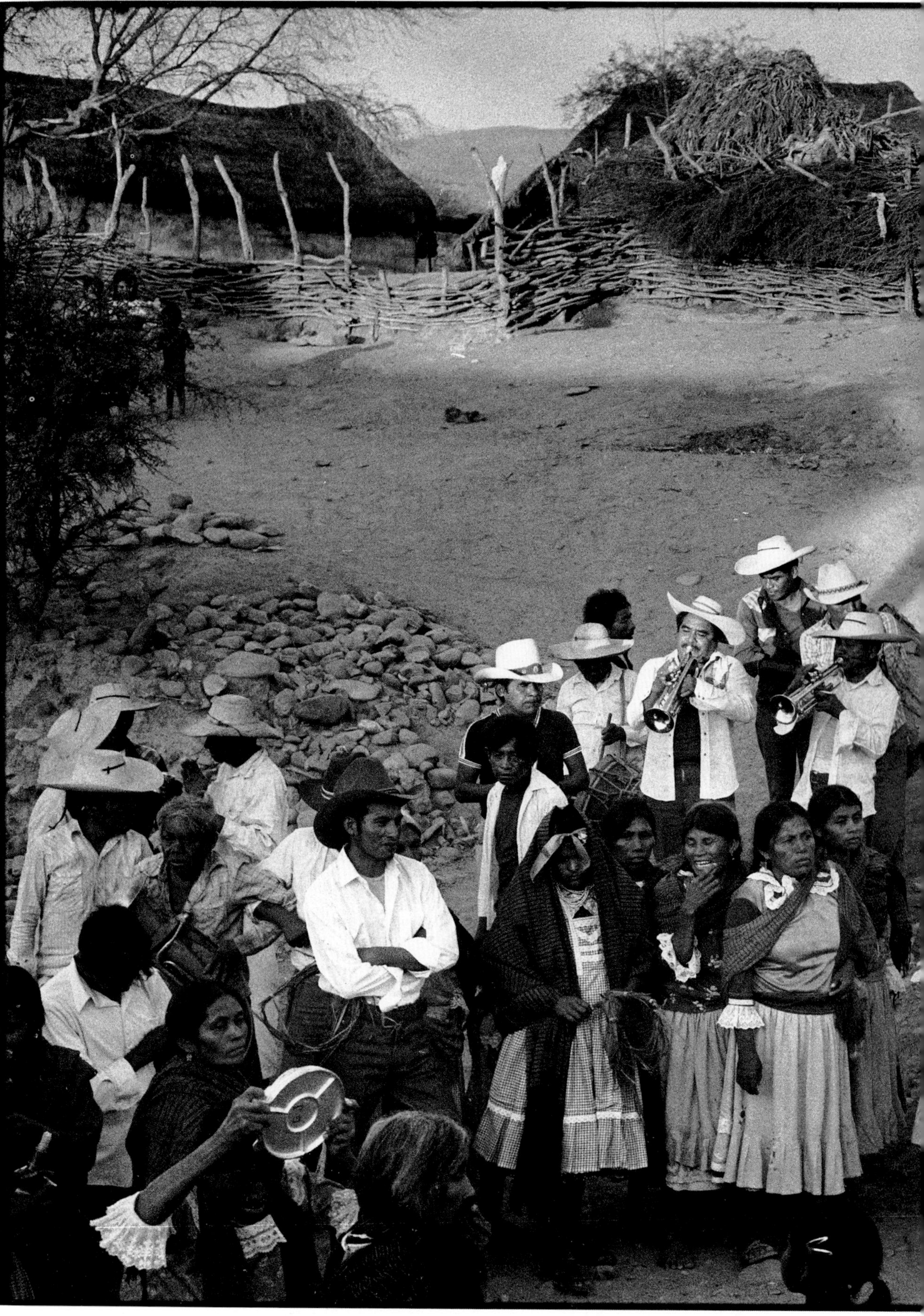

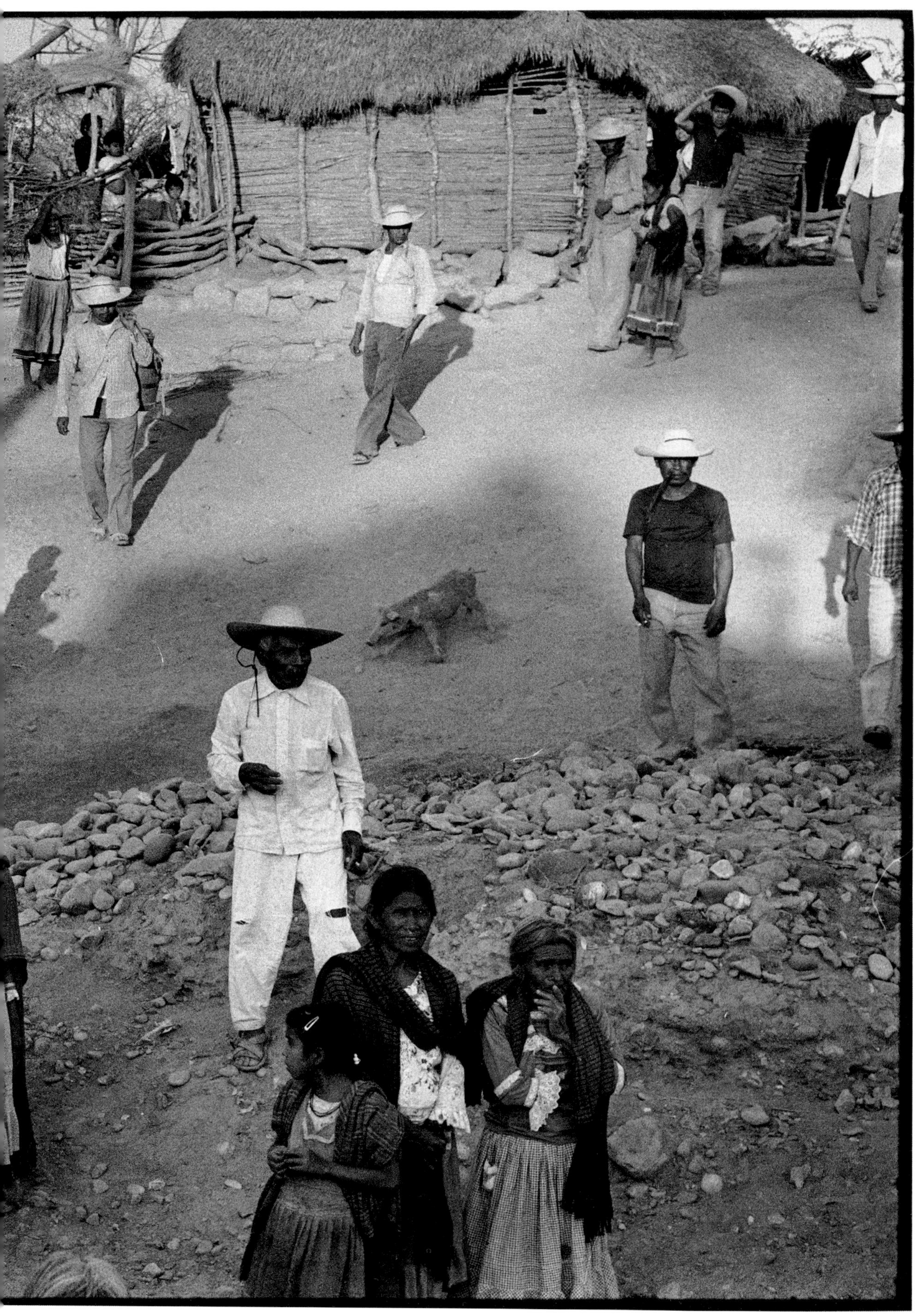

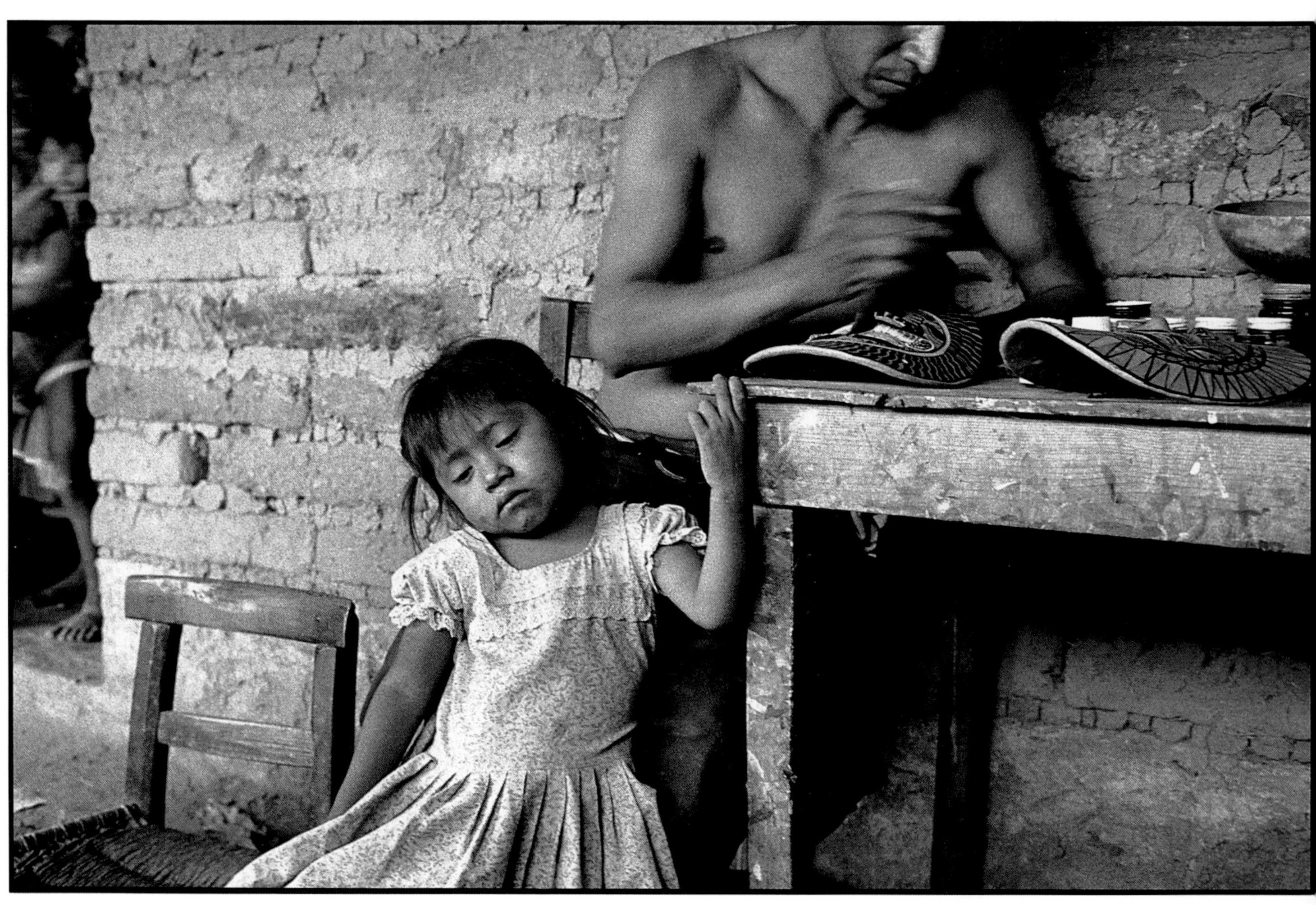

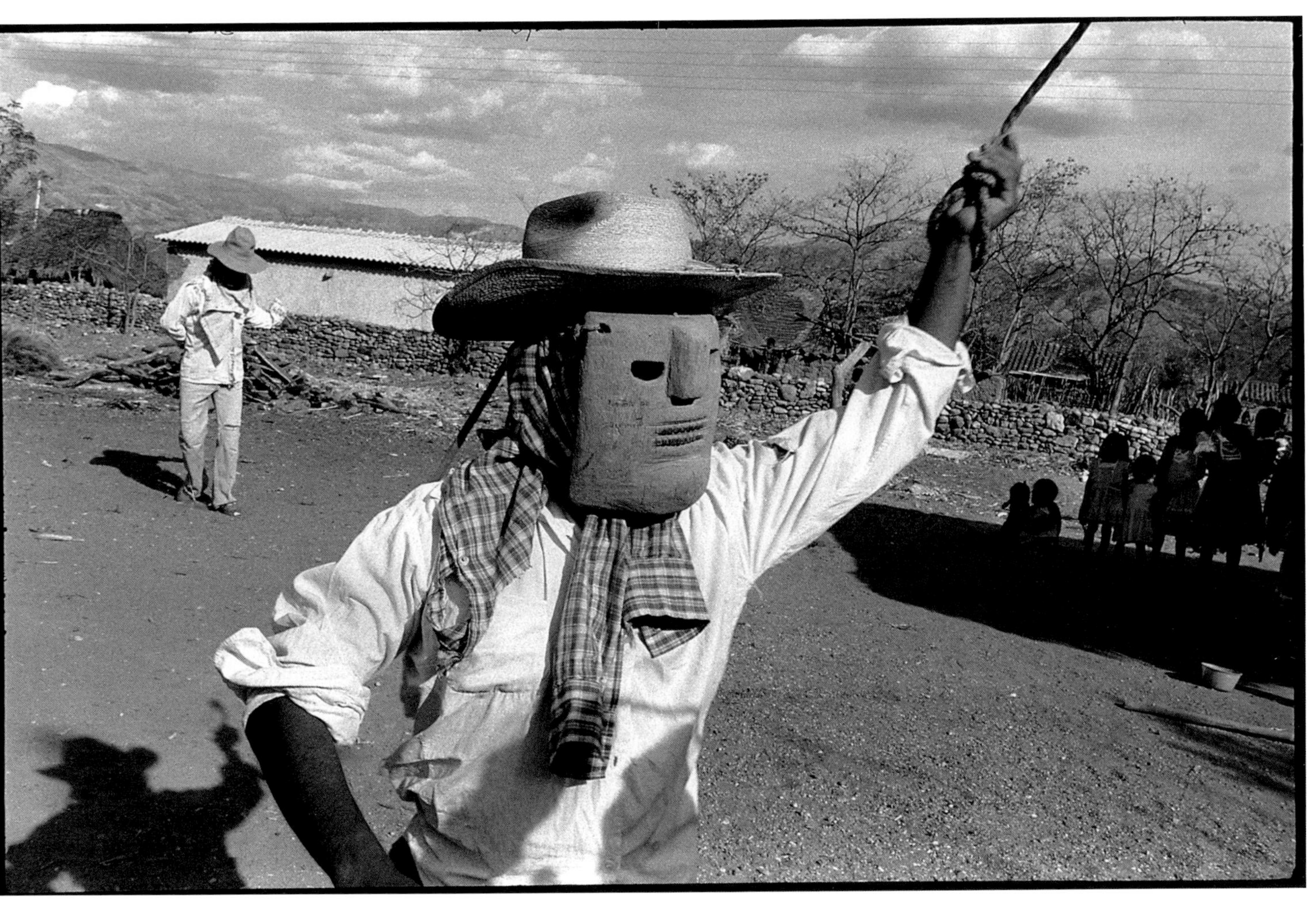

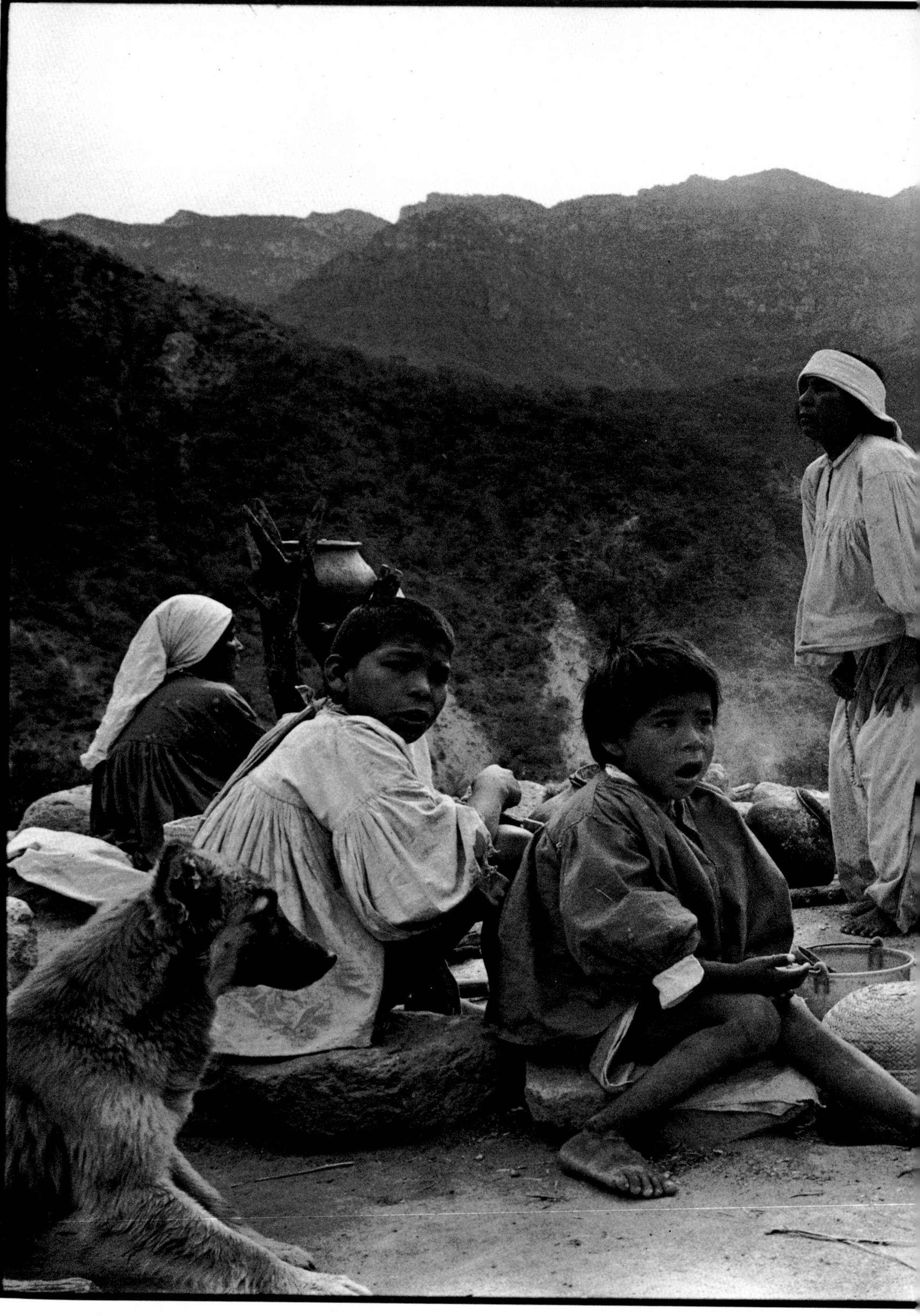

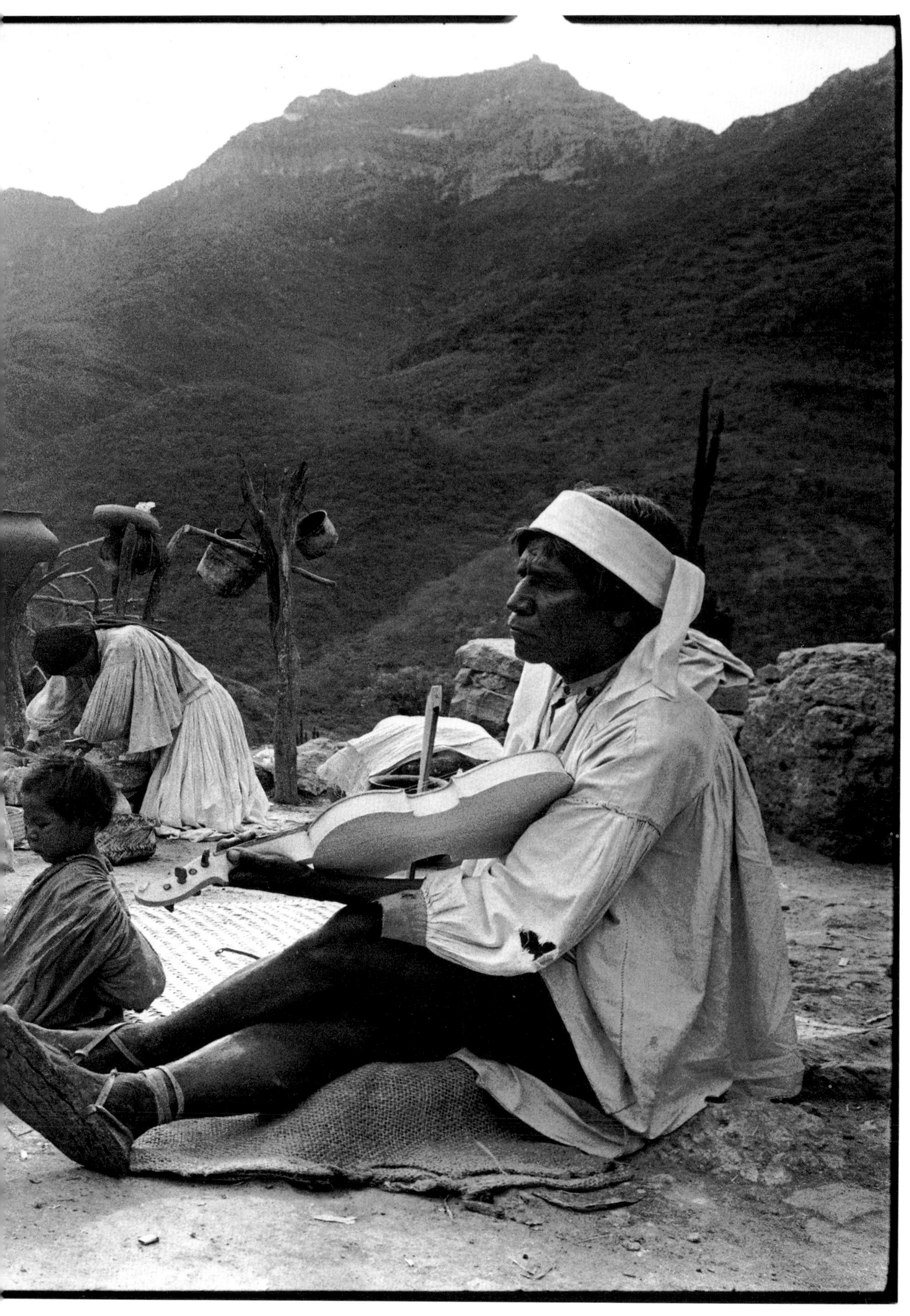

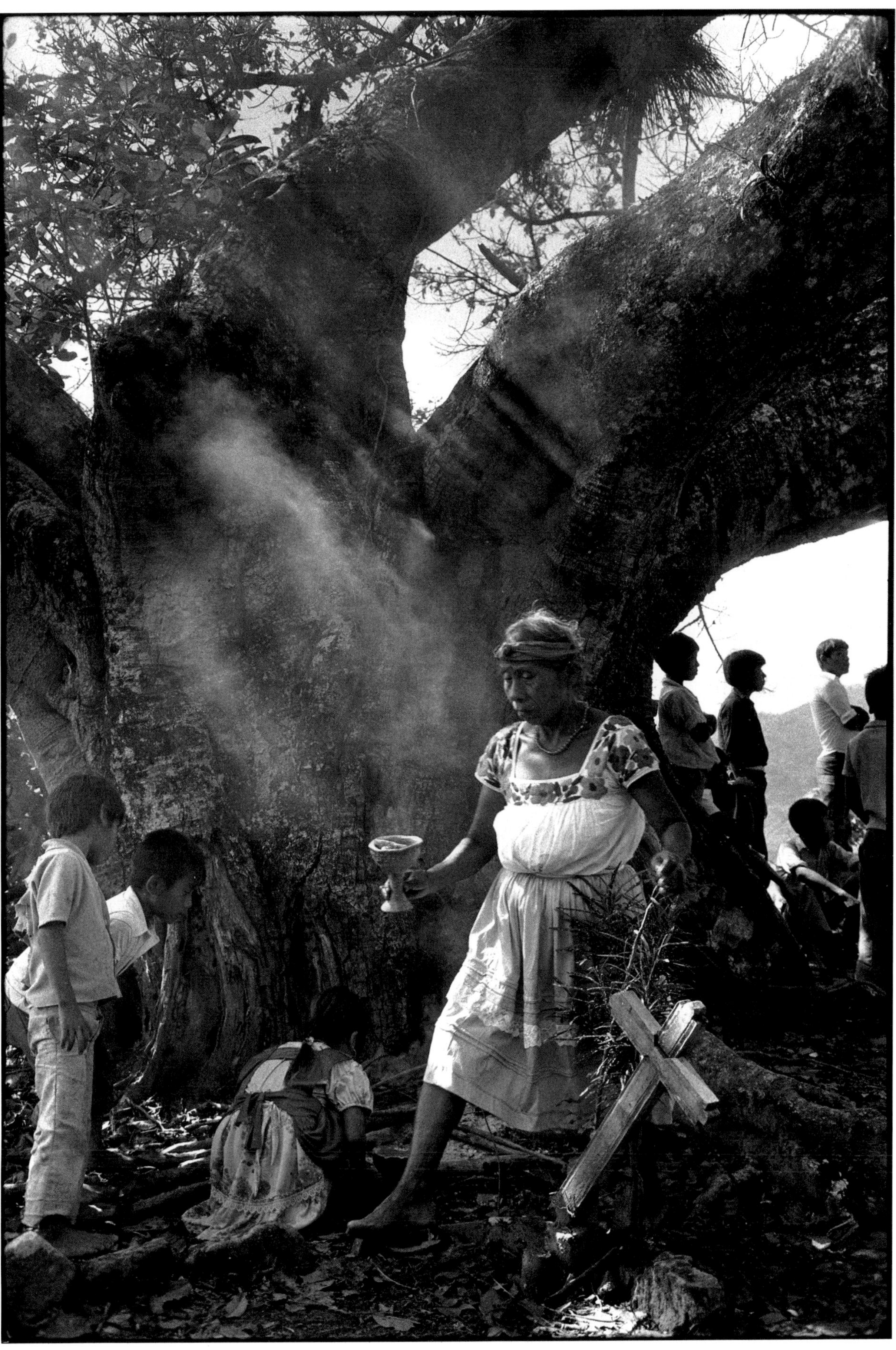

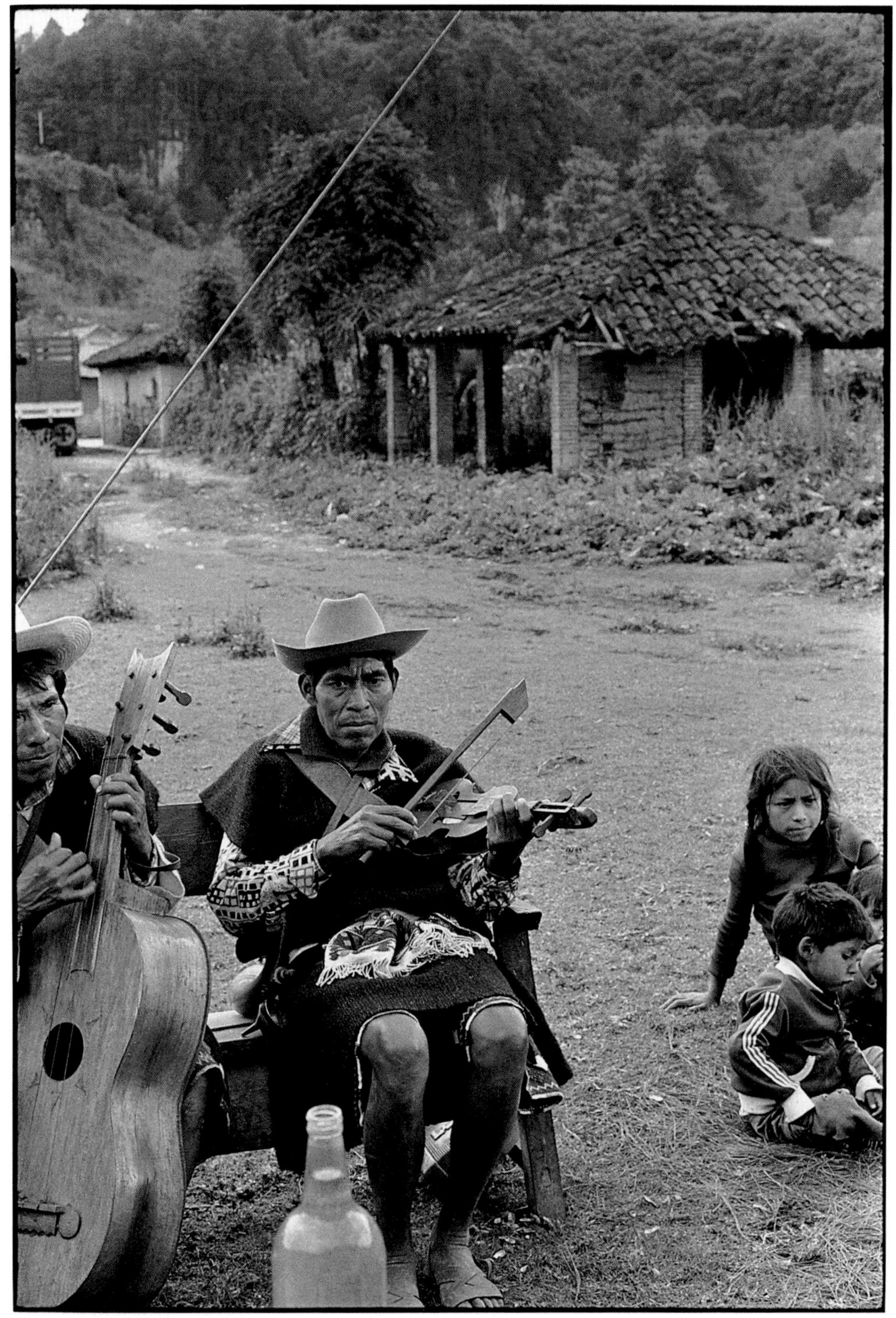

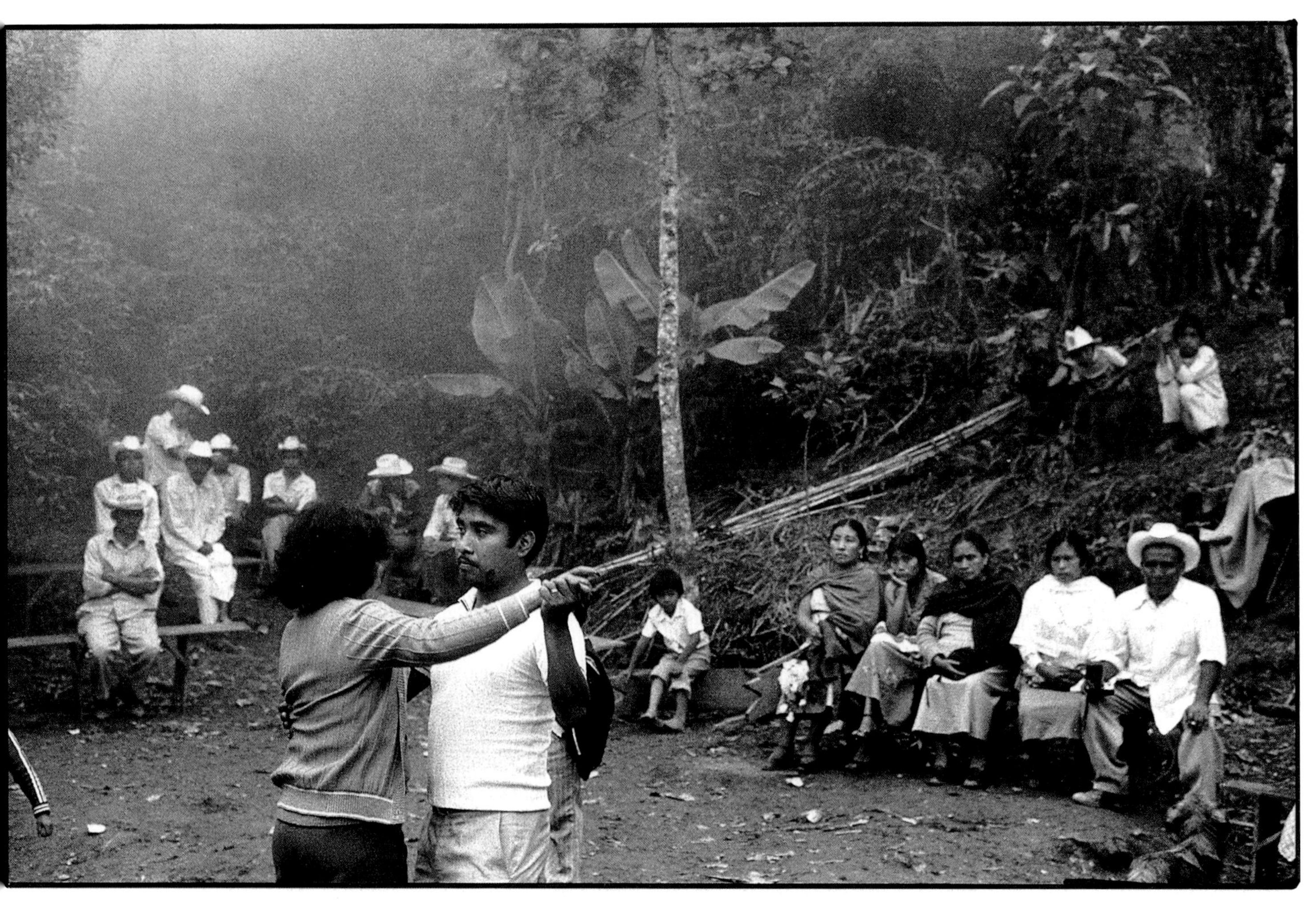

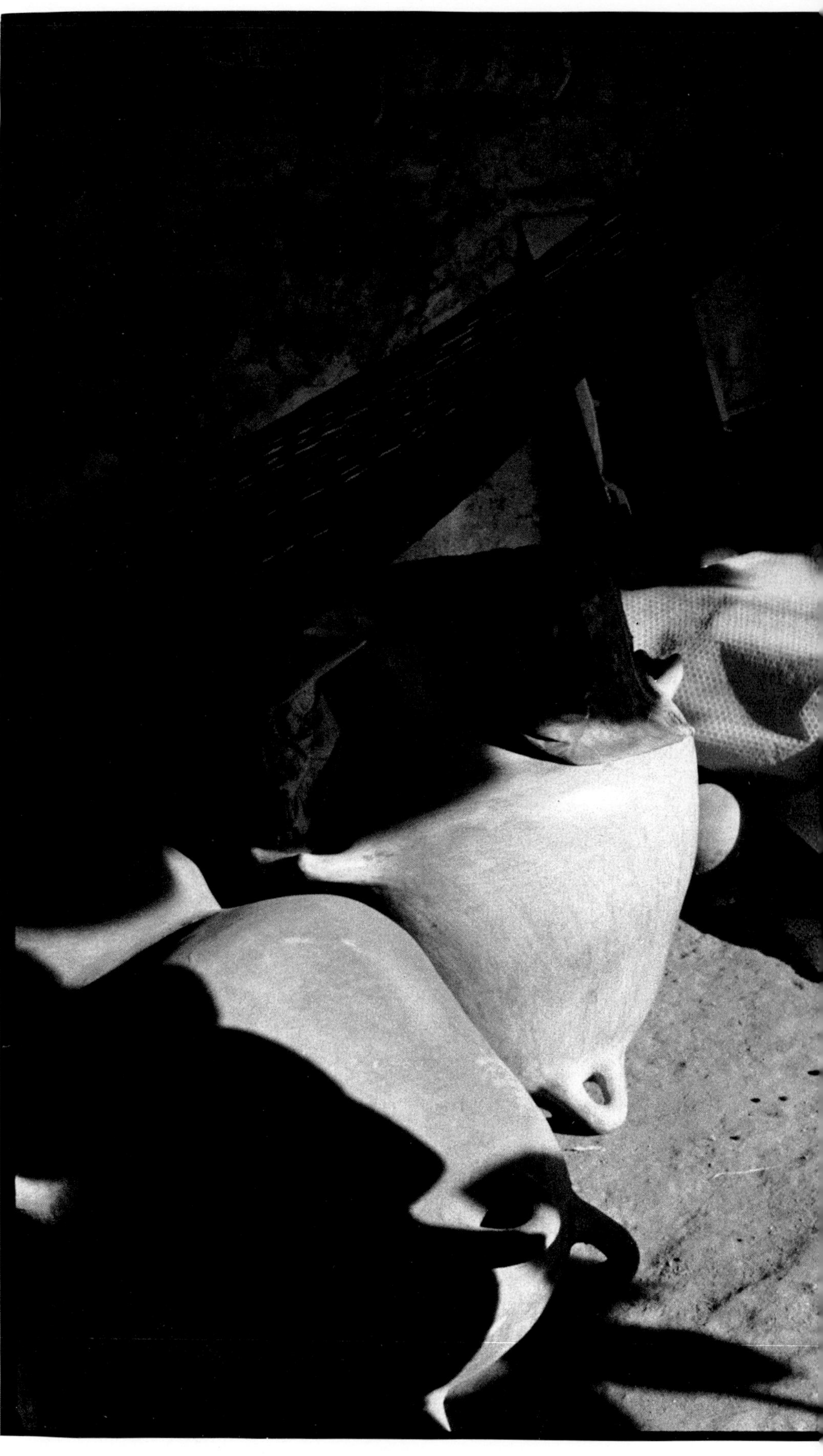

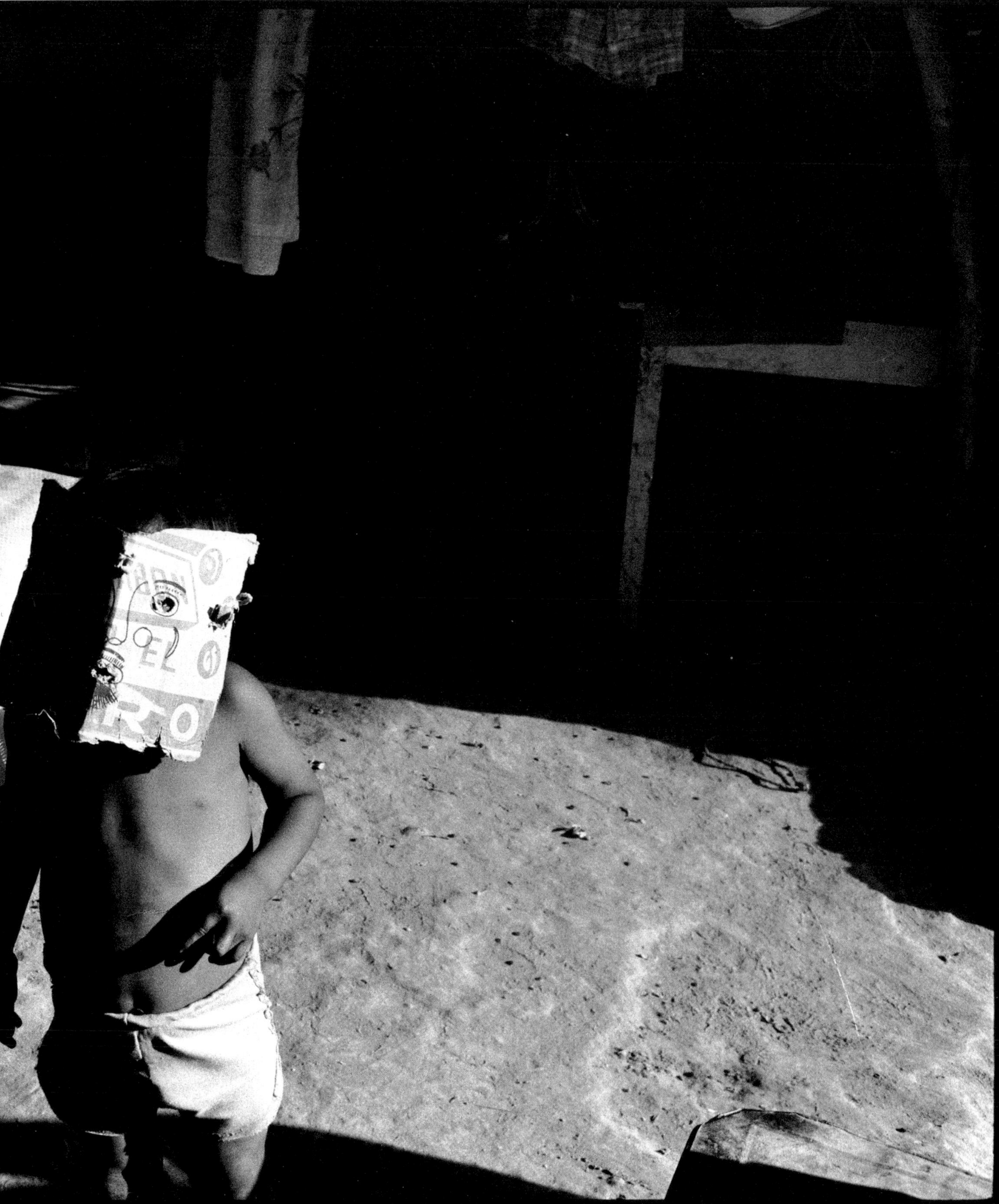
EL
RO

Existence

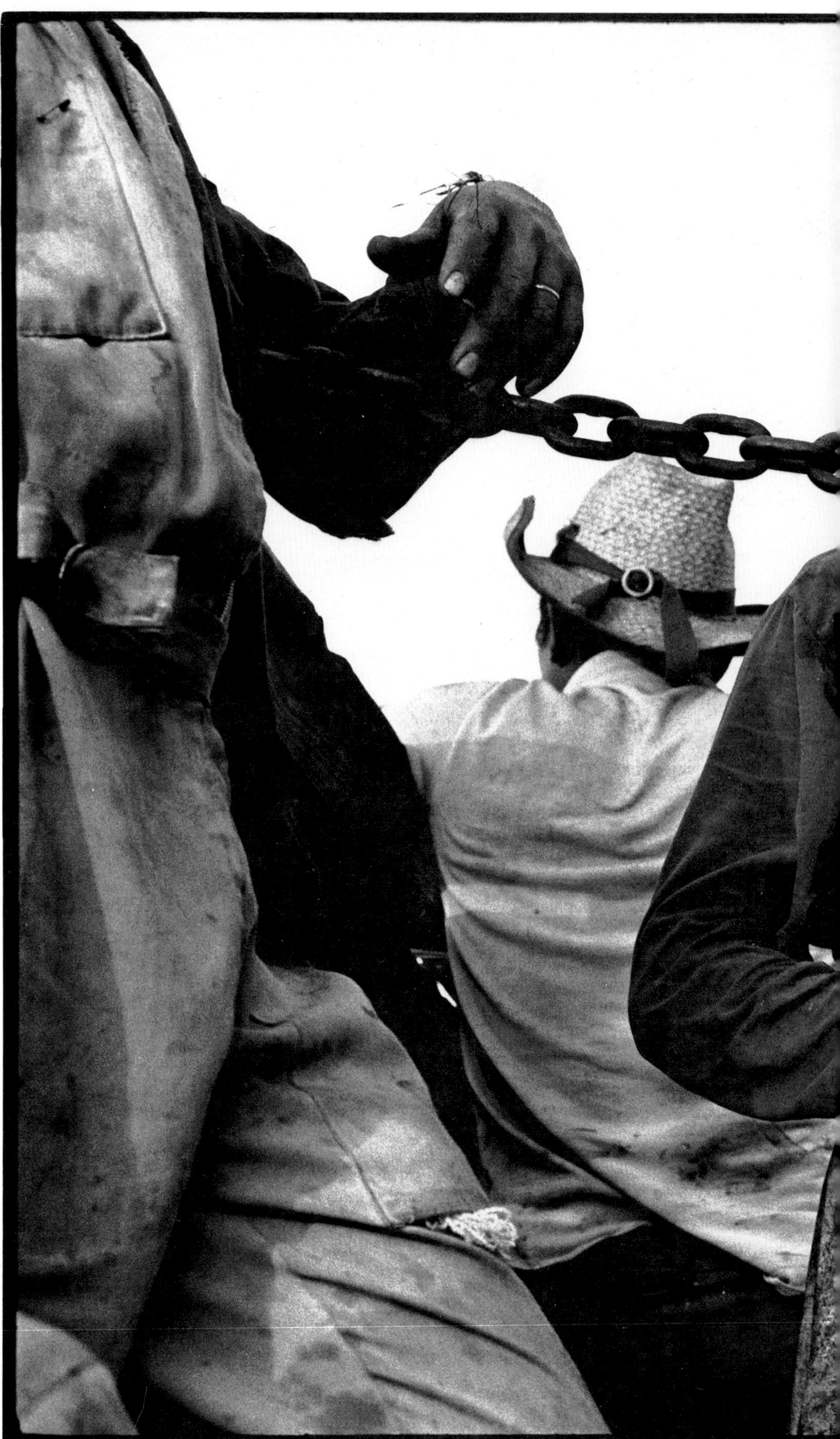

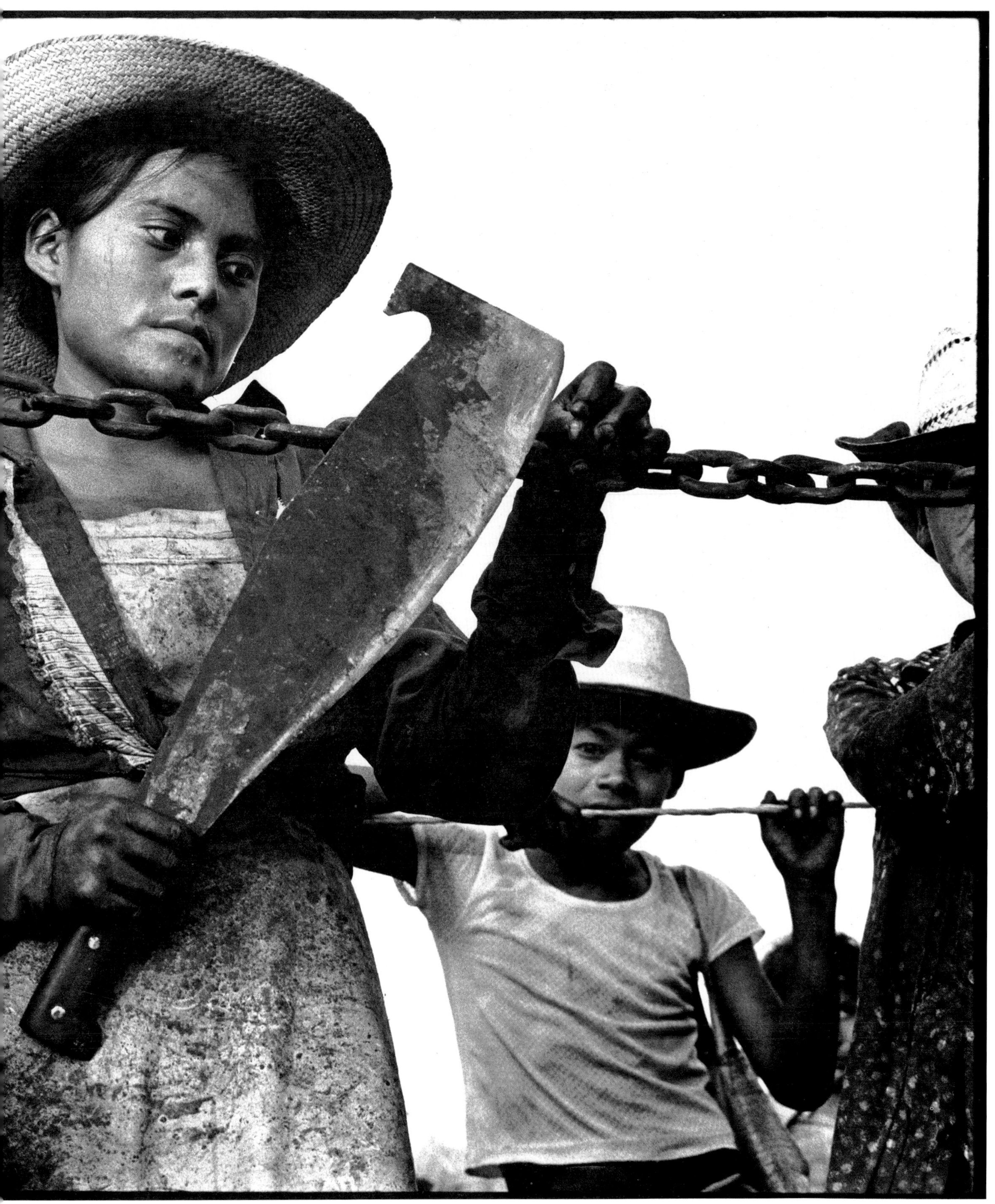

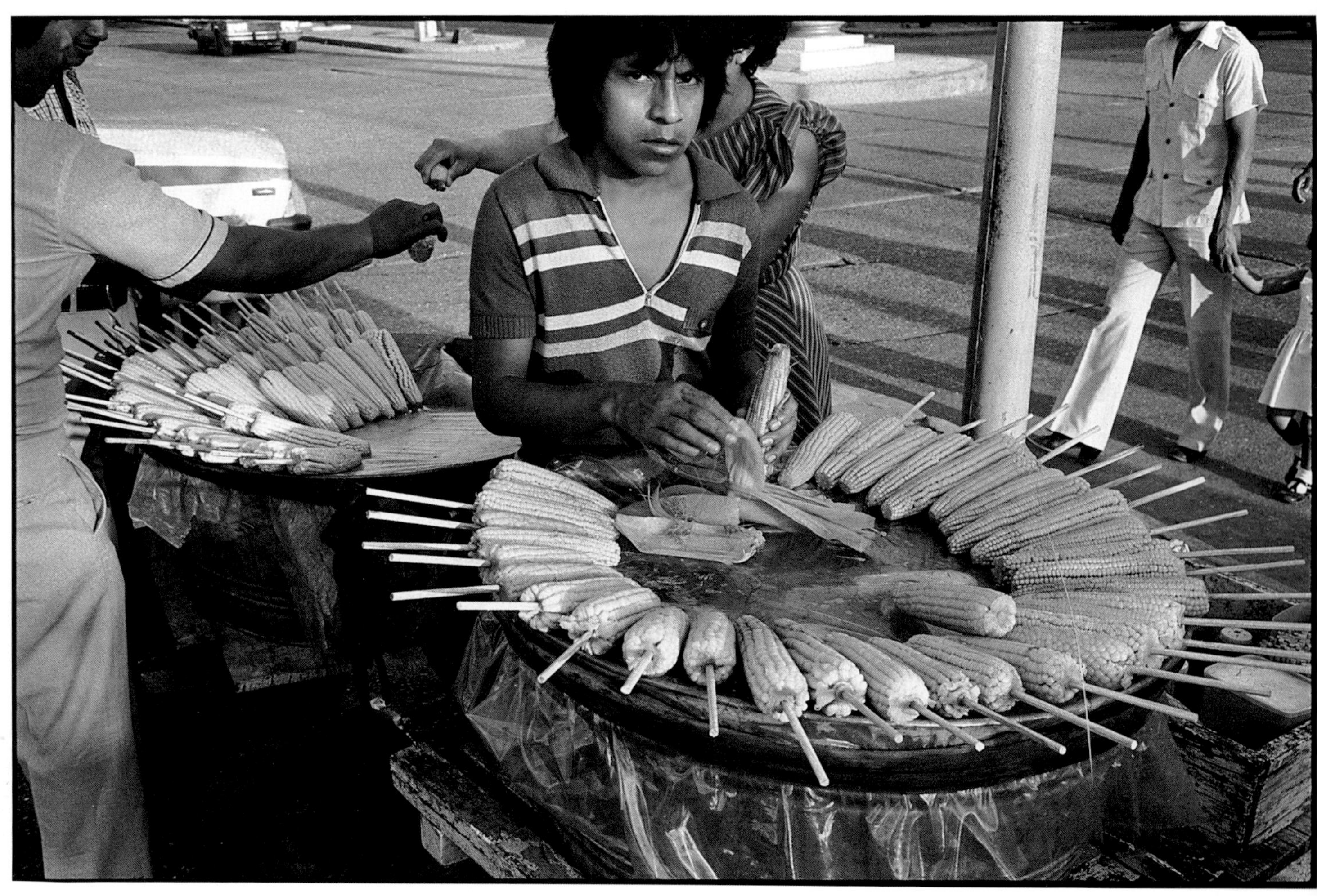

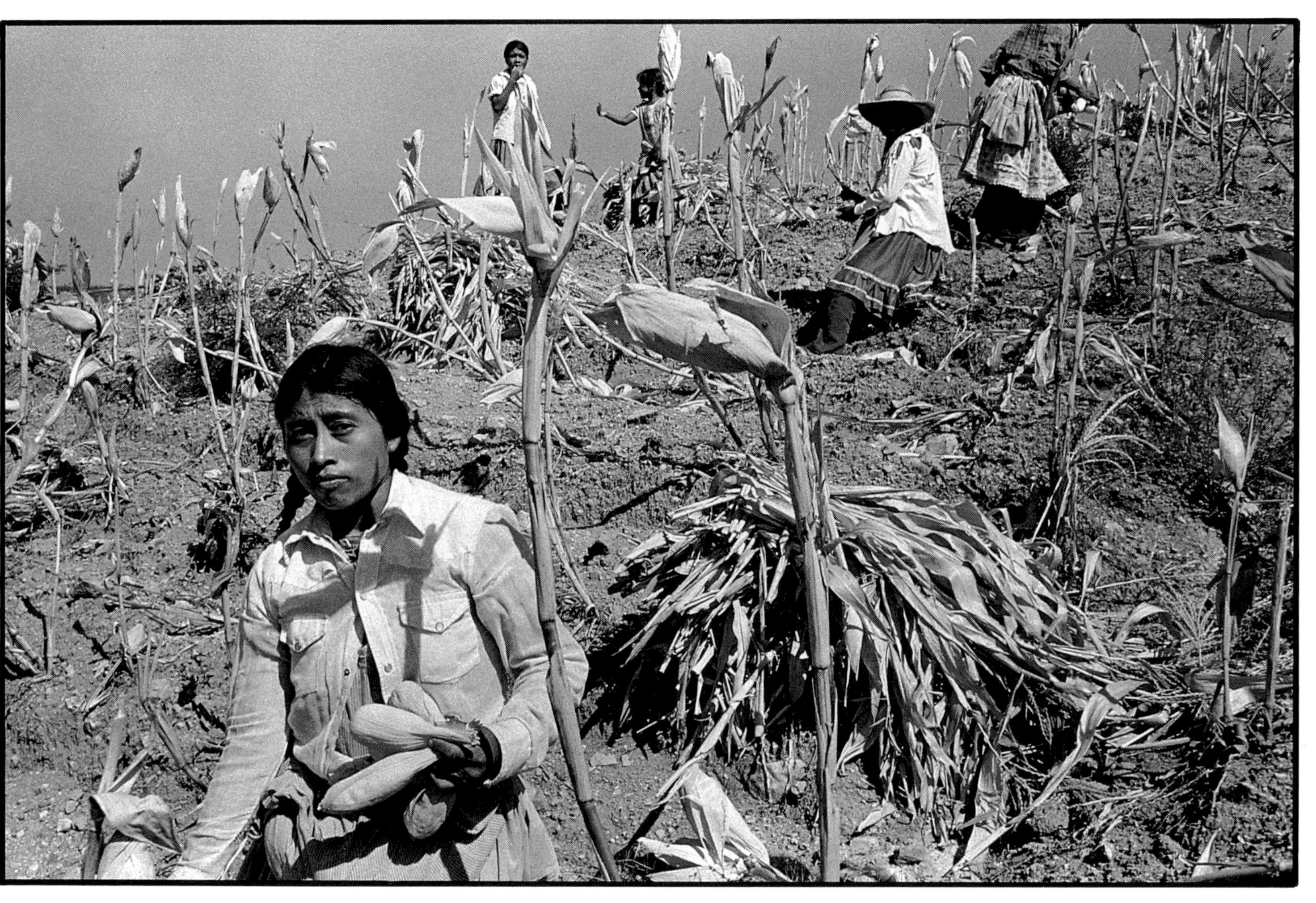

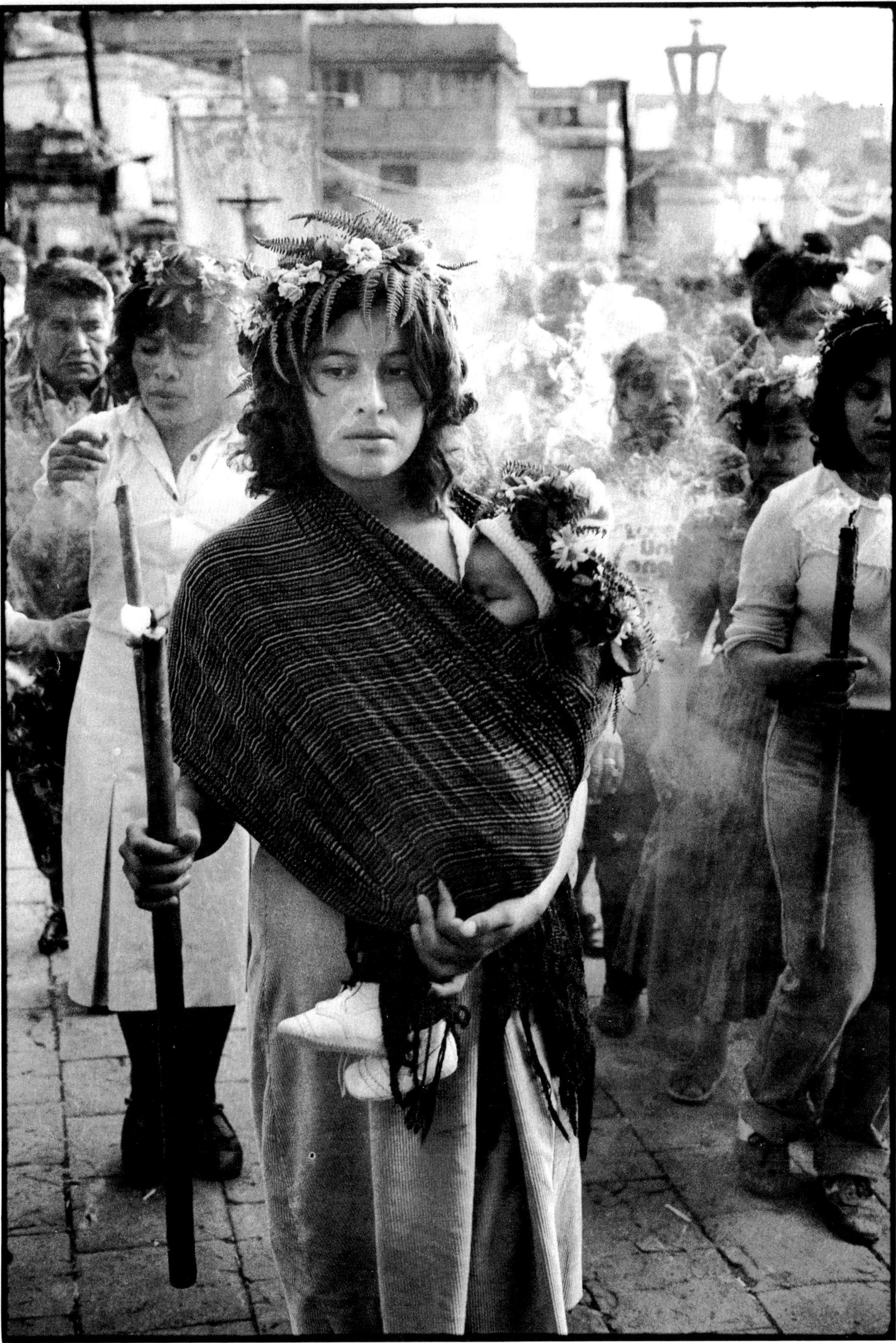

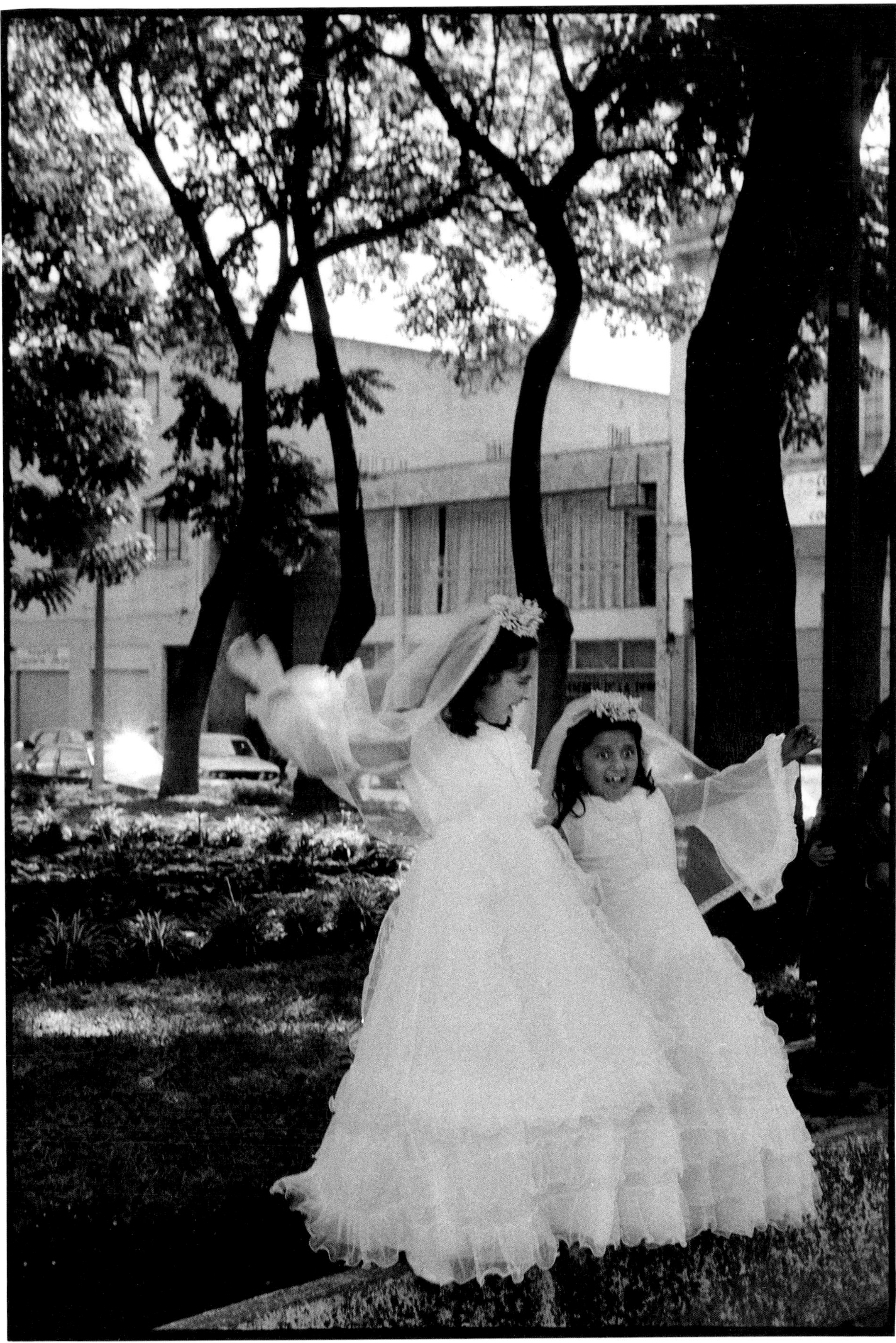

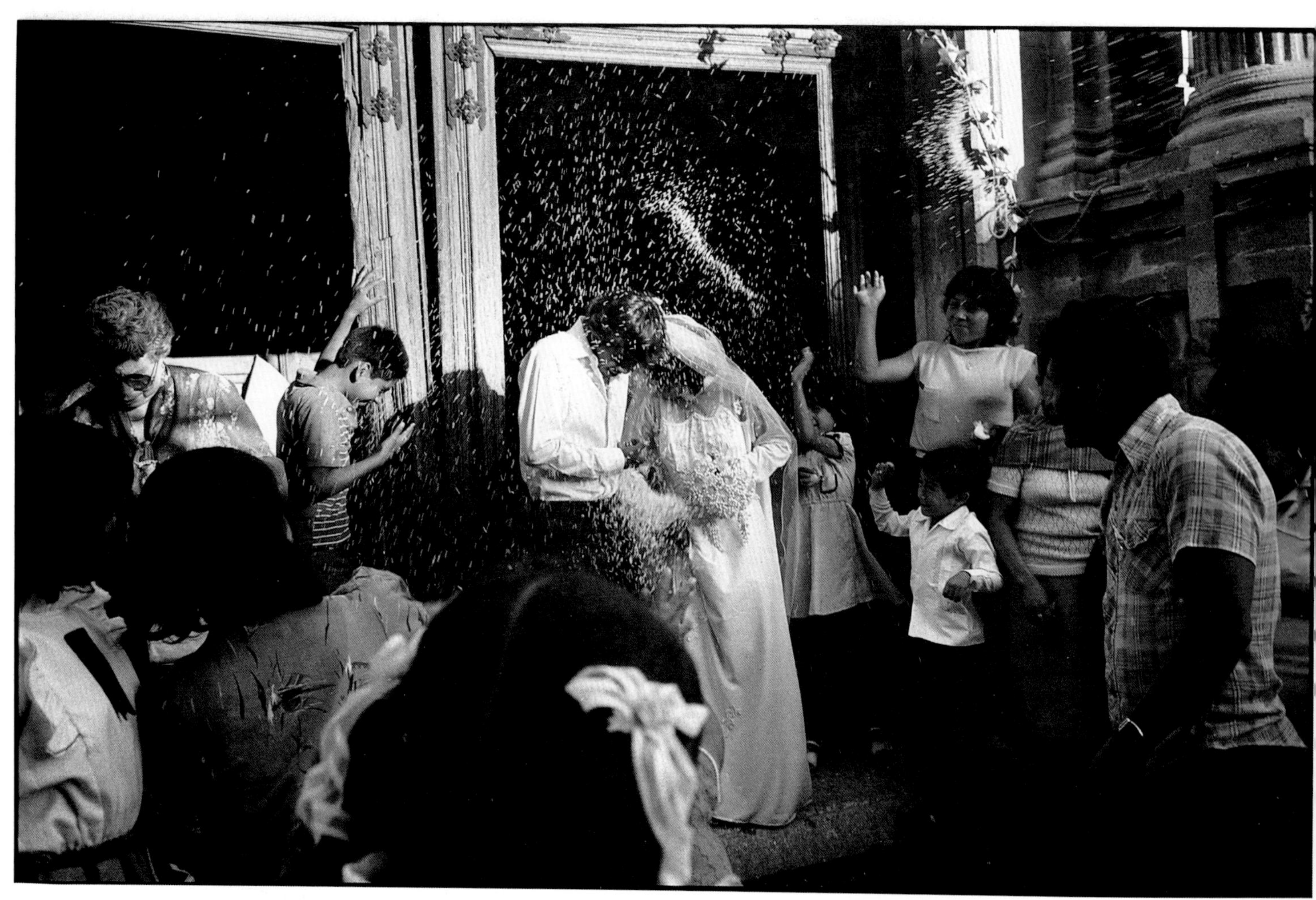

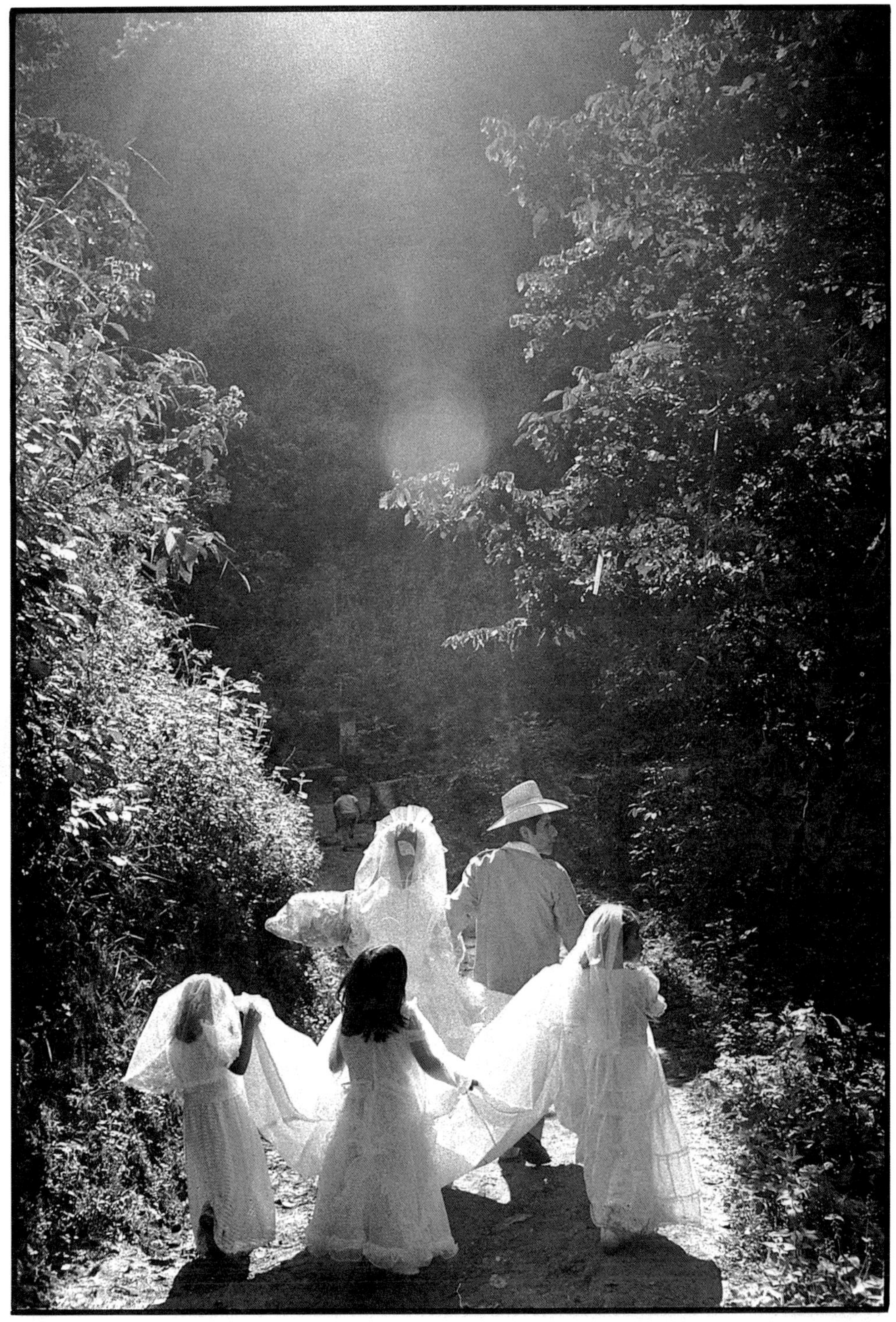

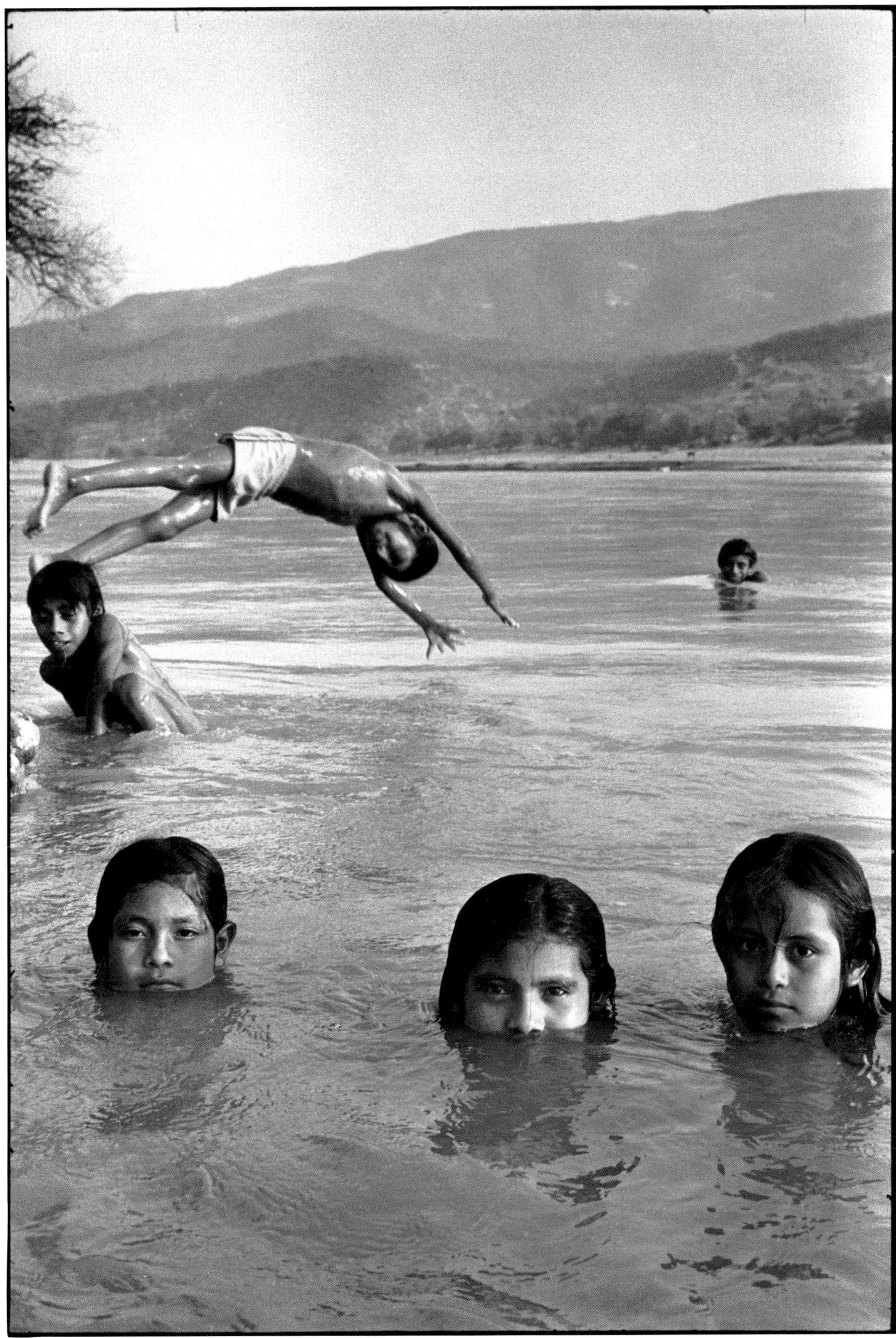

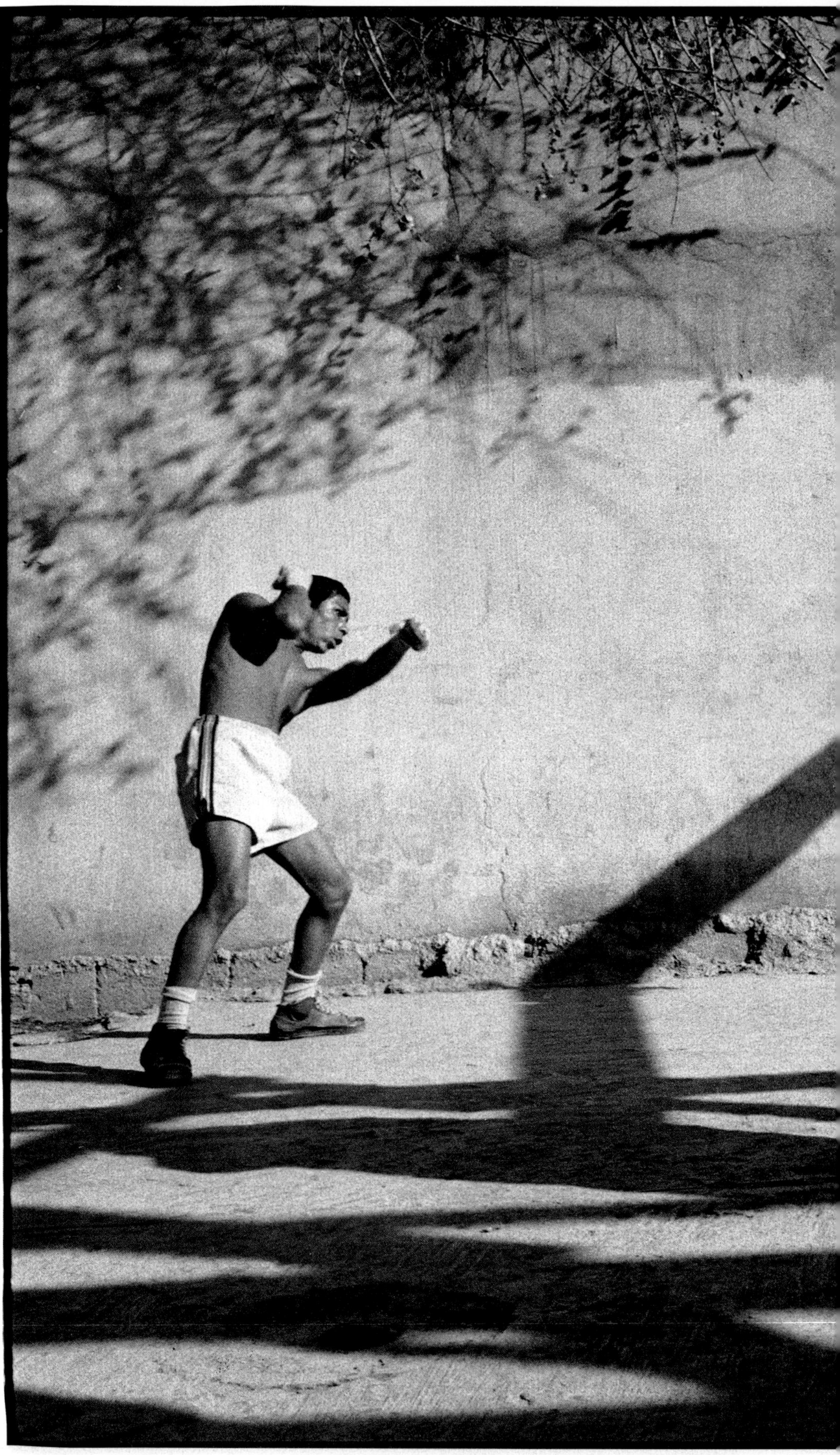

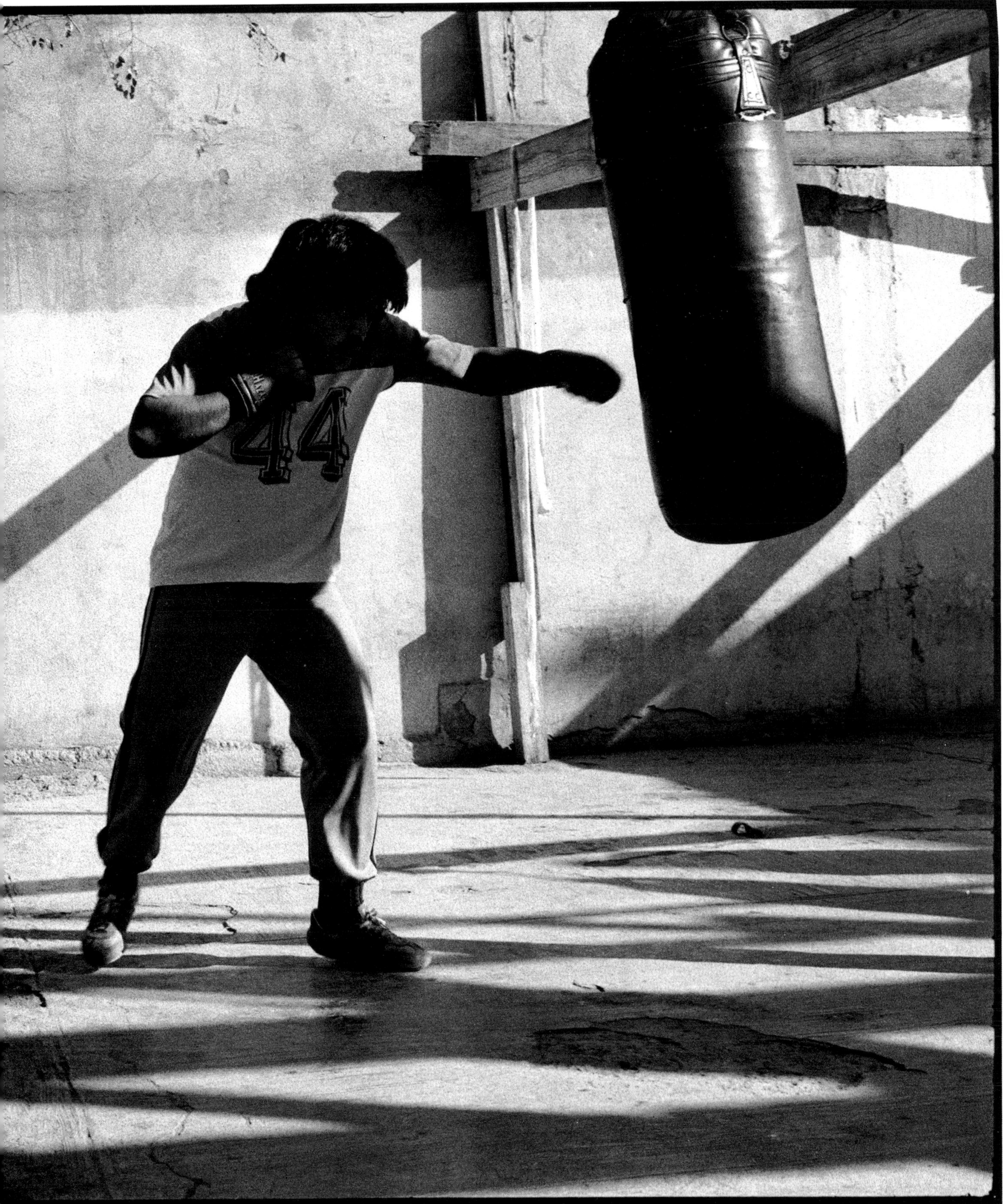
44

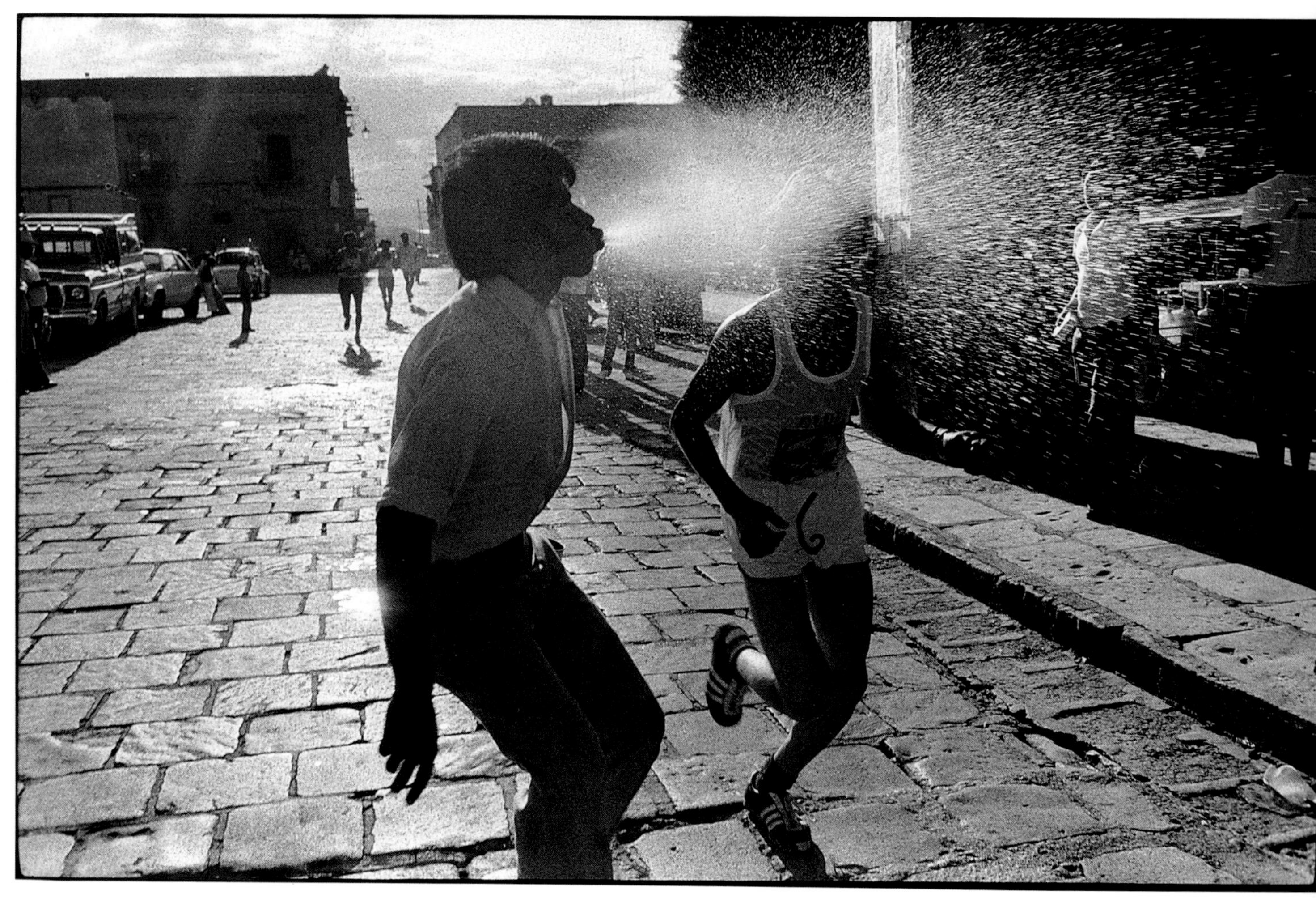

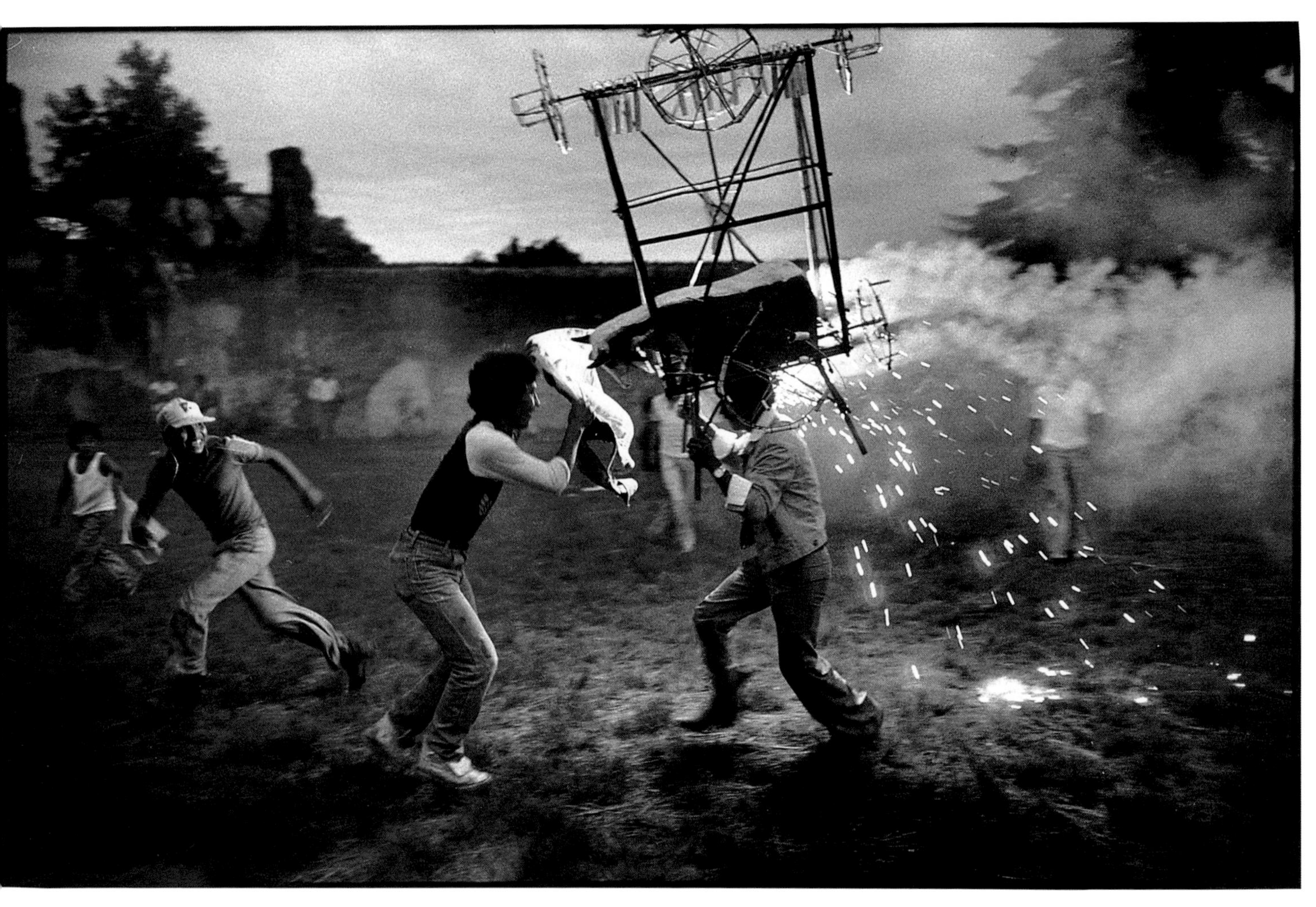

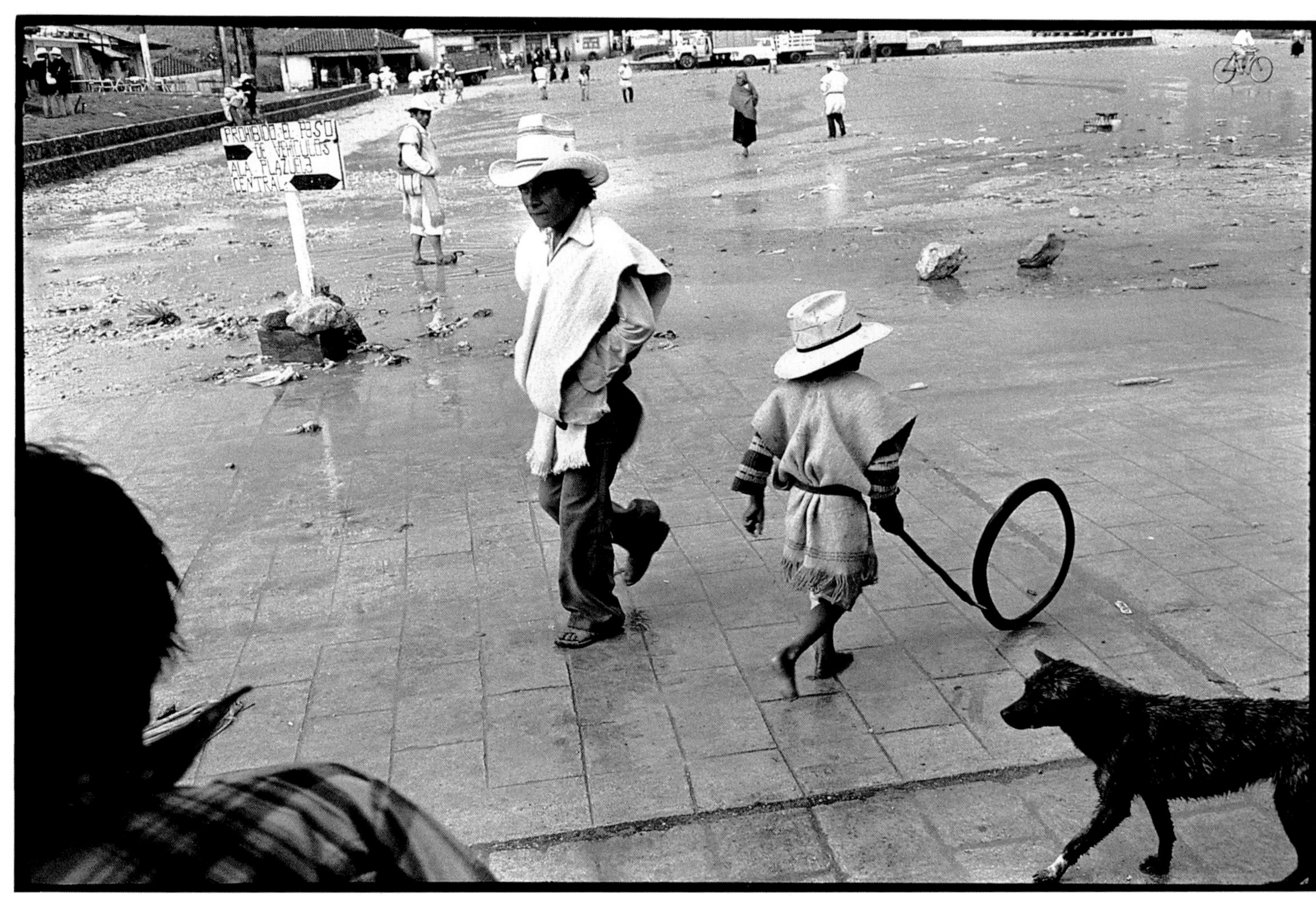
PROHIBIDO EL PASO
DE VEHICULOS
ALA PLAZUELA
CENTRAL

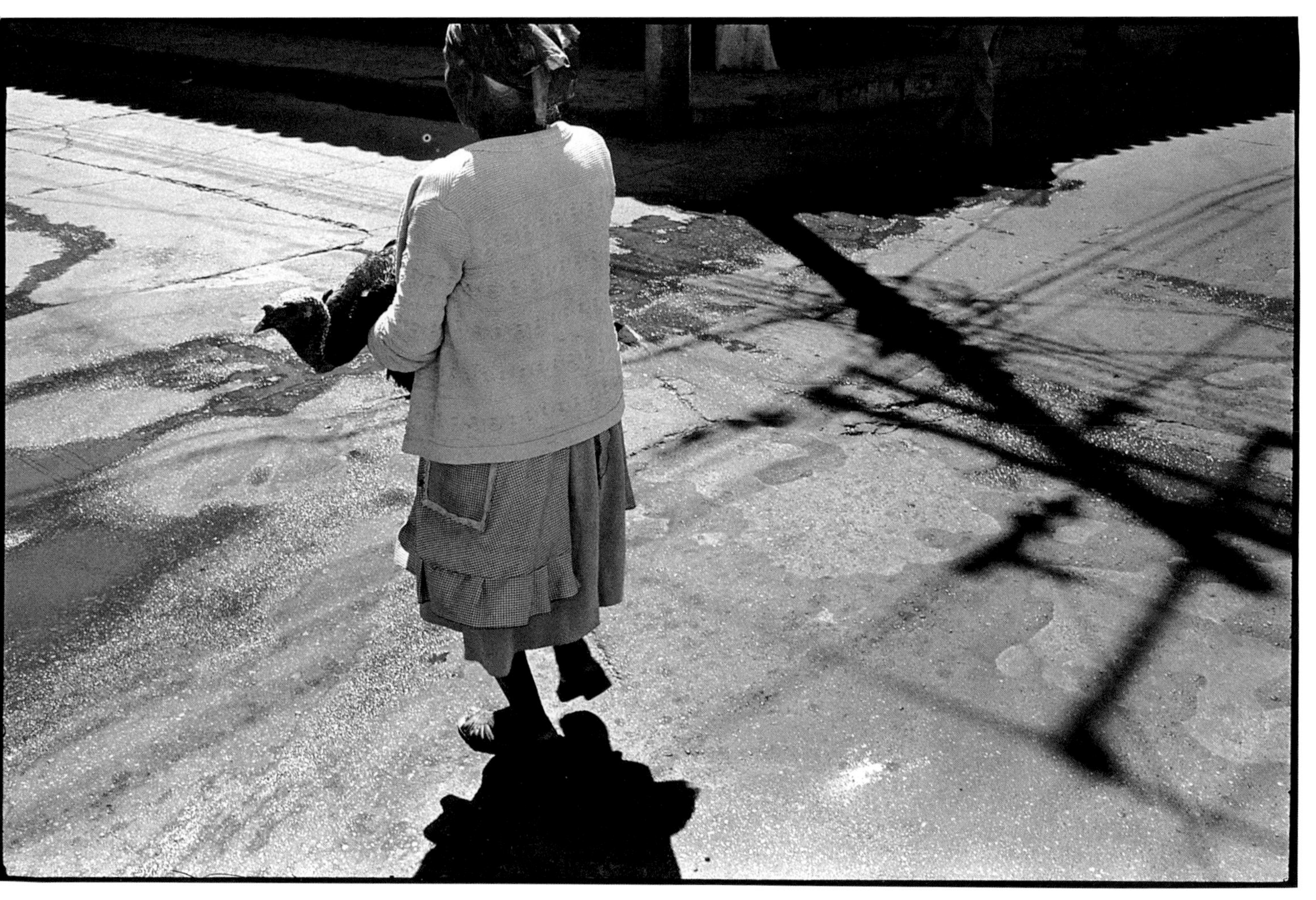

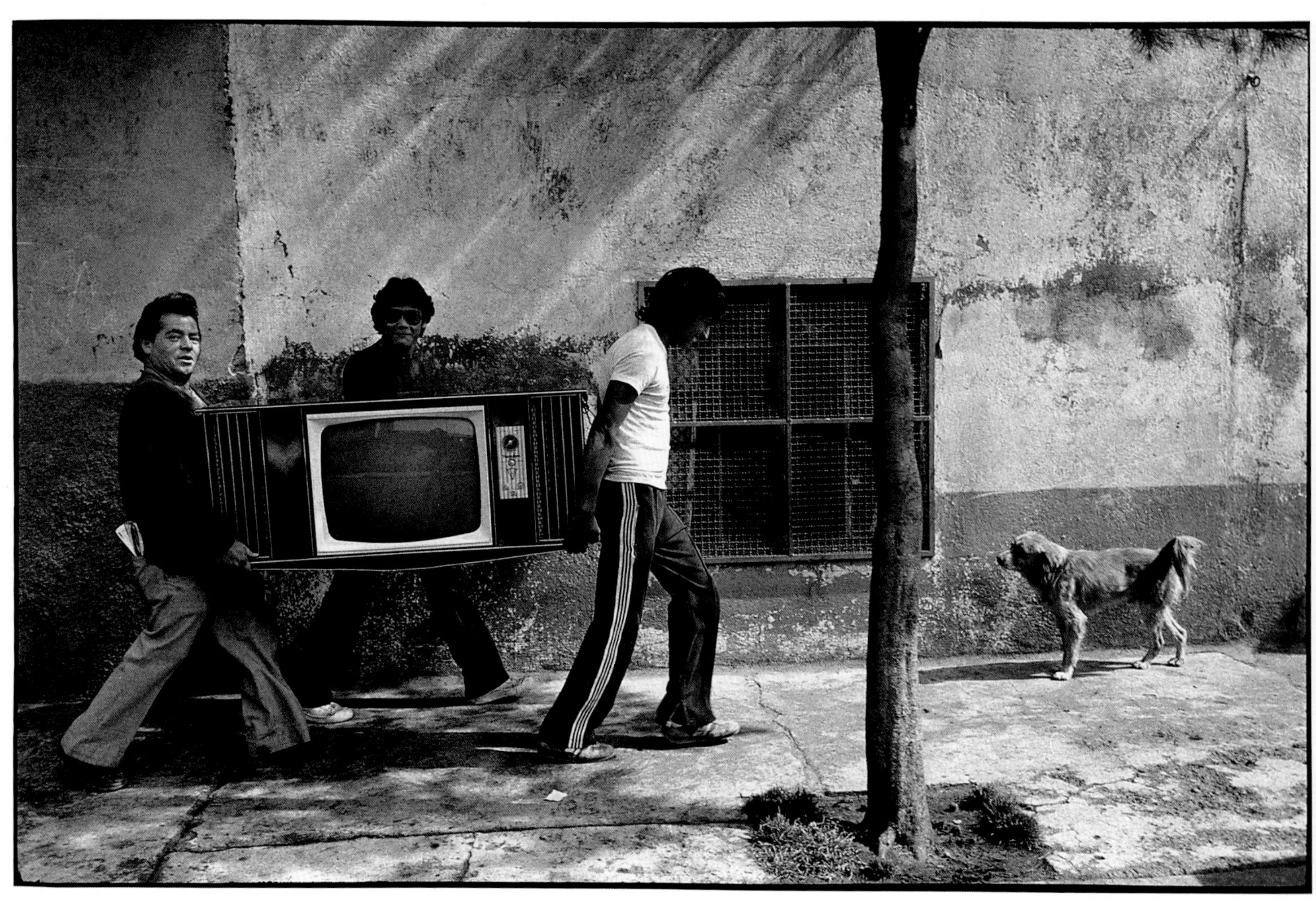

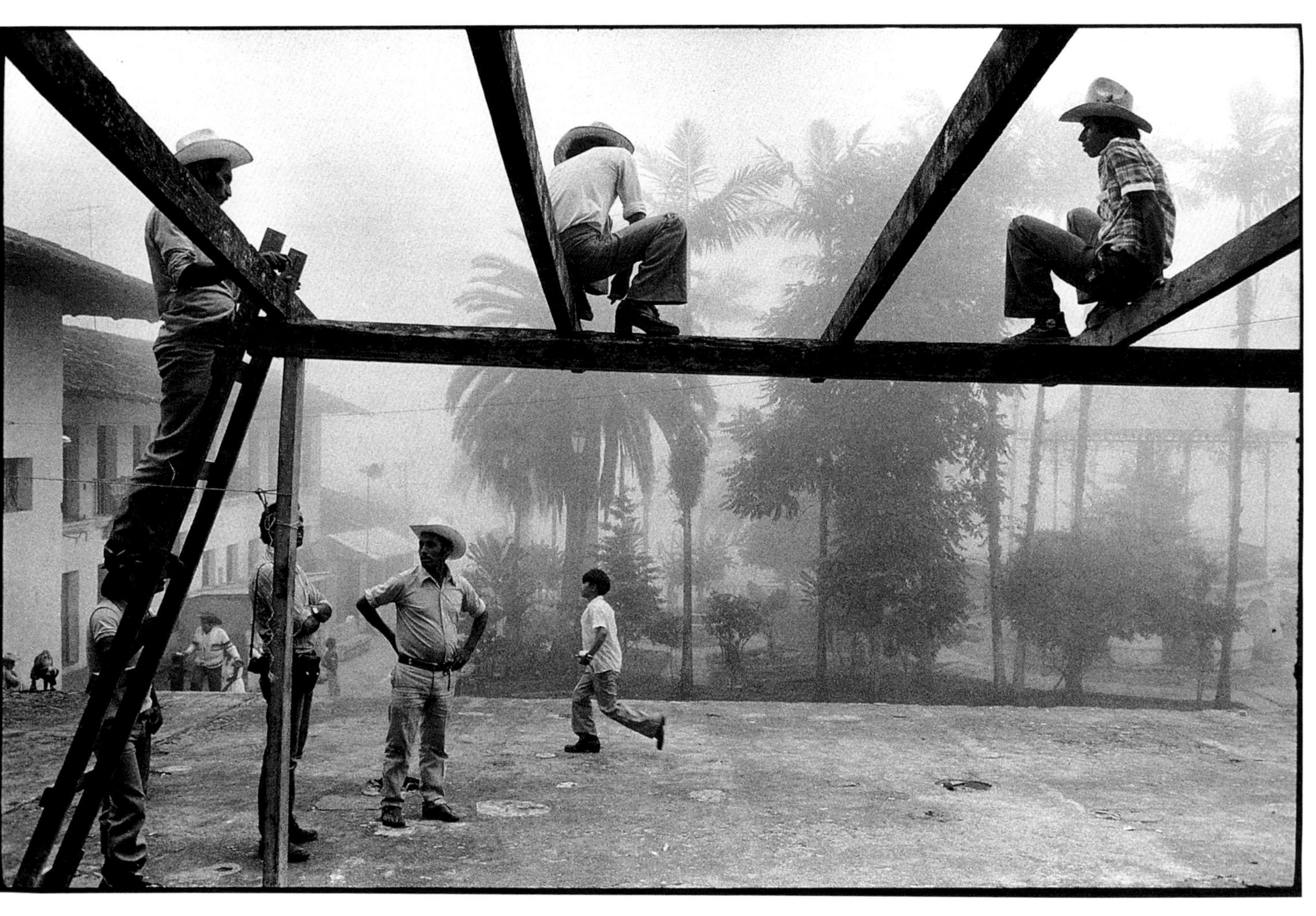

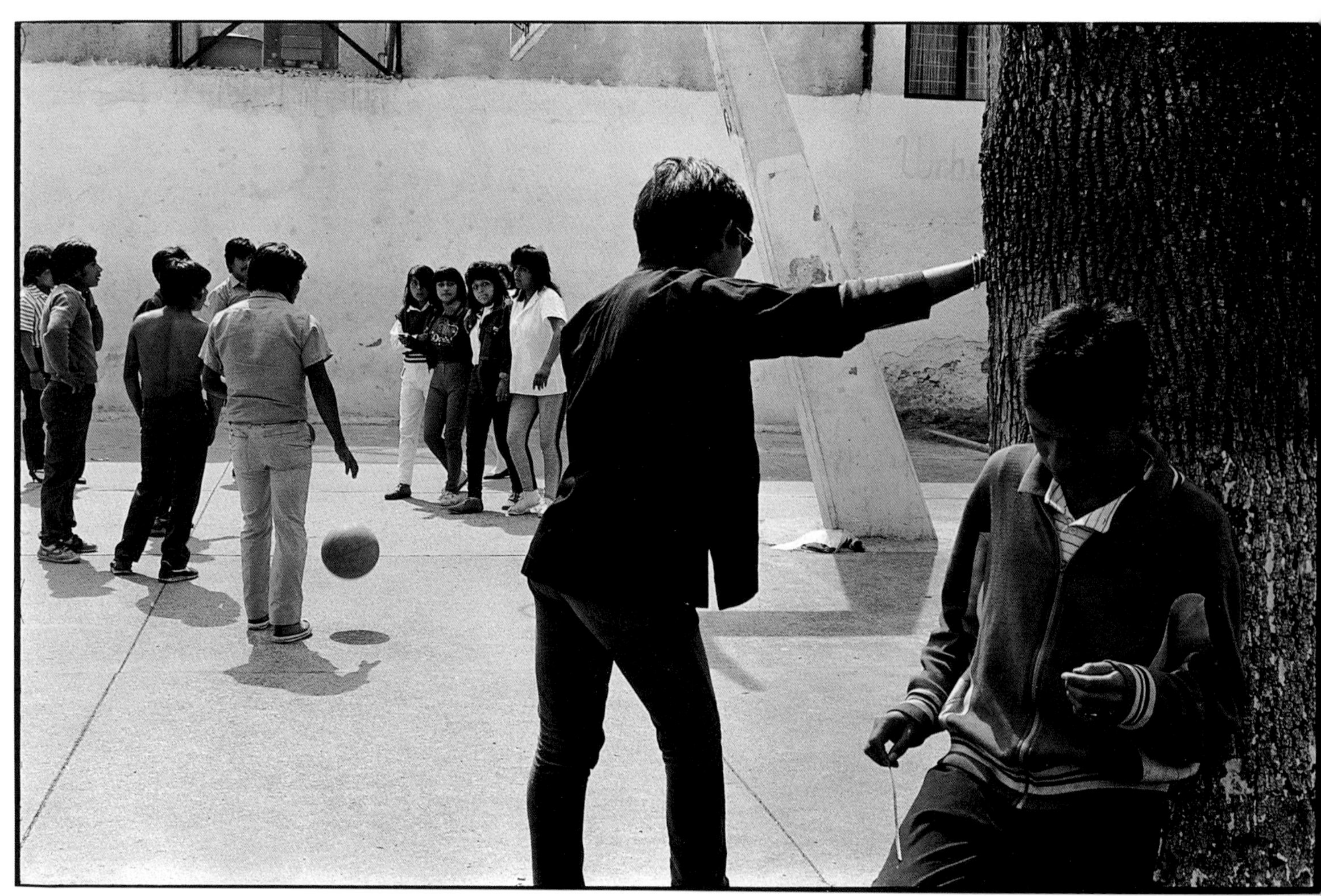

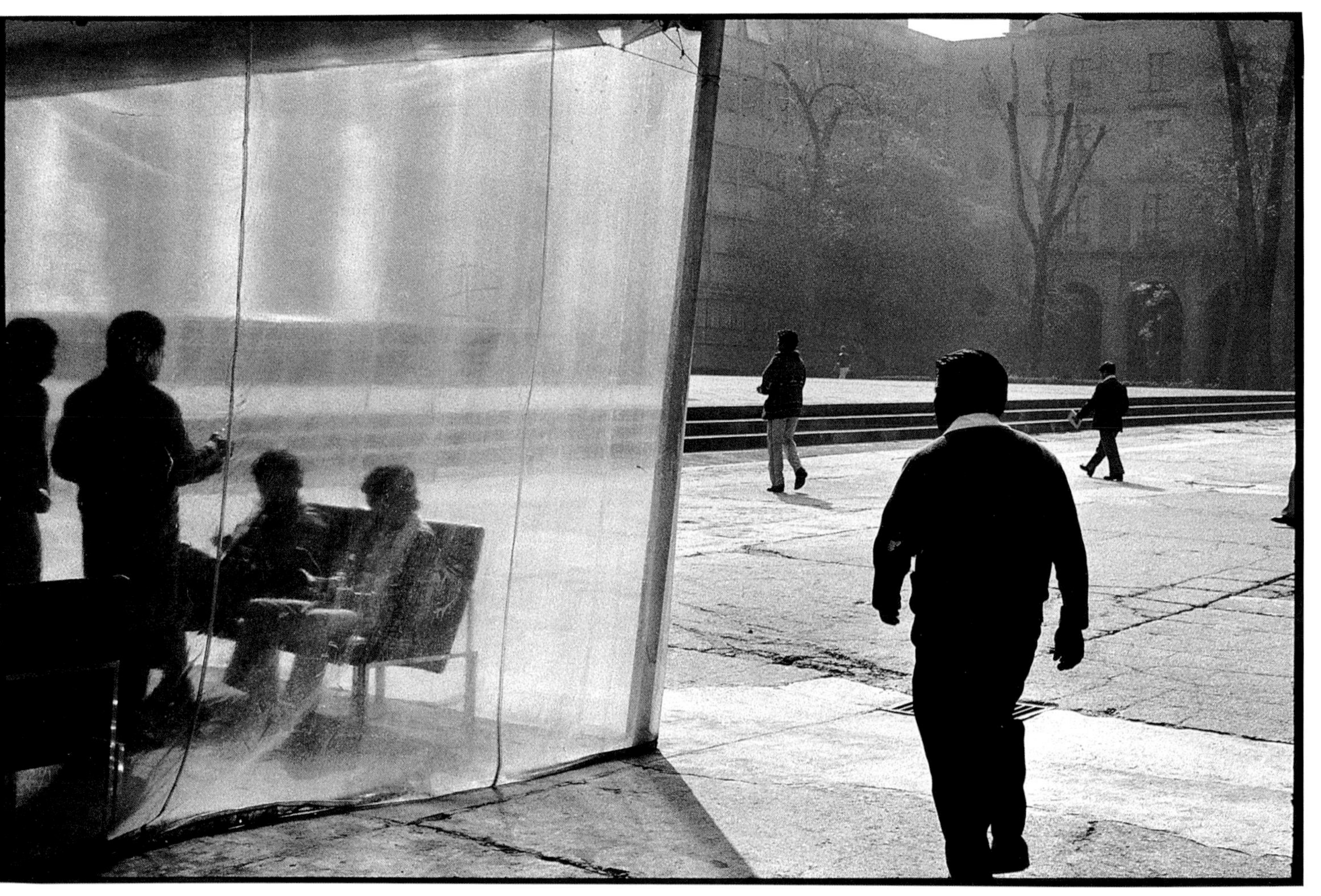

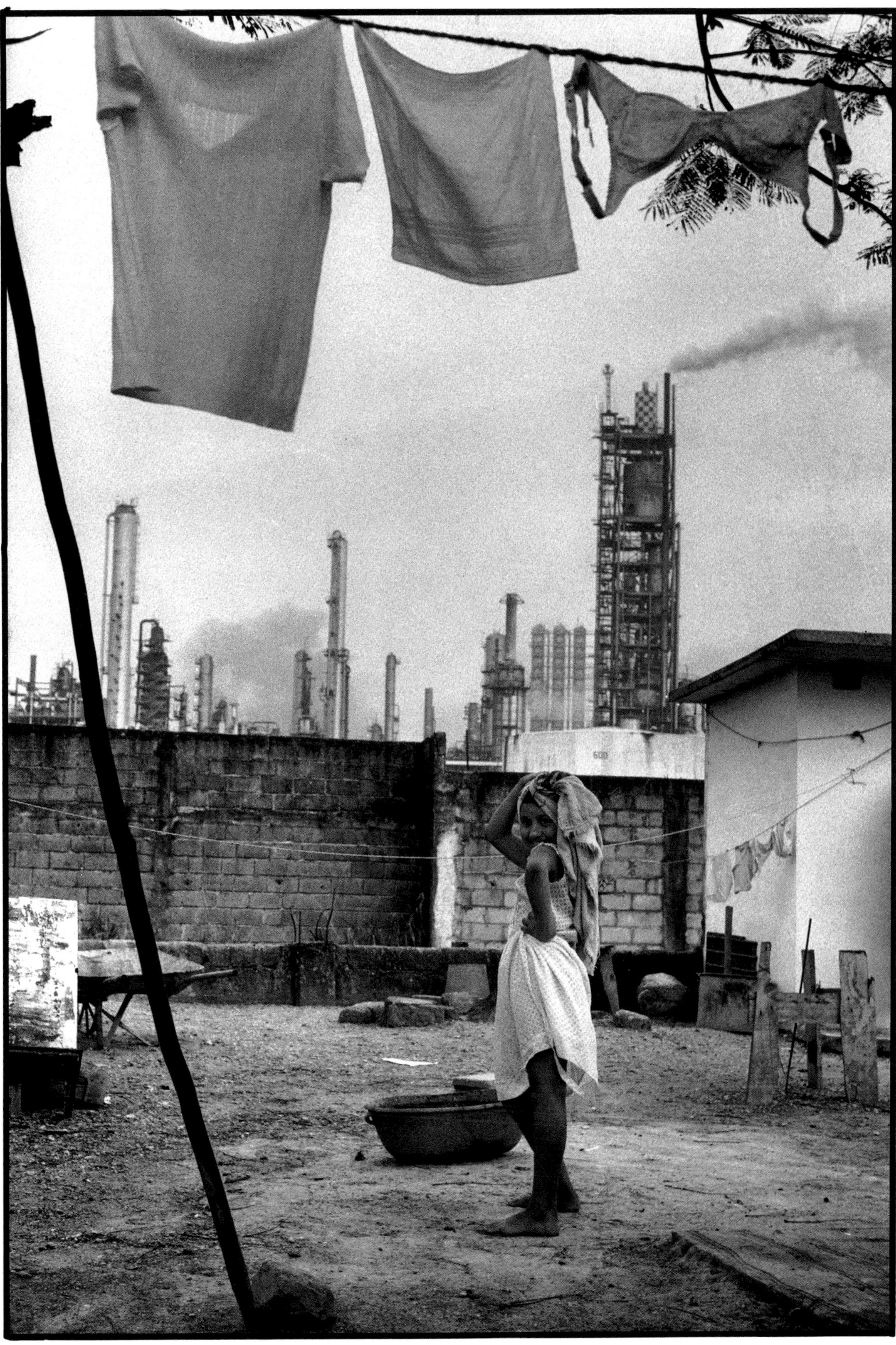
500

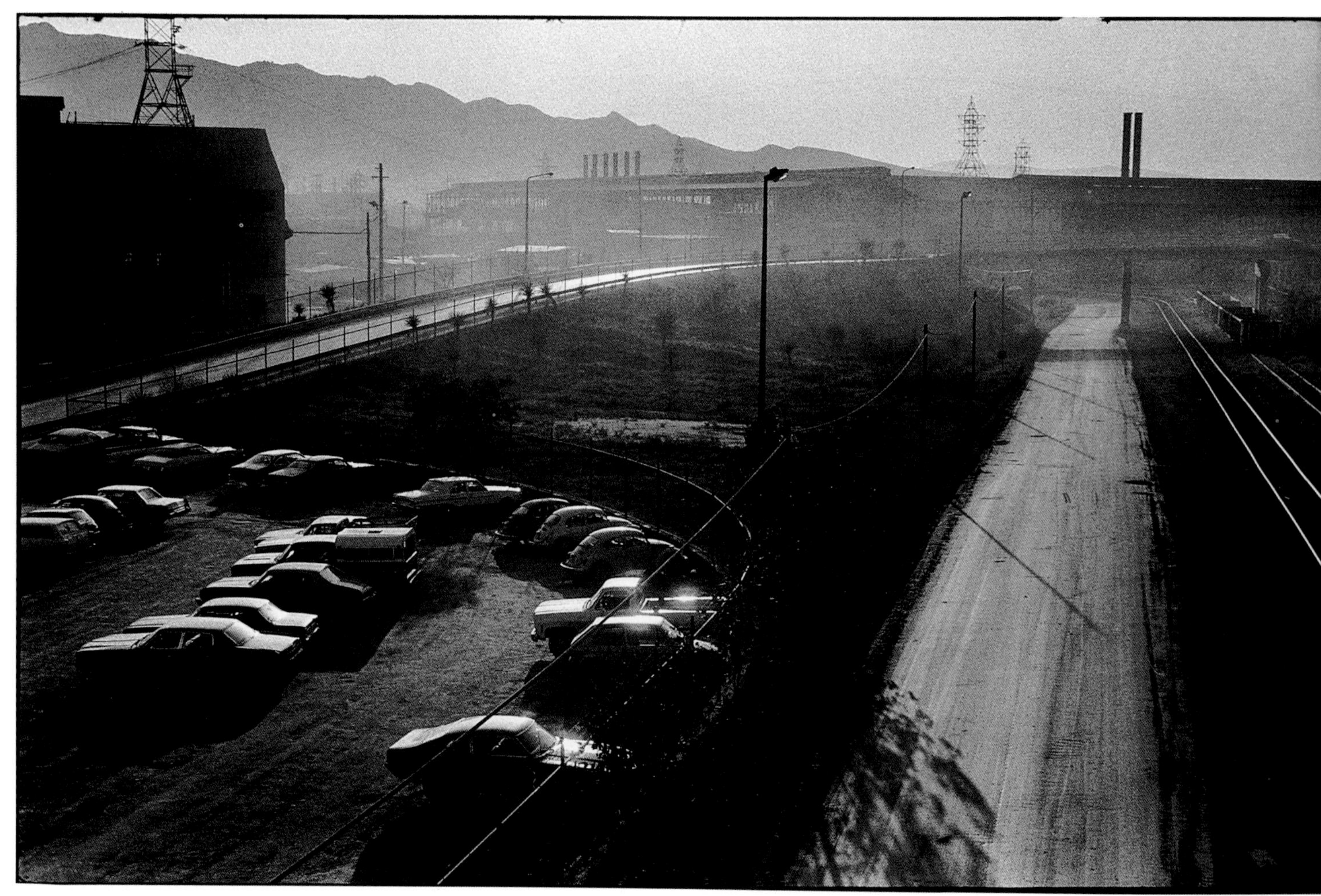

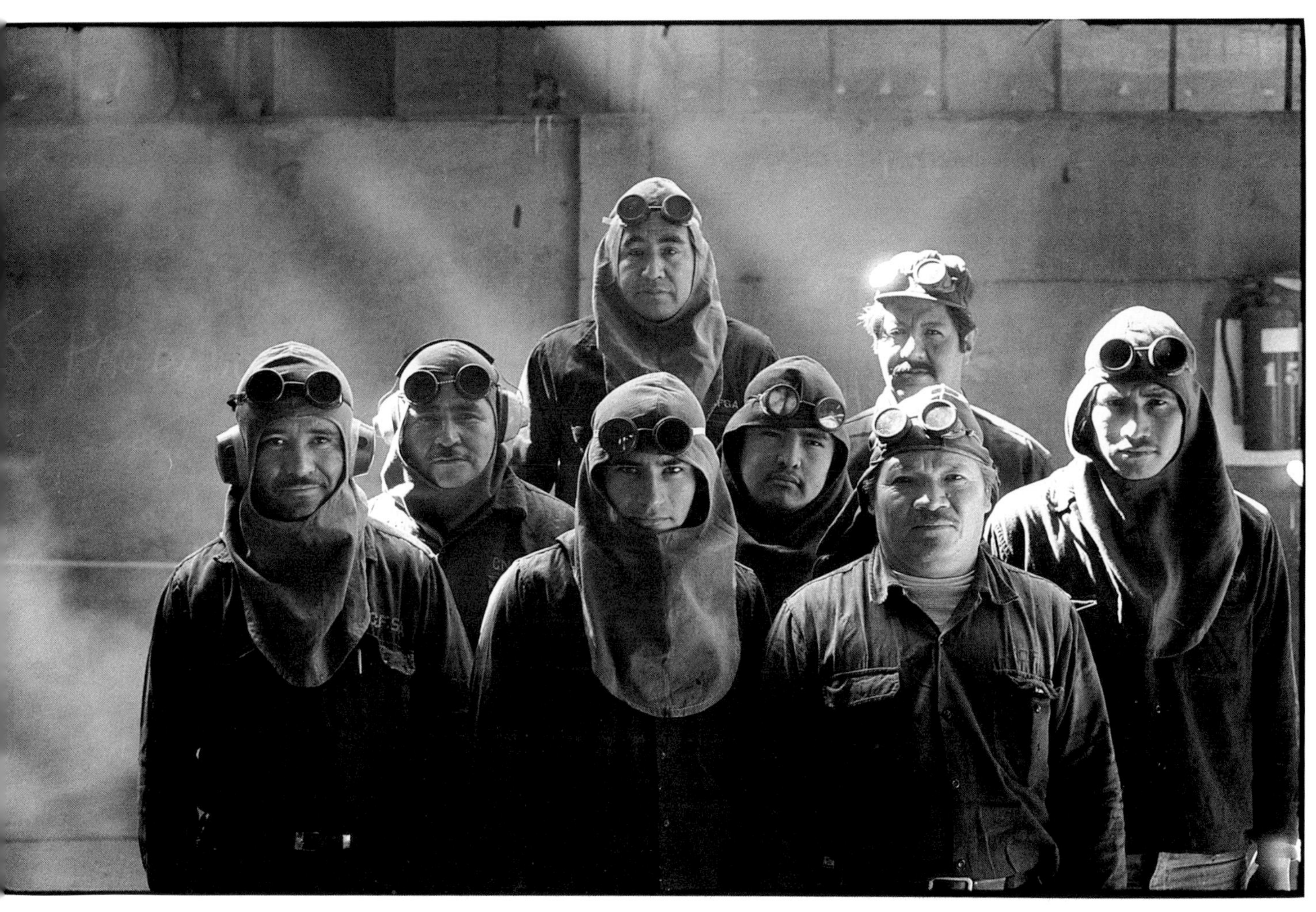

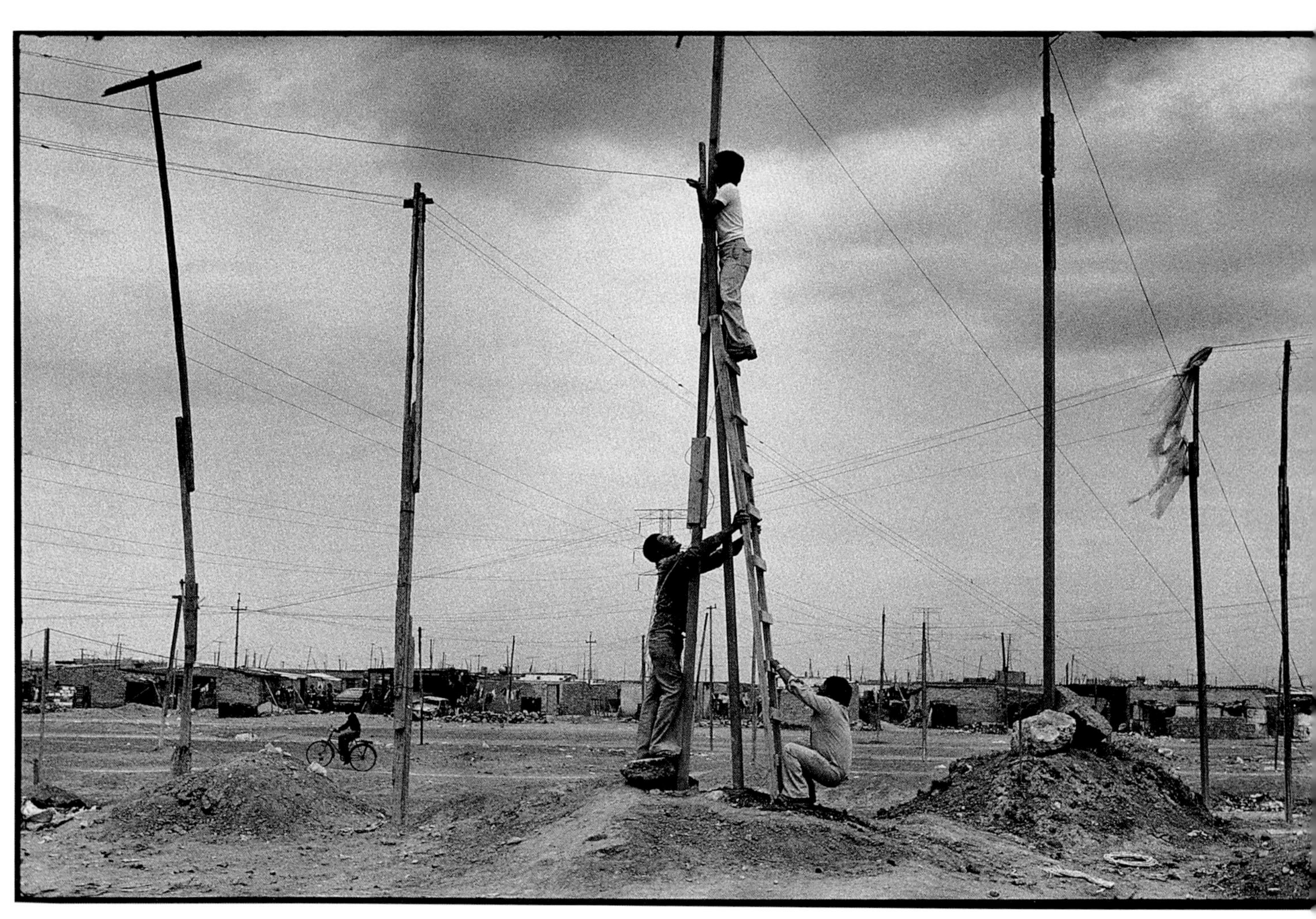

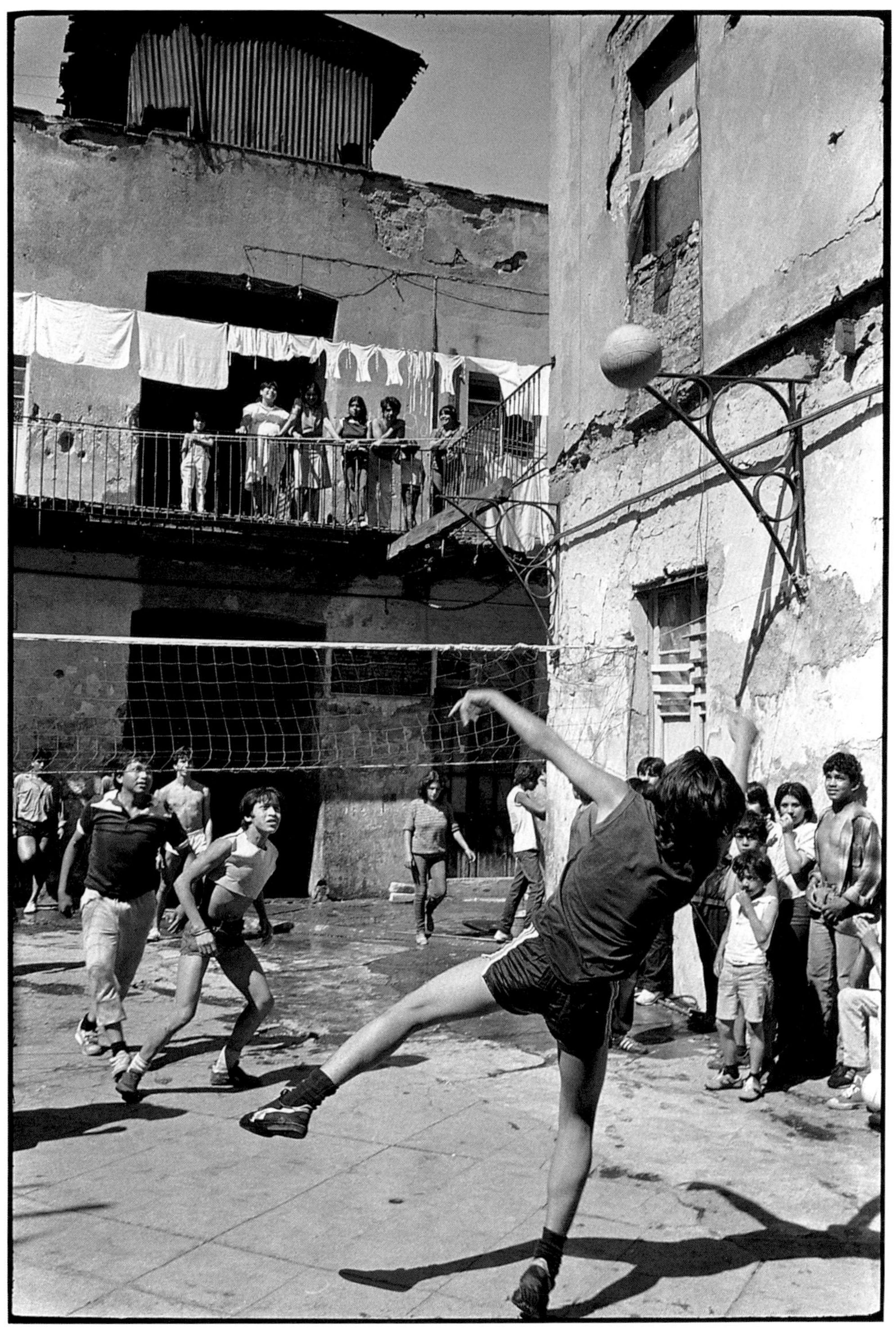

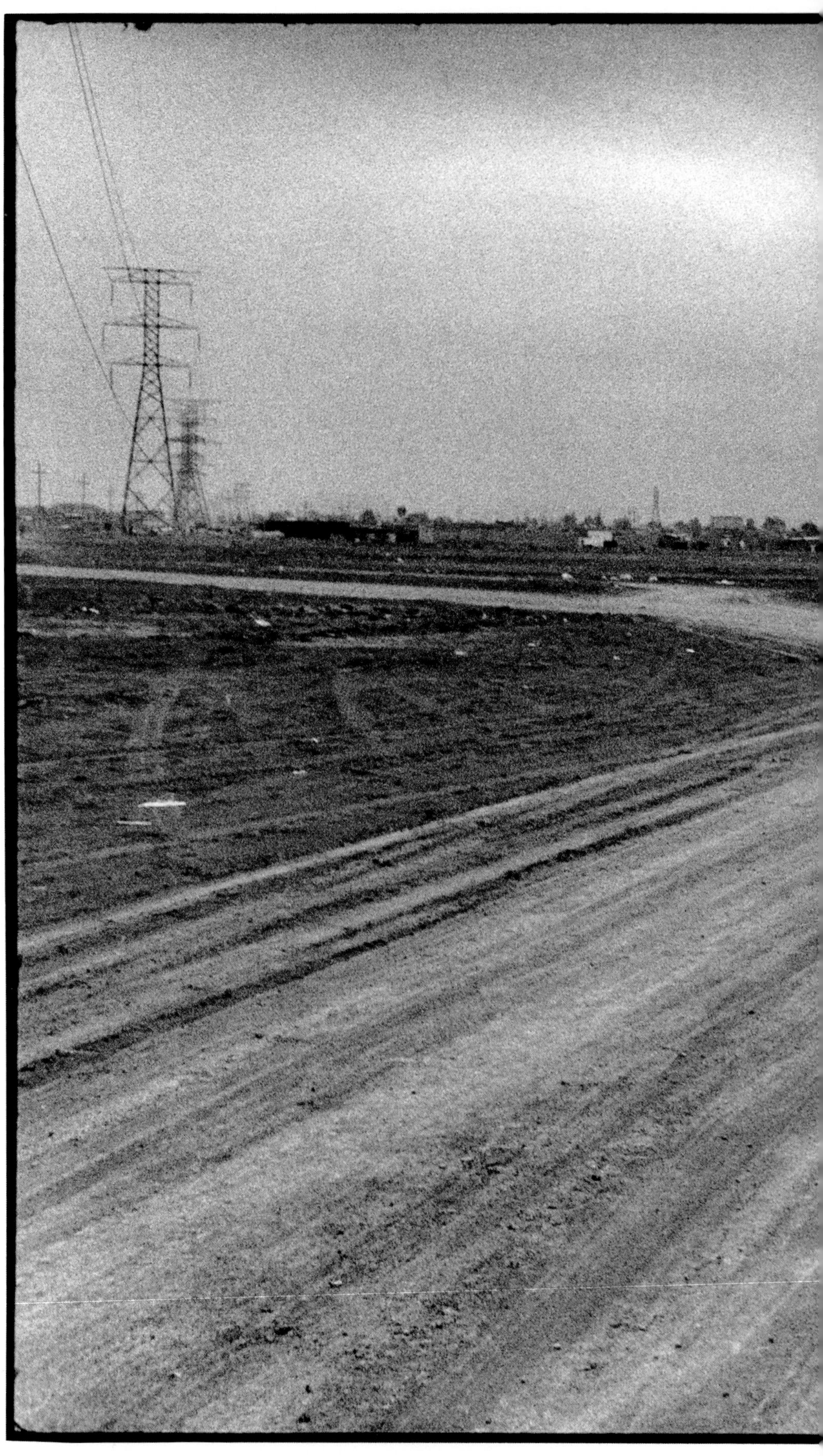

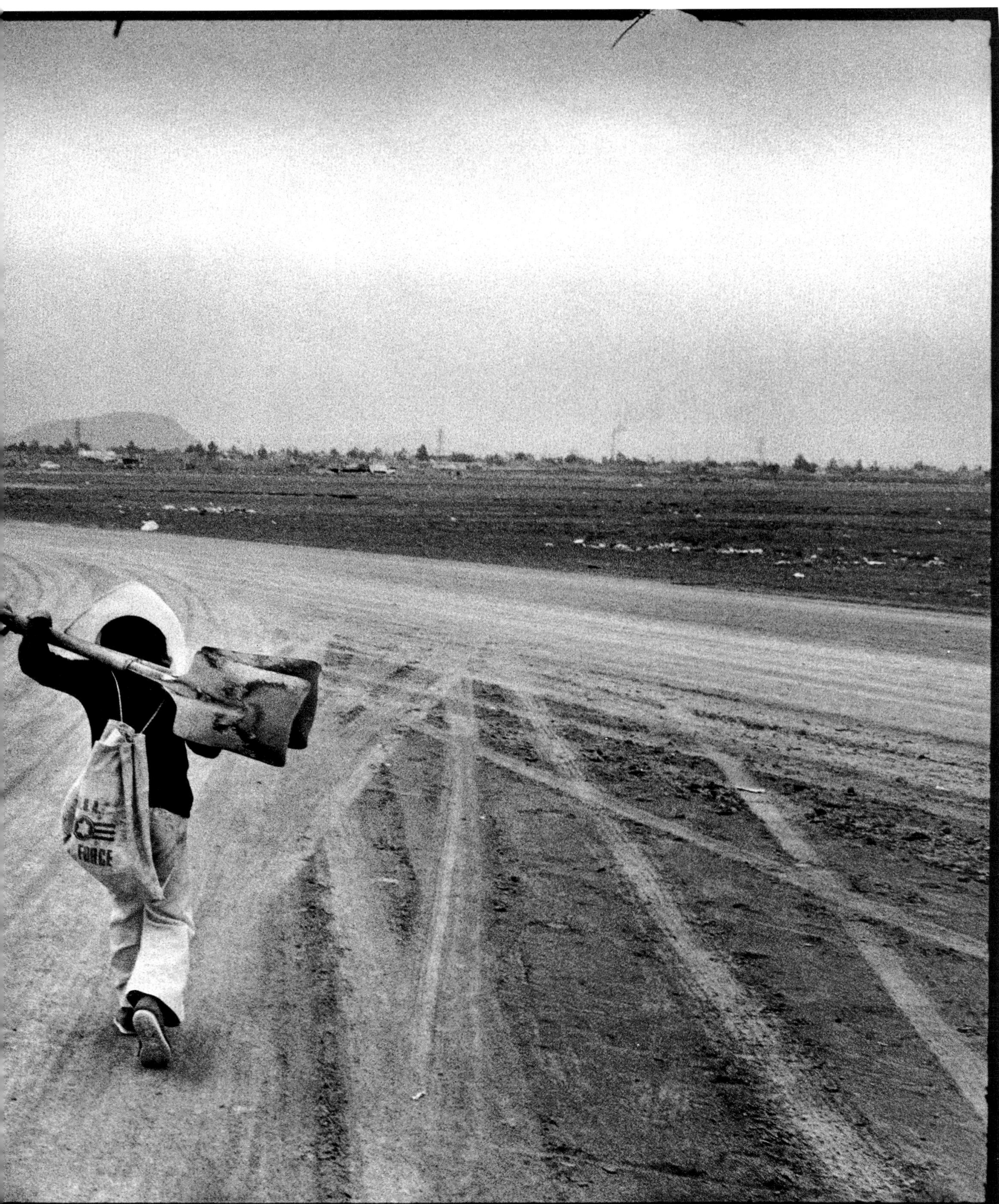
FORCE

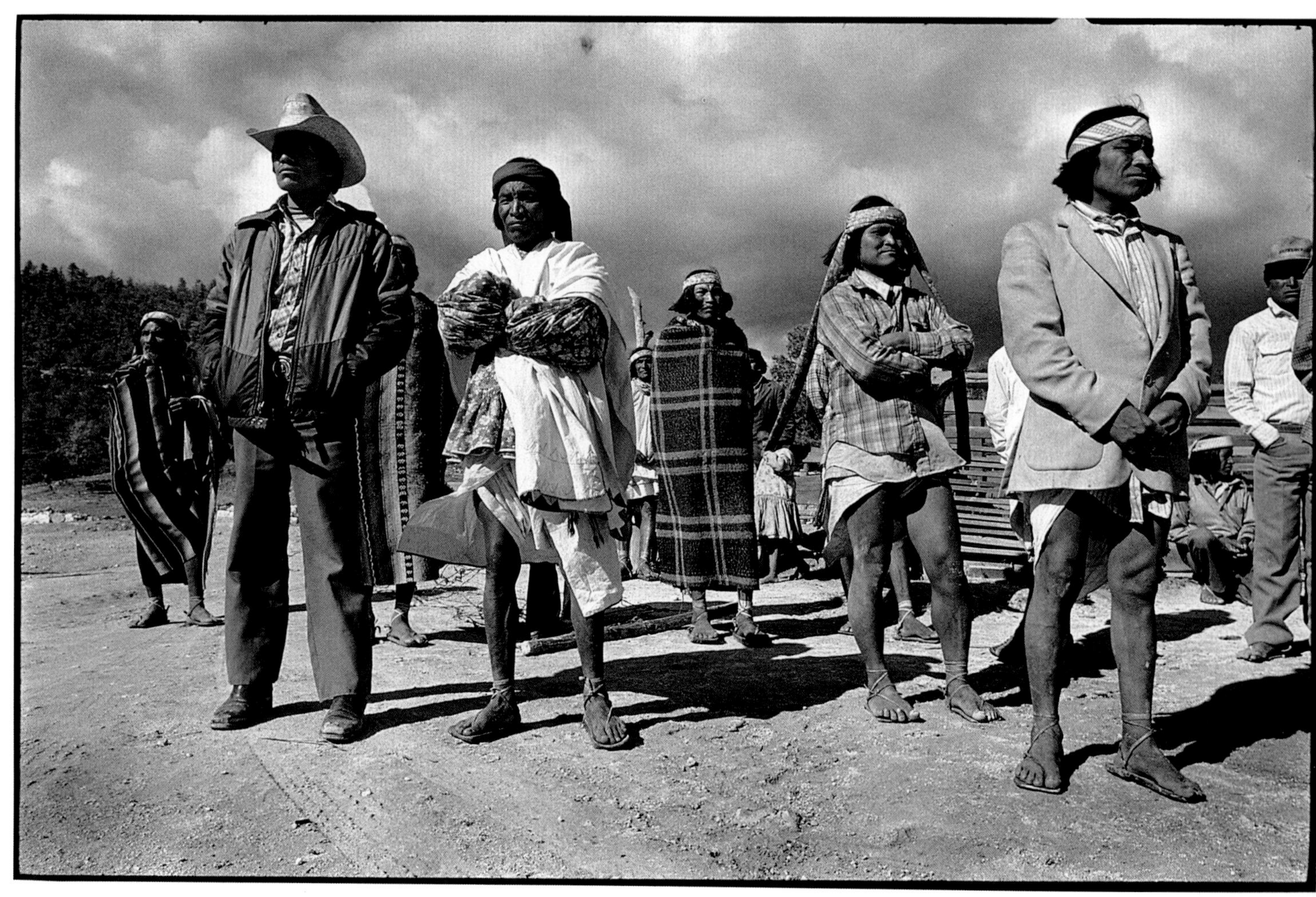

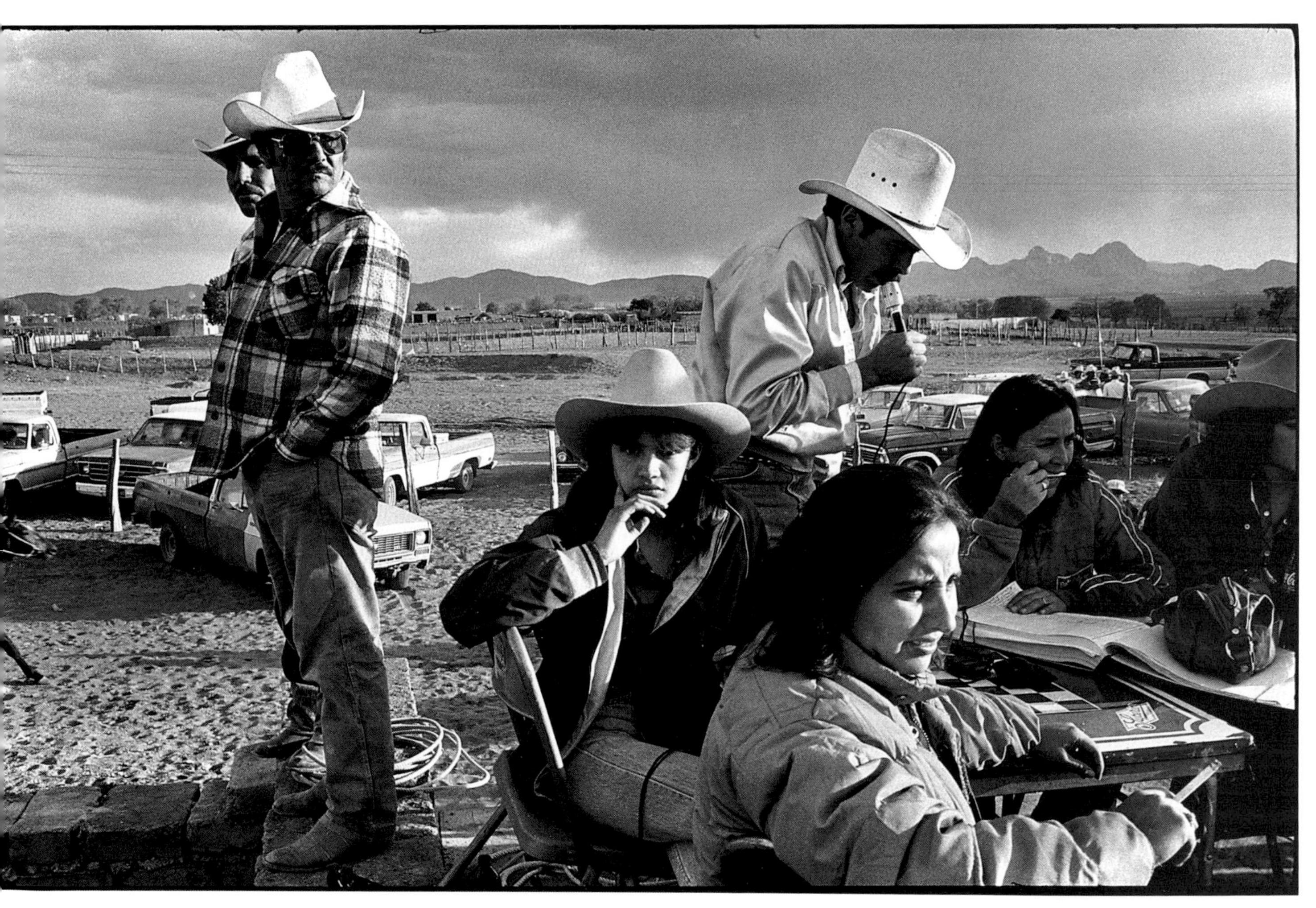

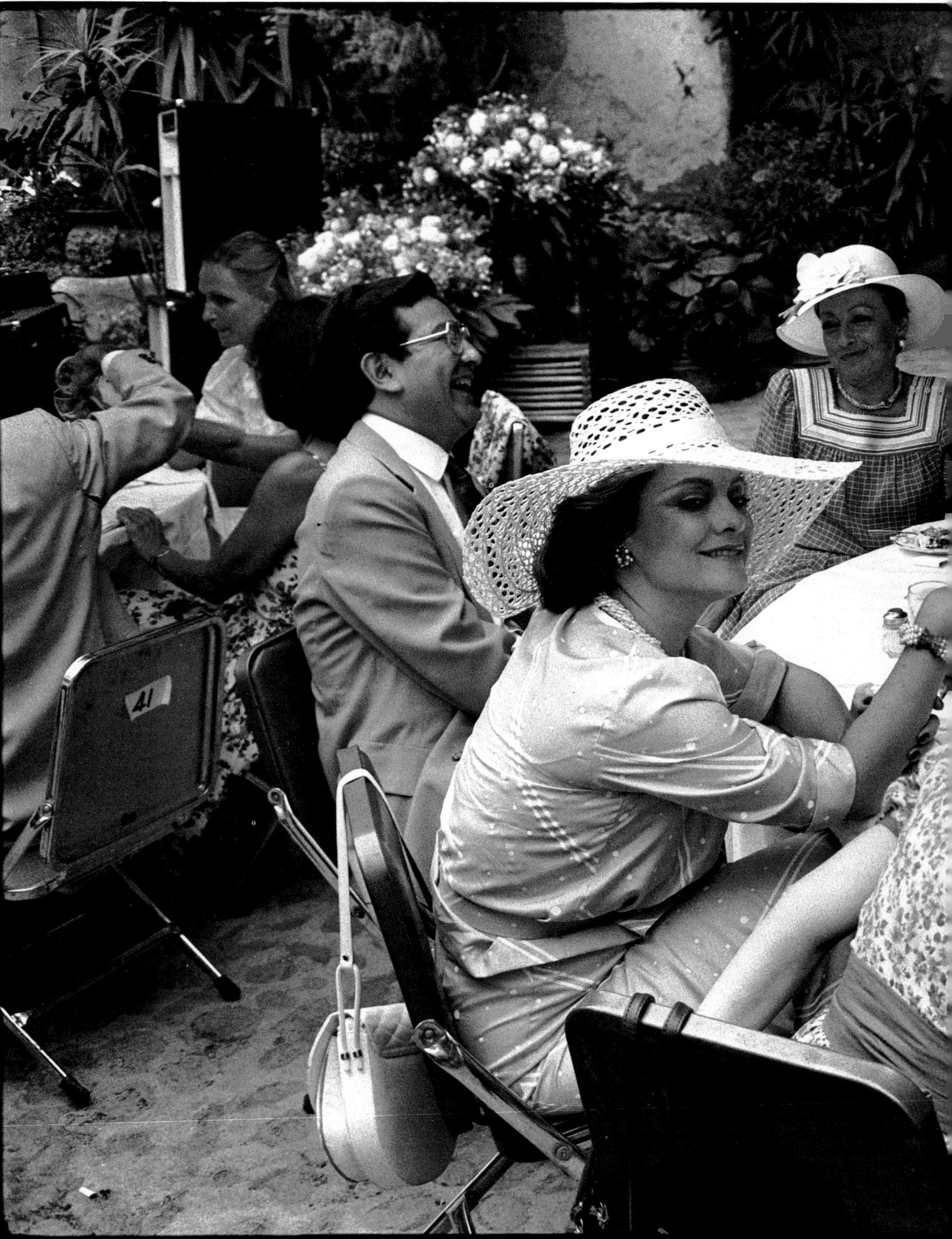
41

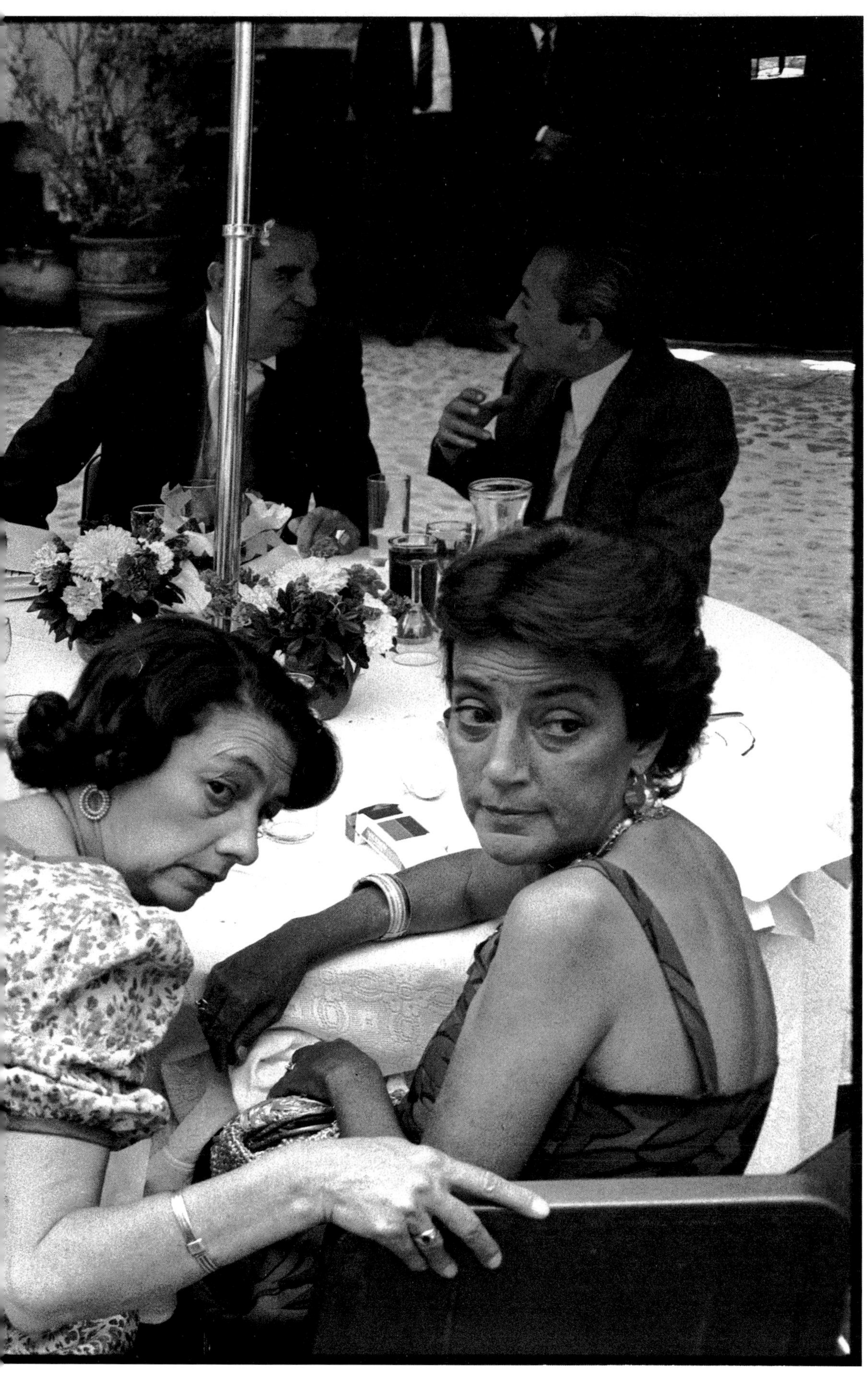

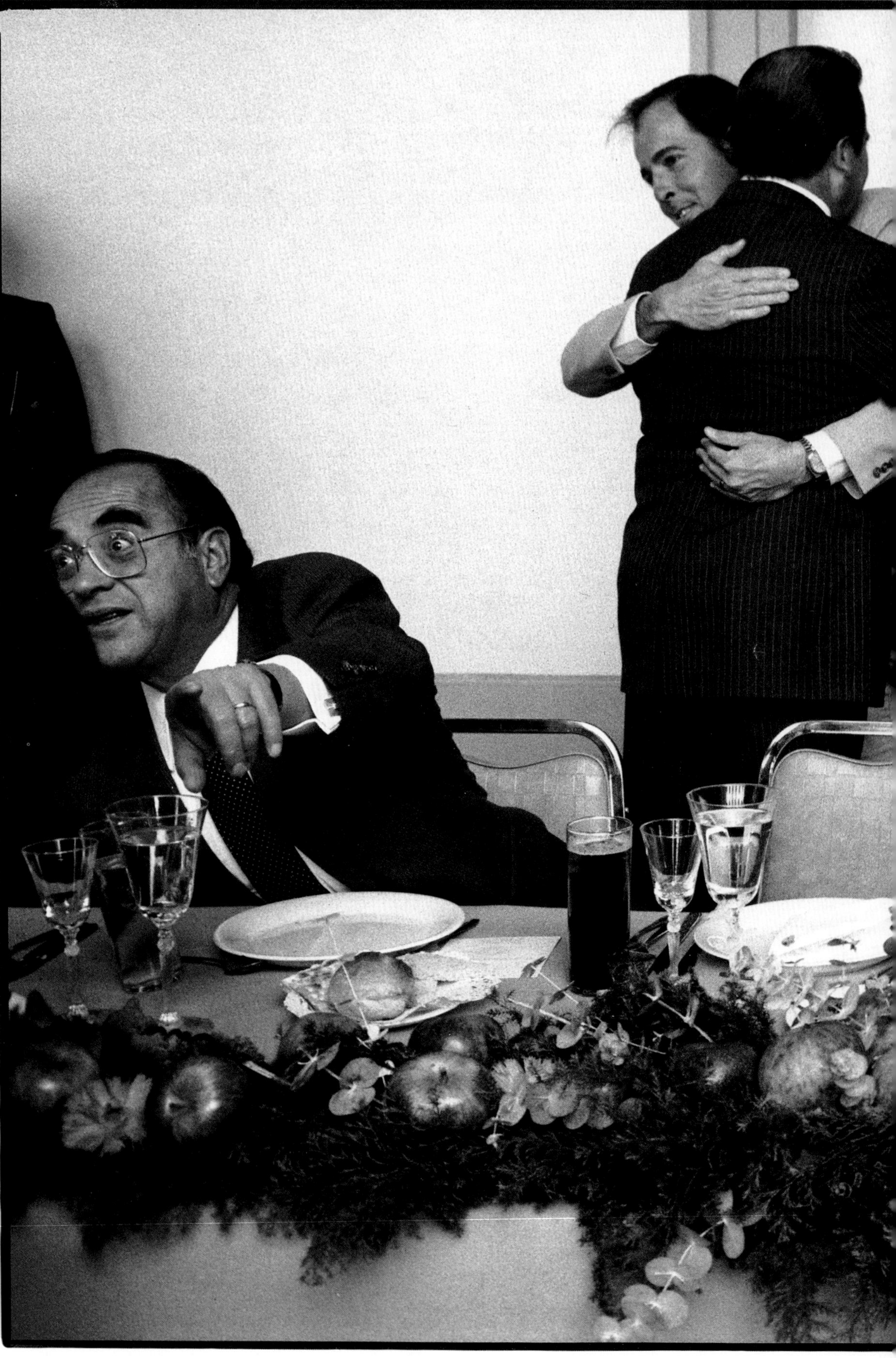

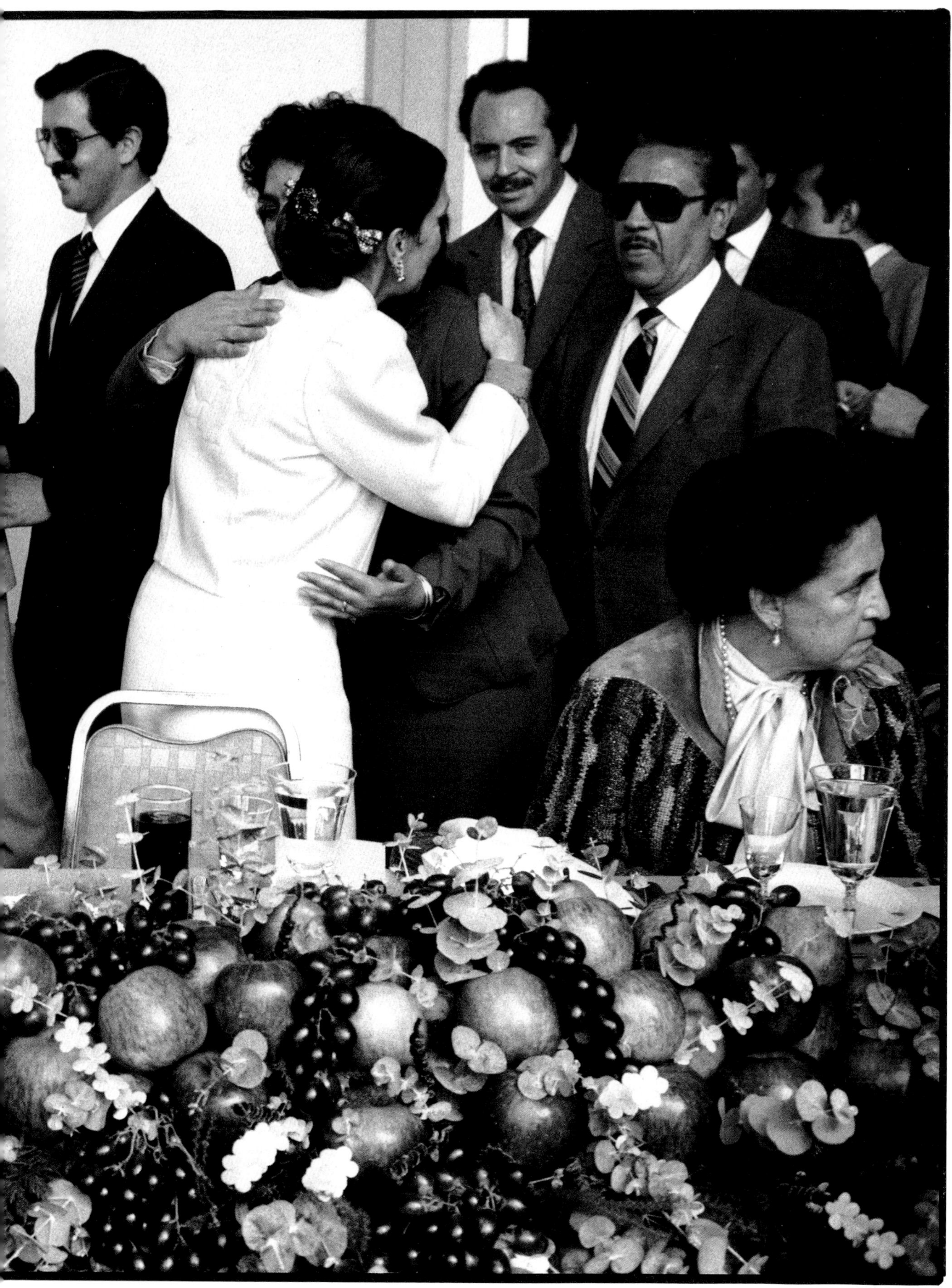

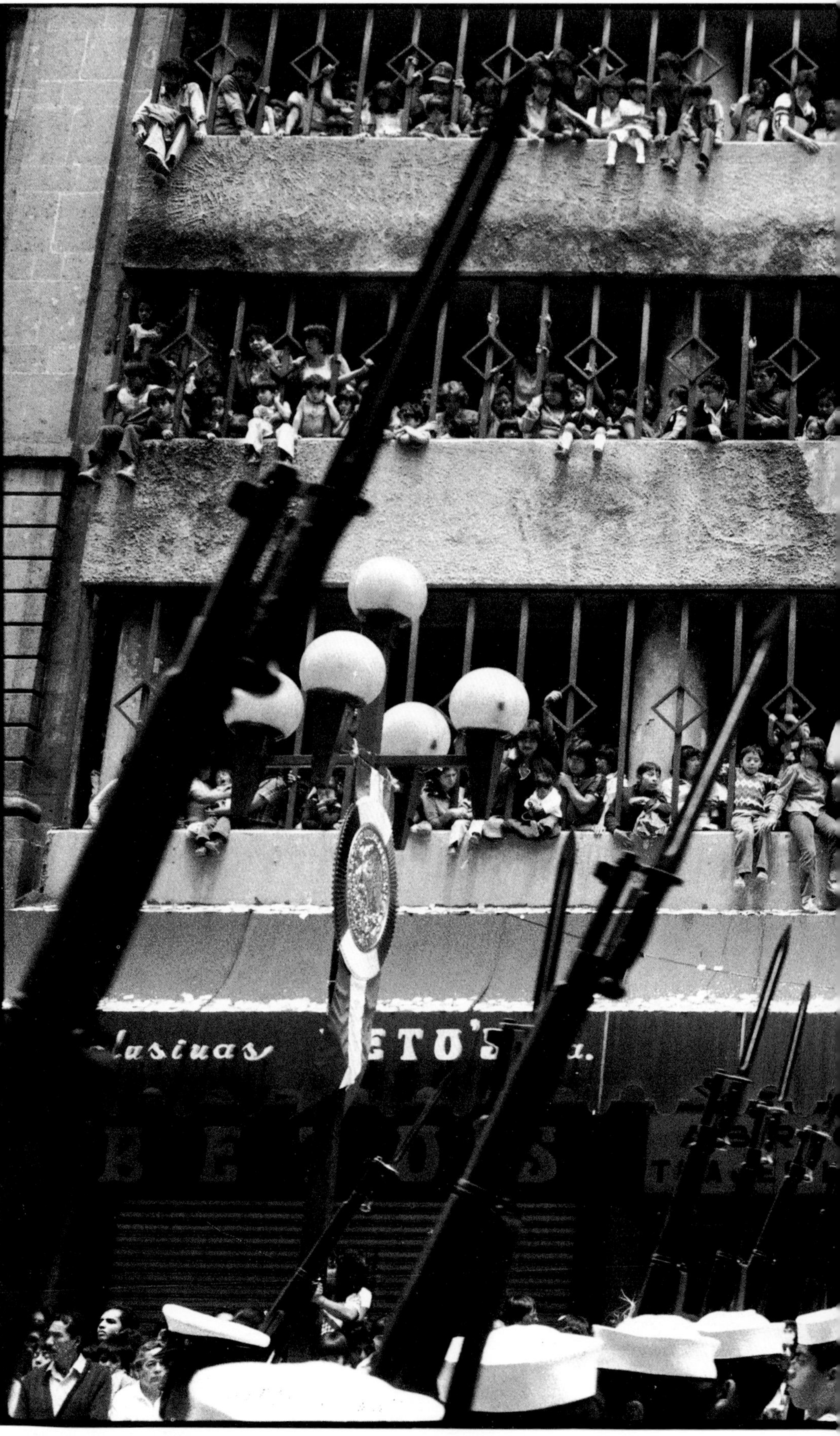

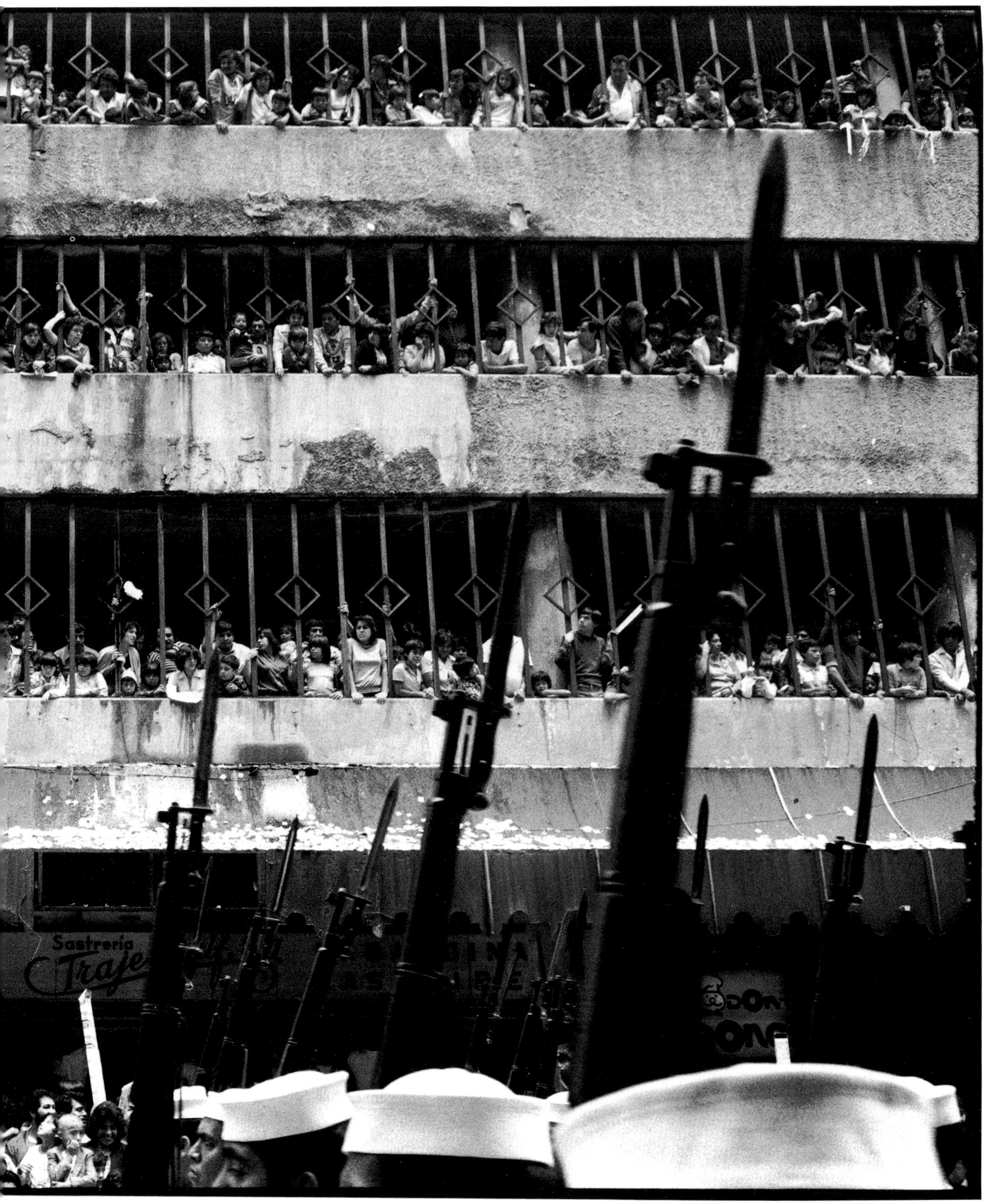
Sastreria
Traje

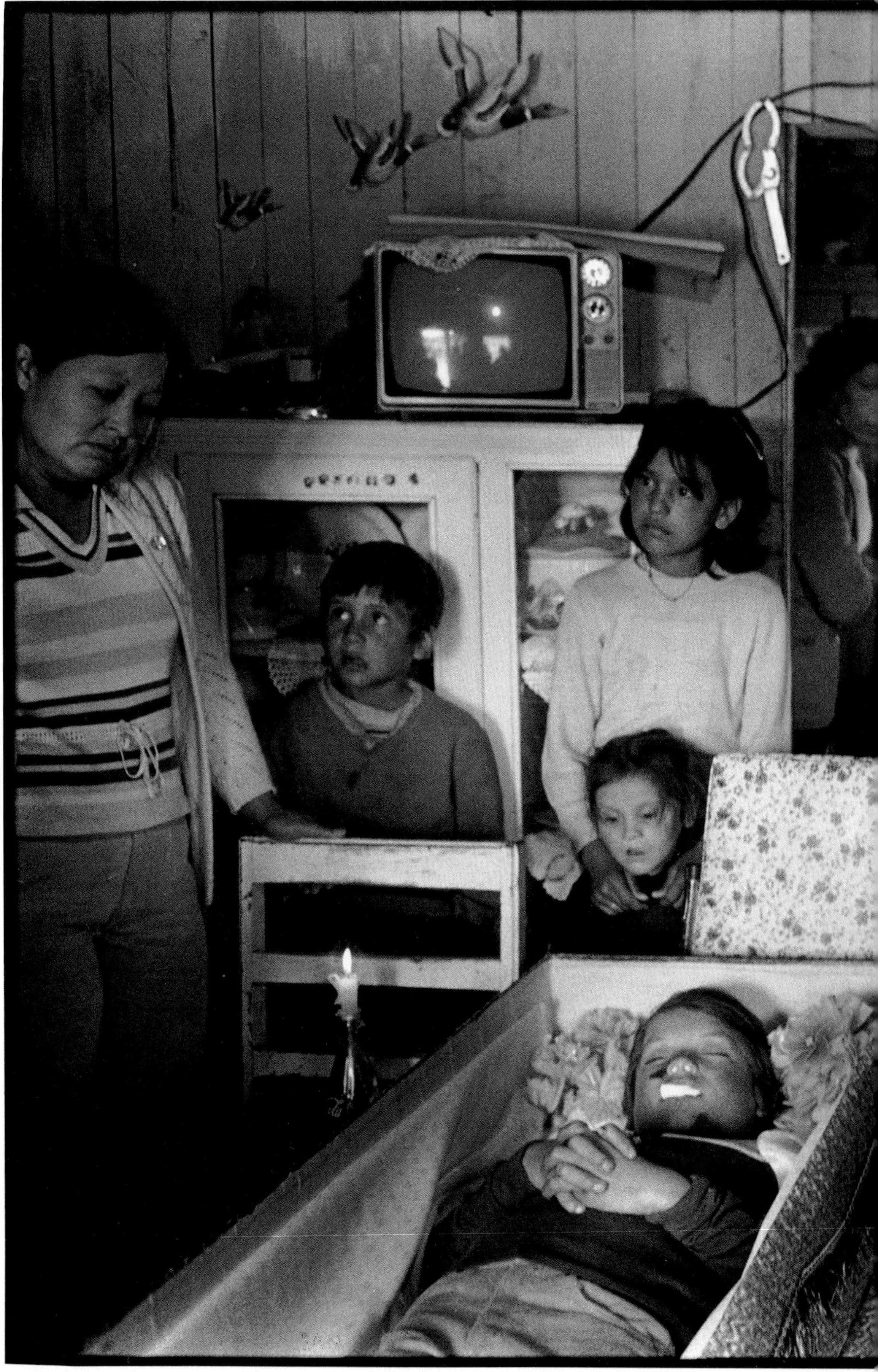

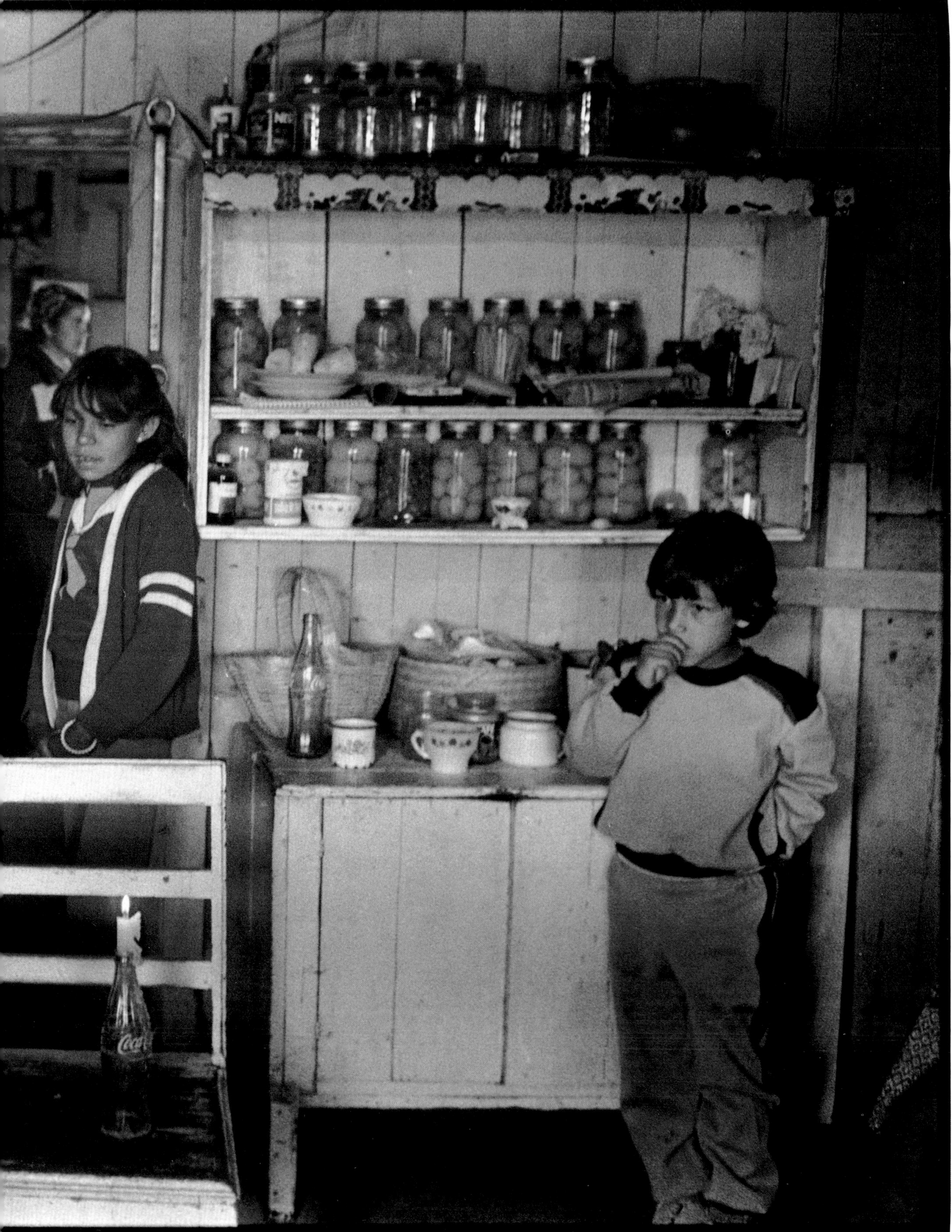
Coca

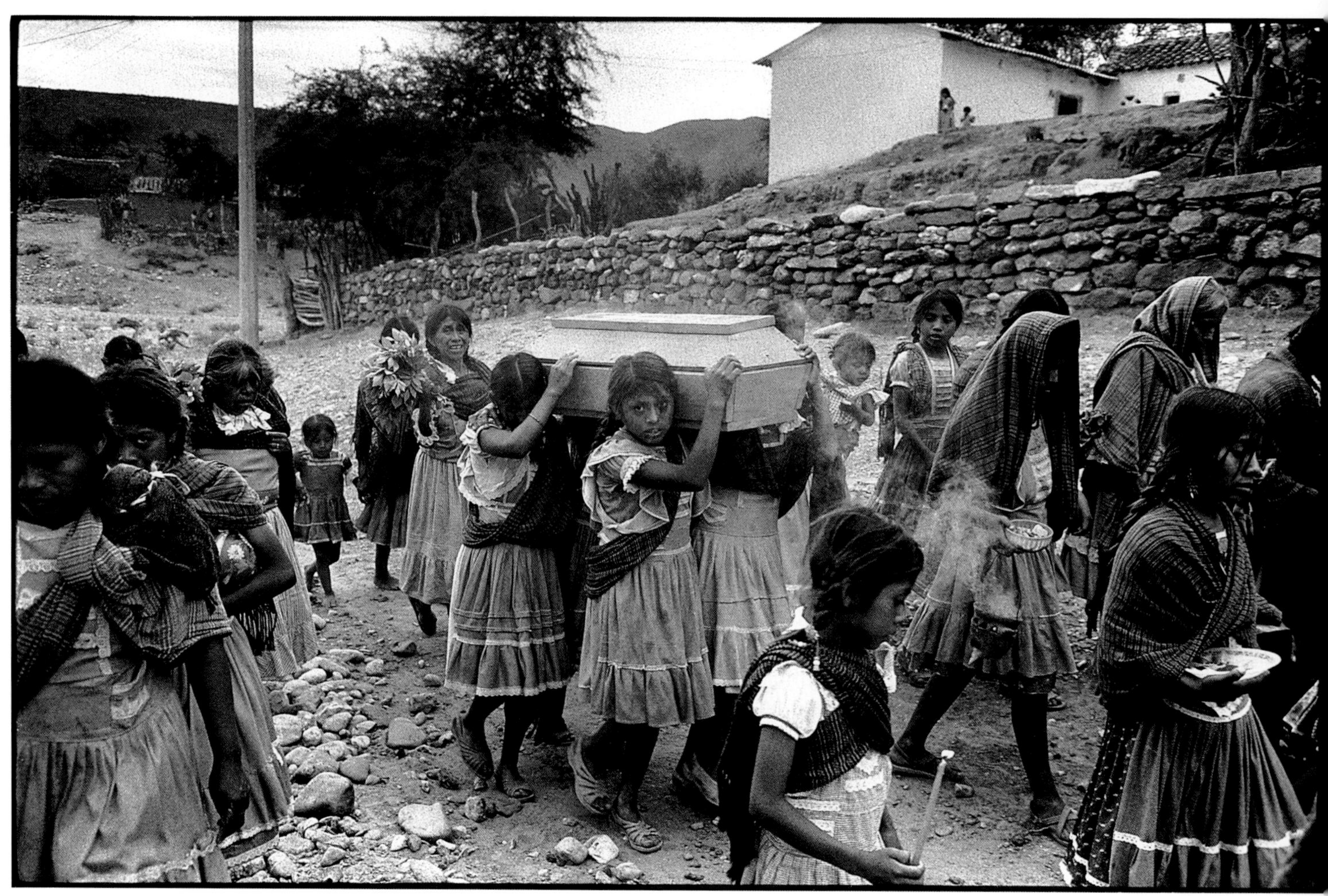

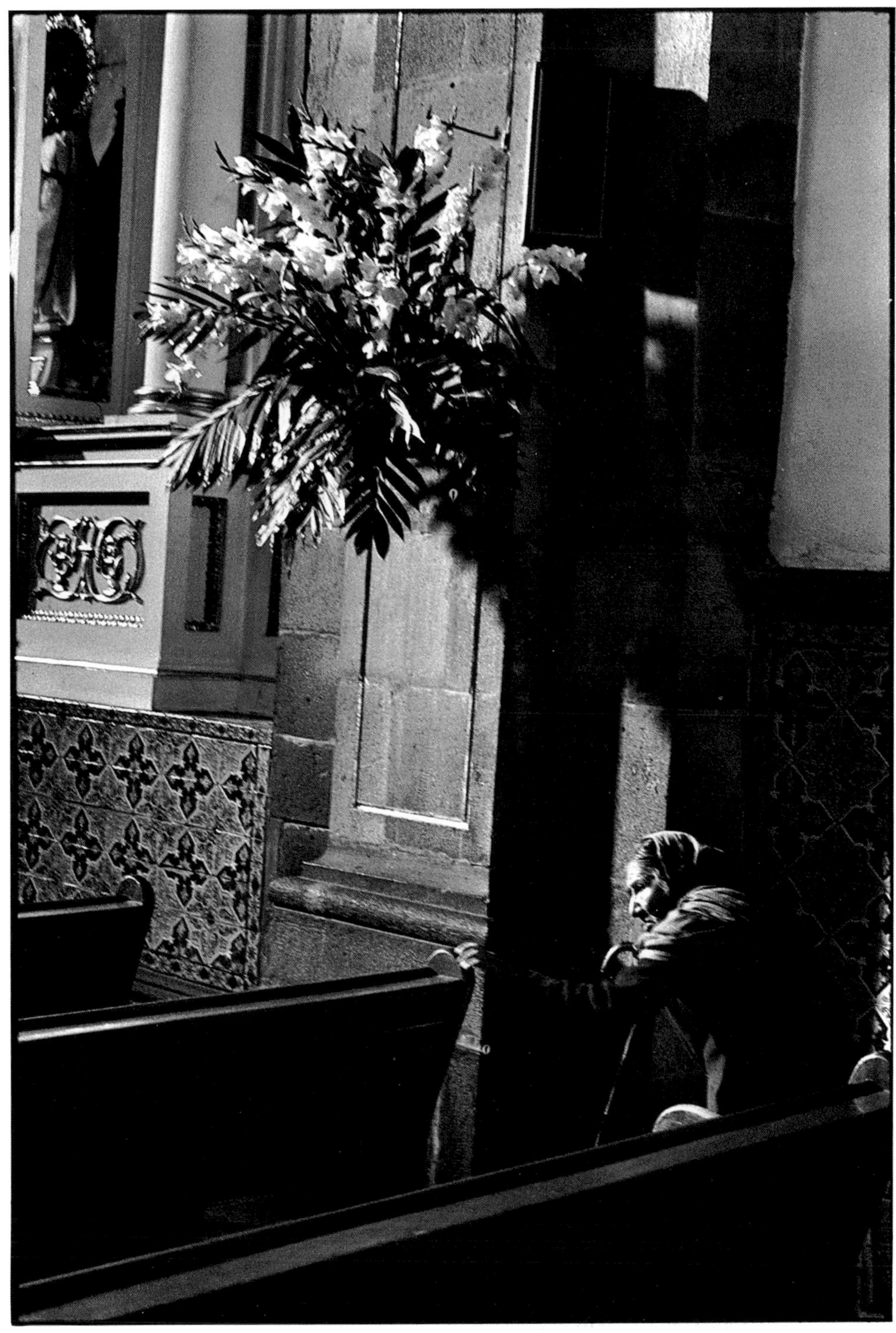

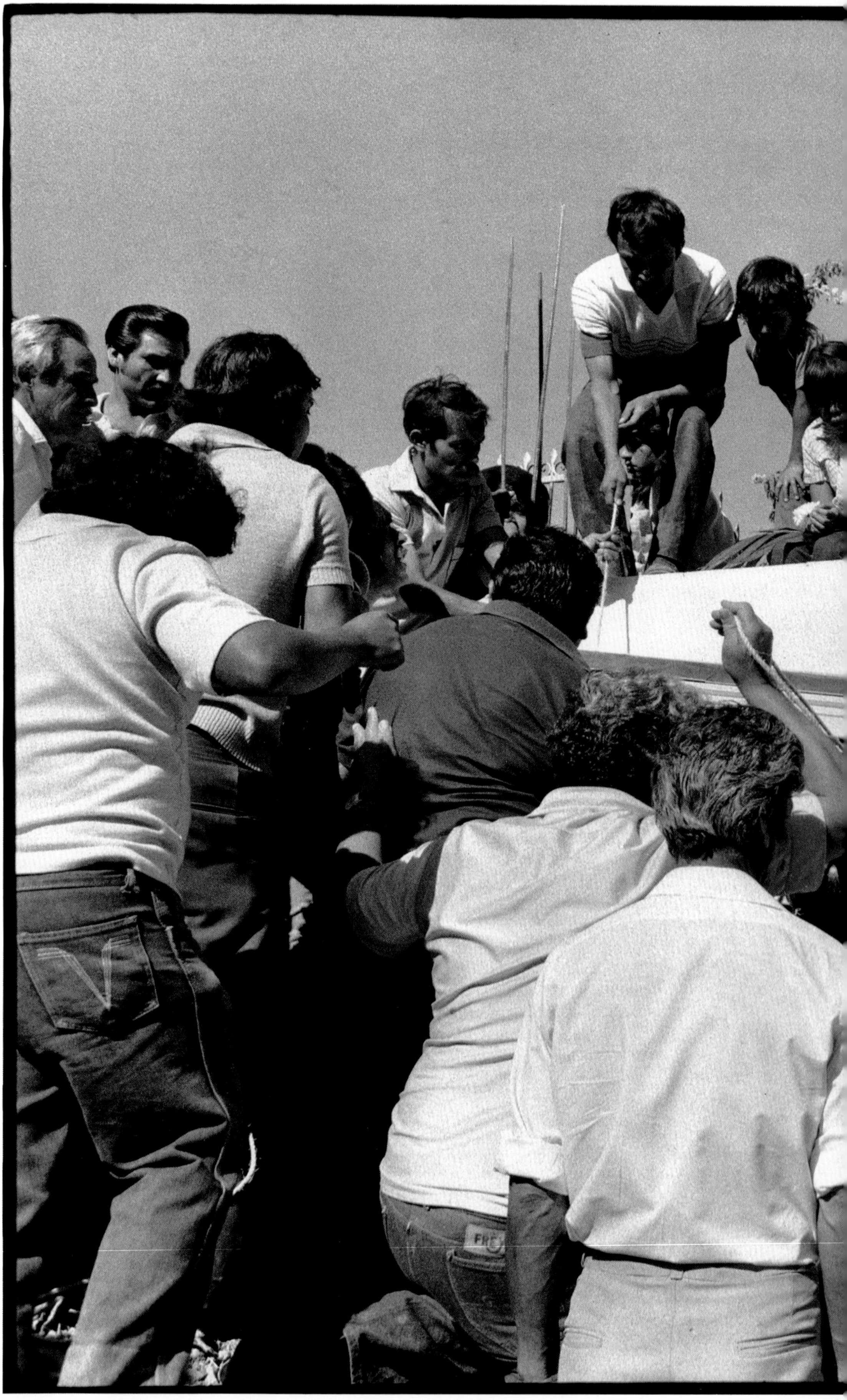

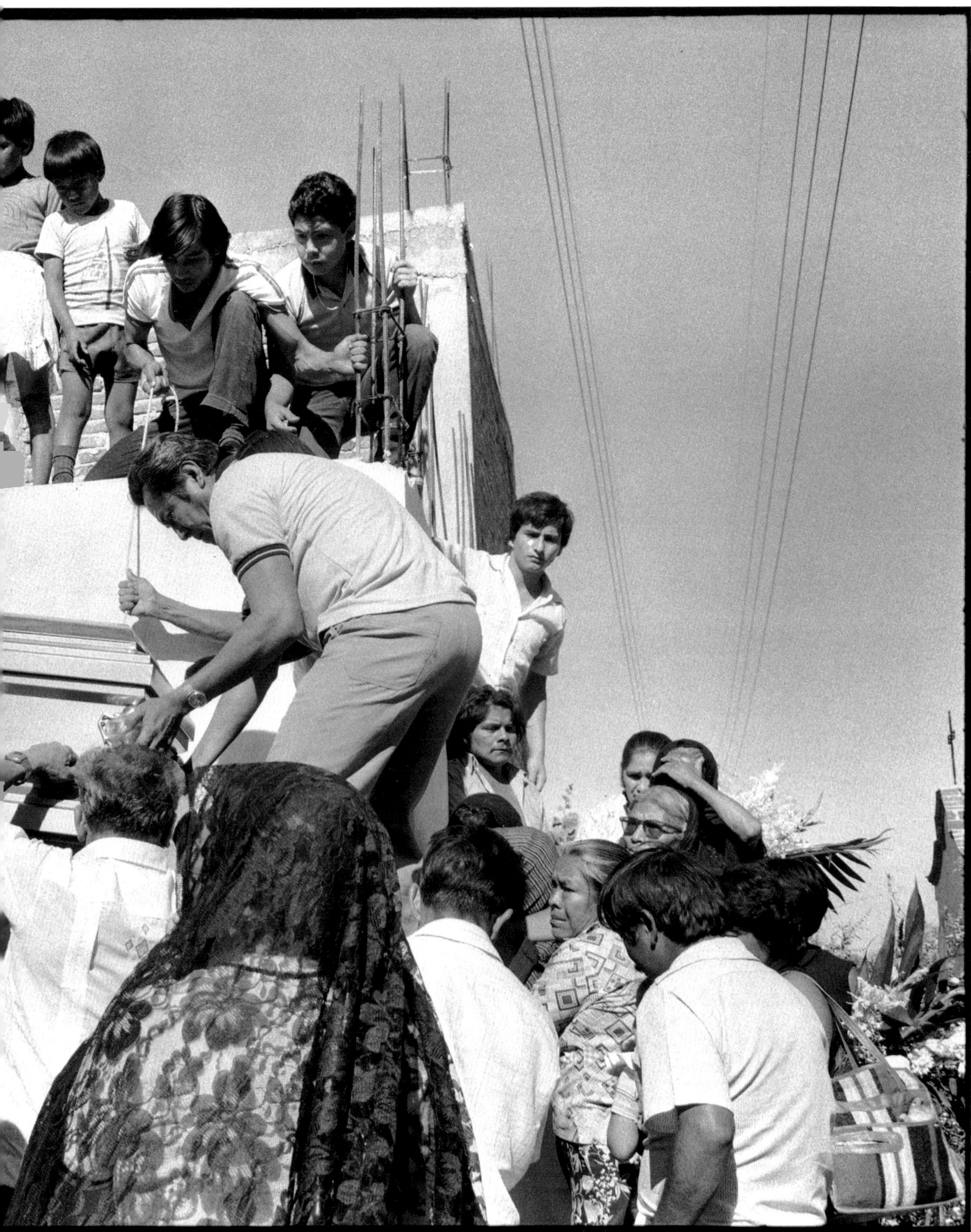

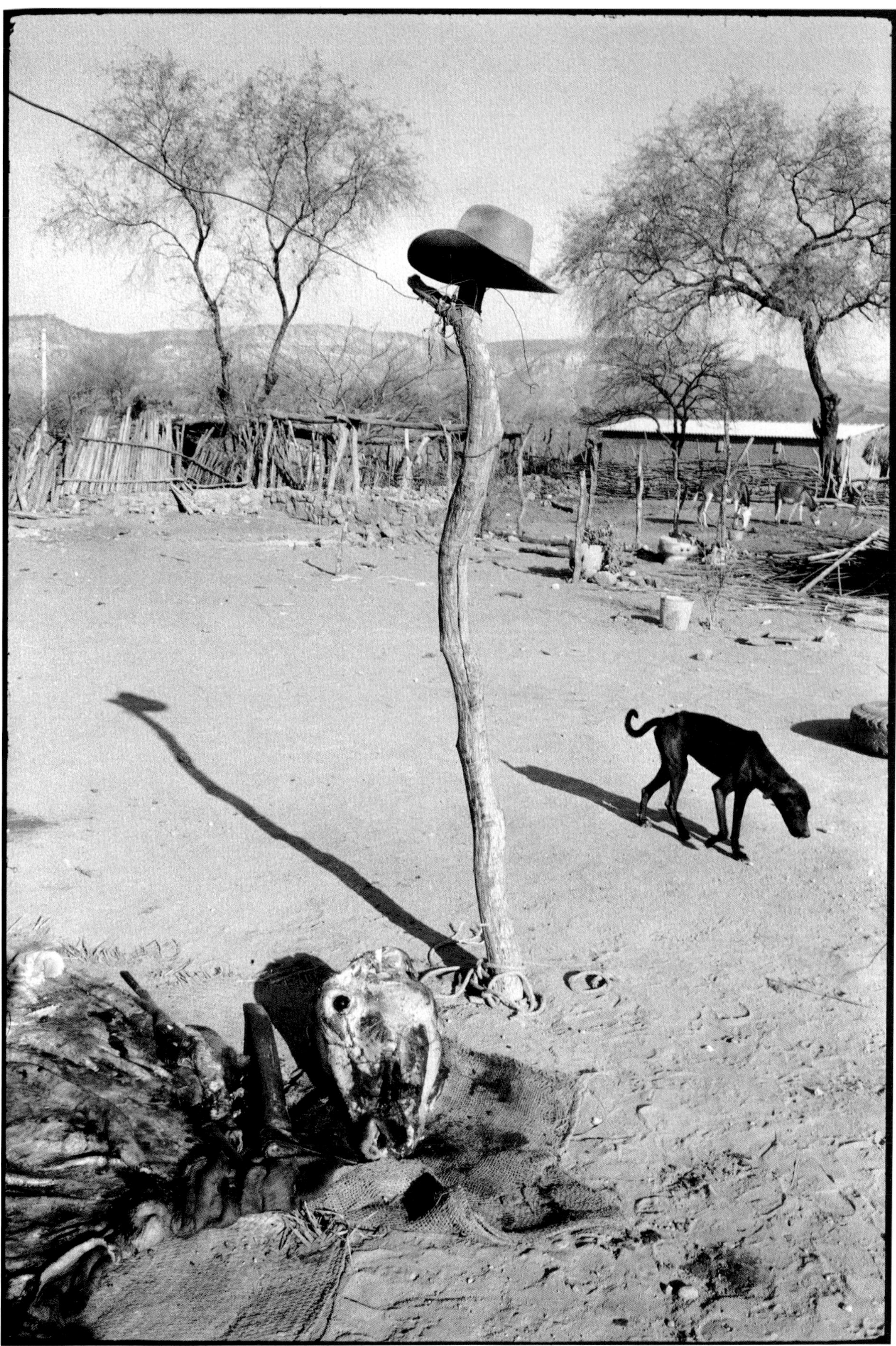

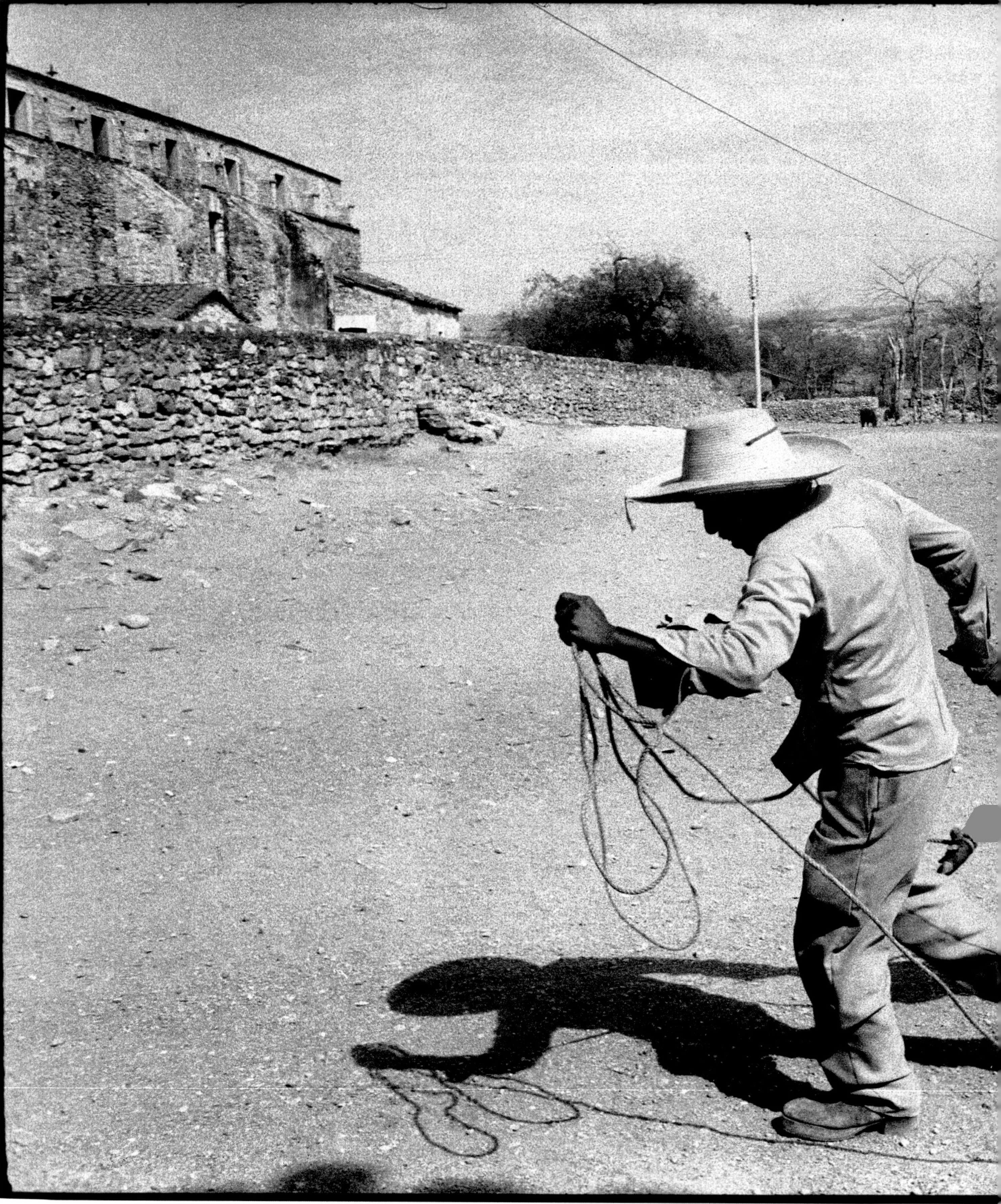

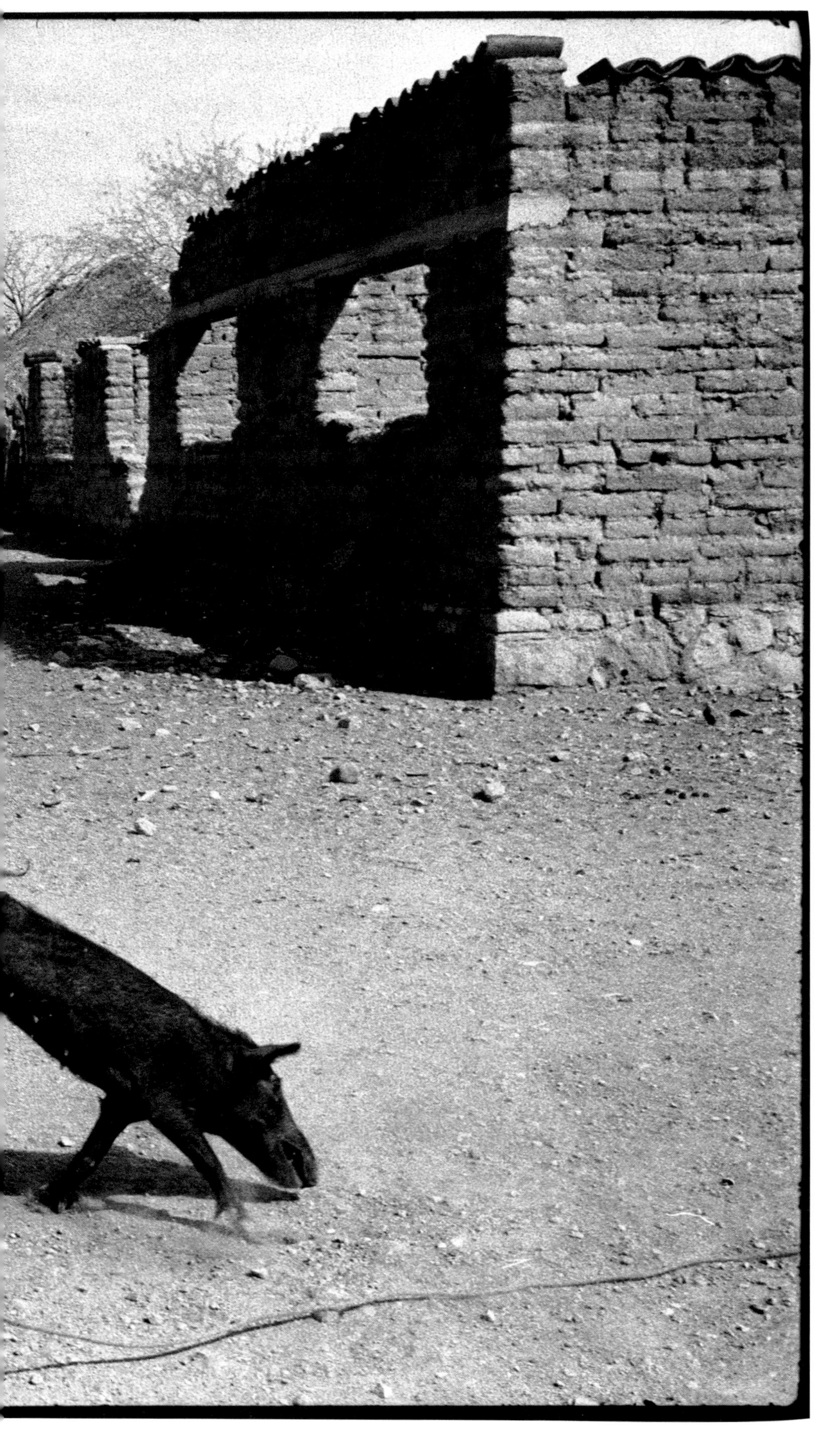

Eternity

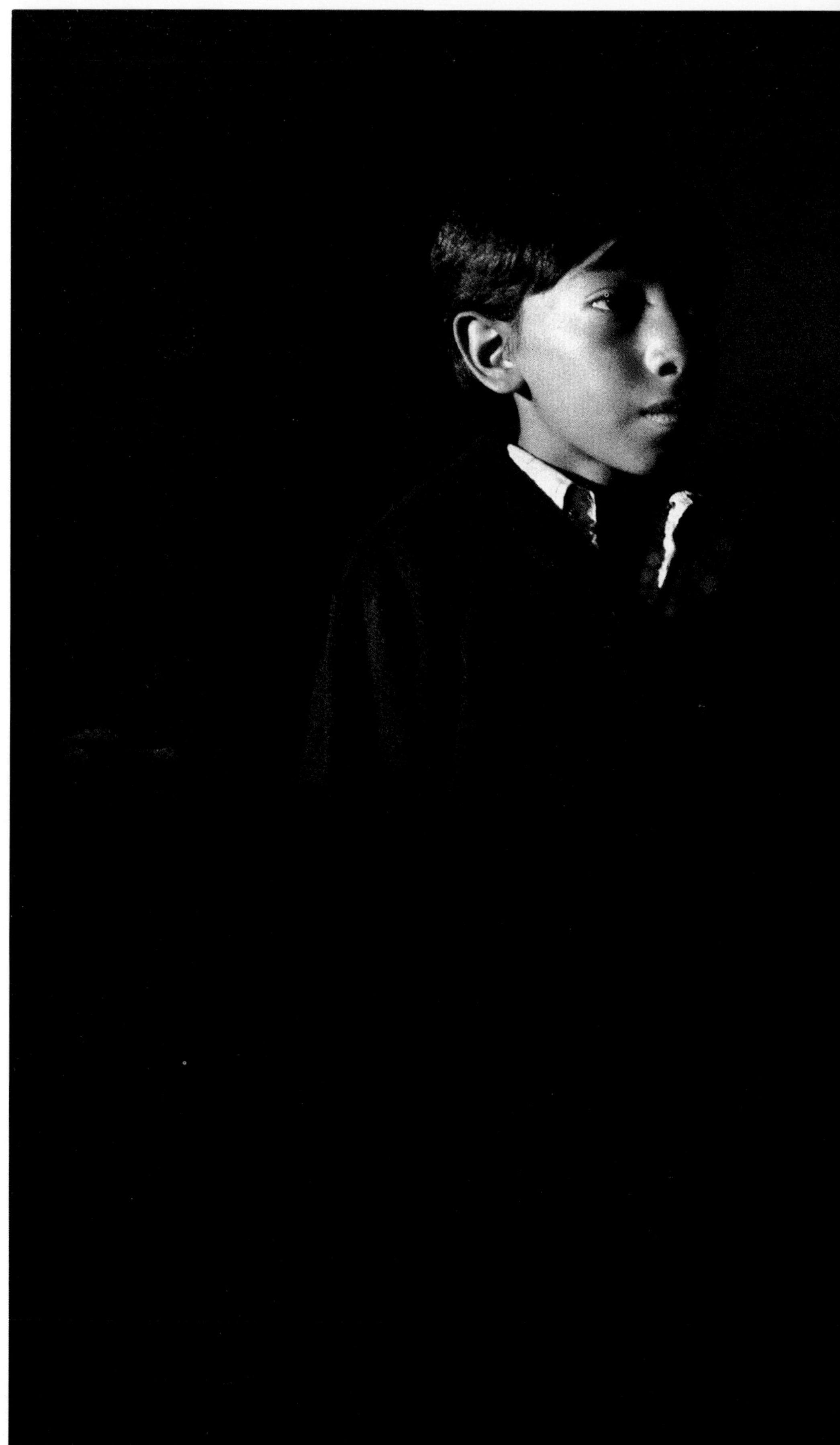

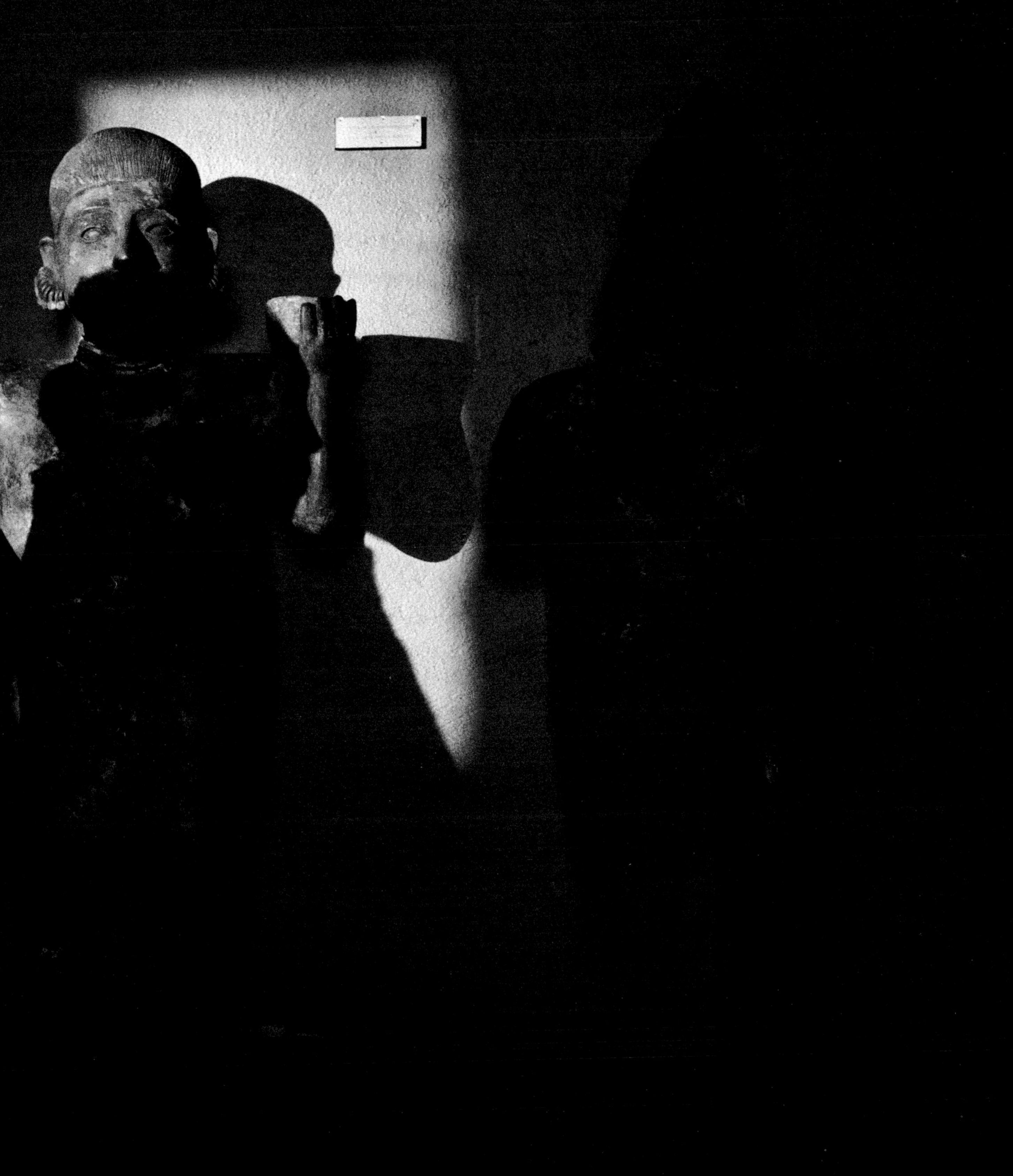

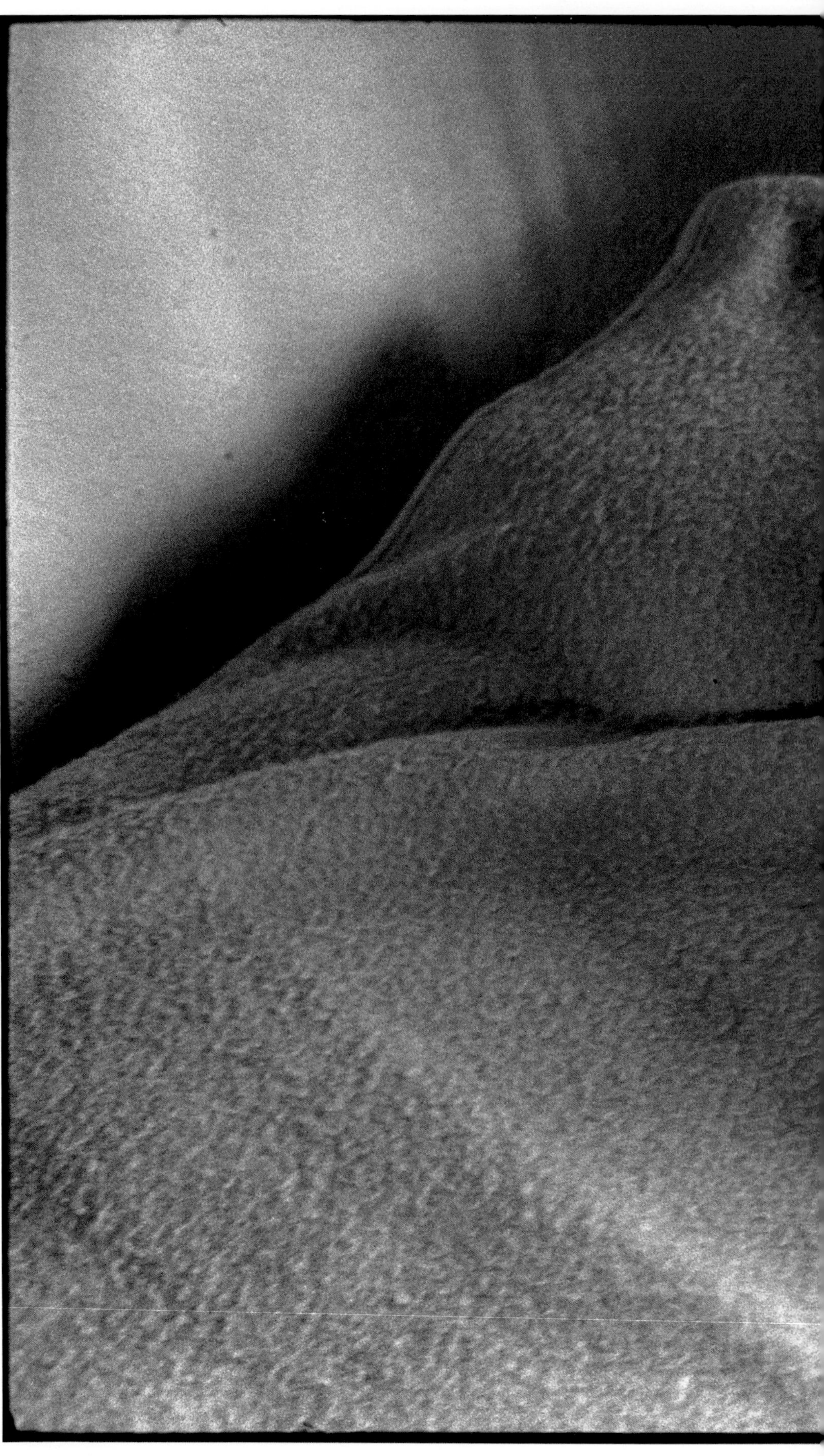

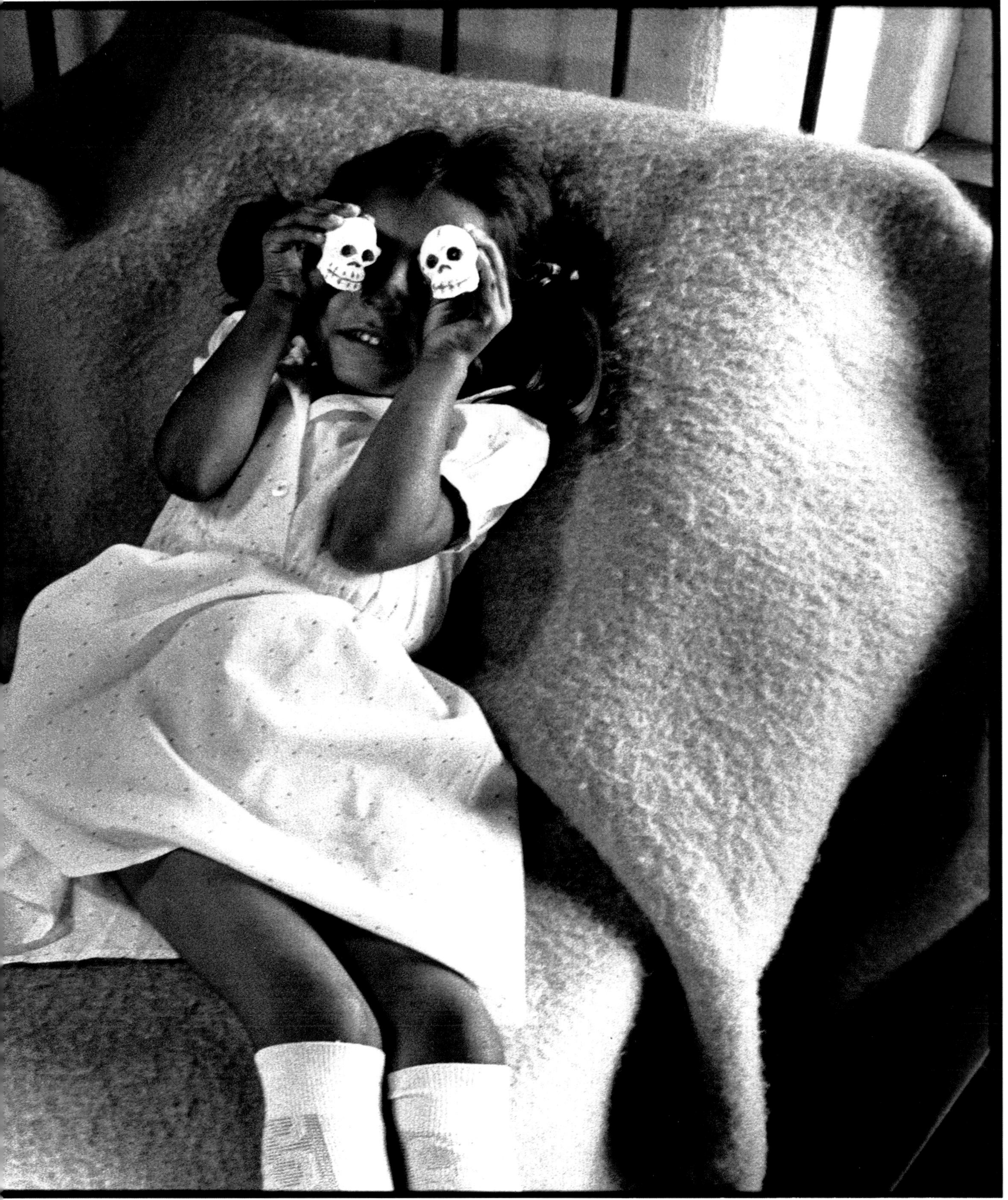

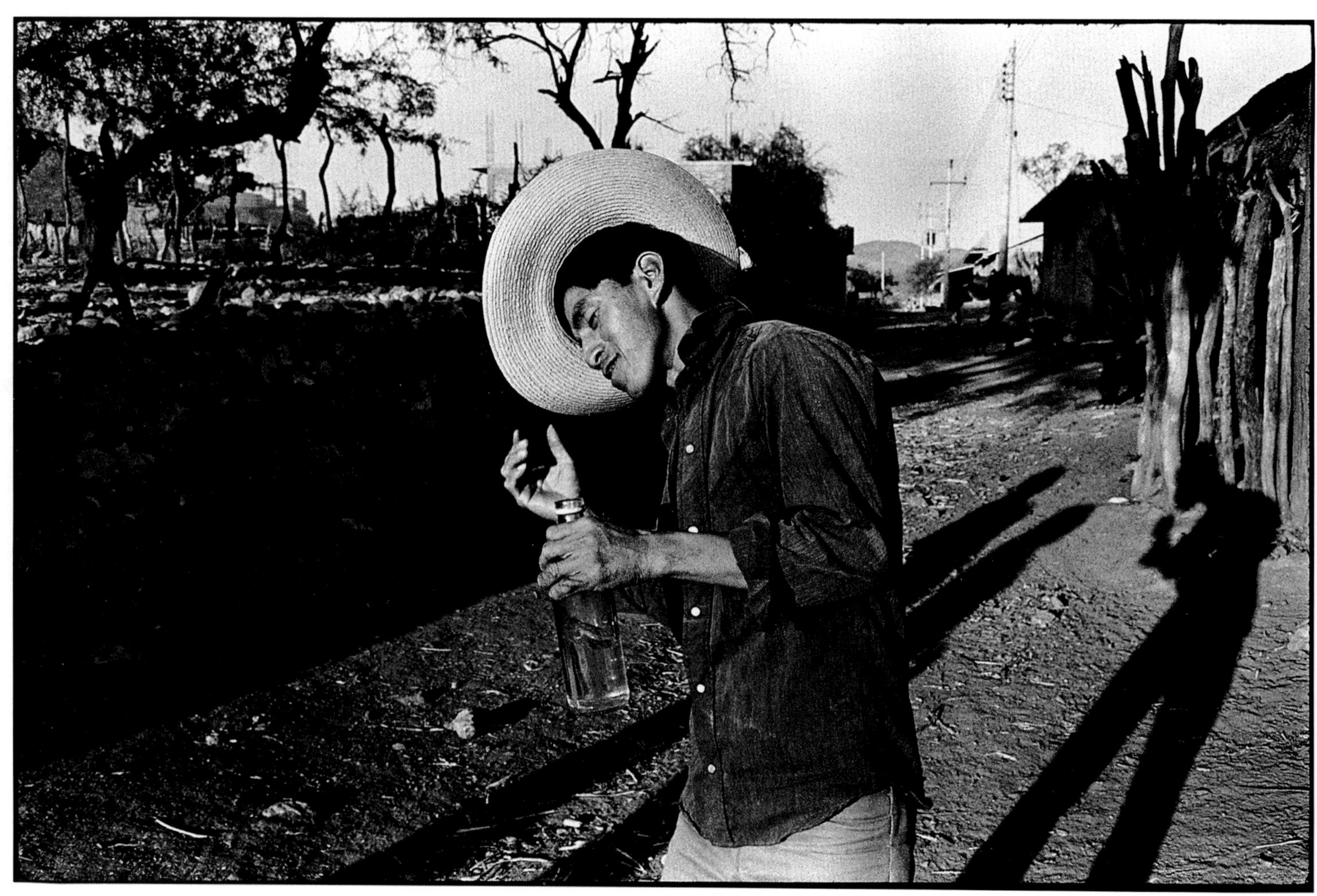

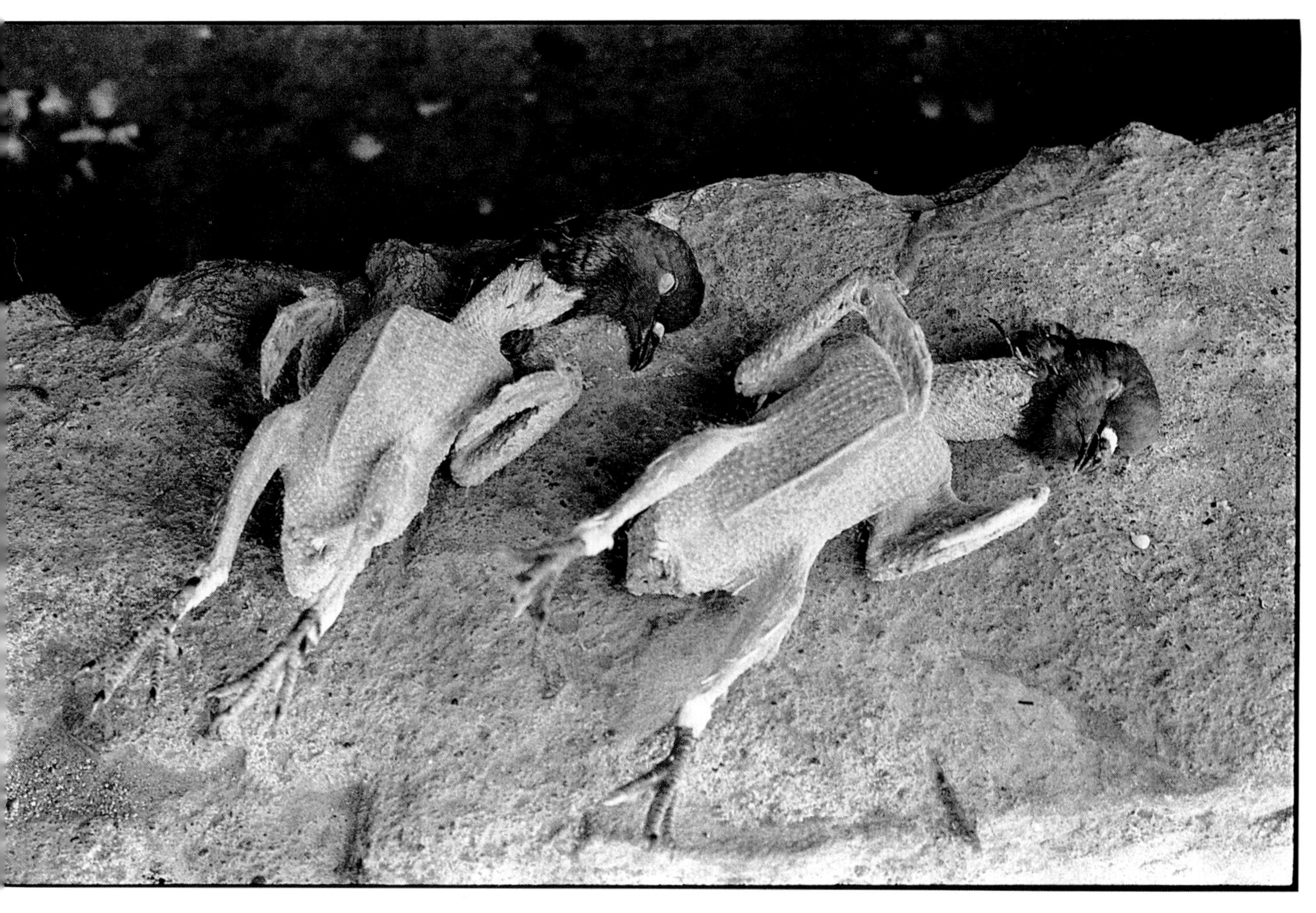

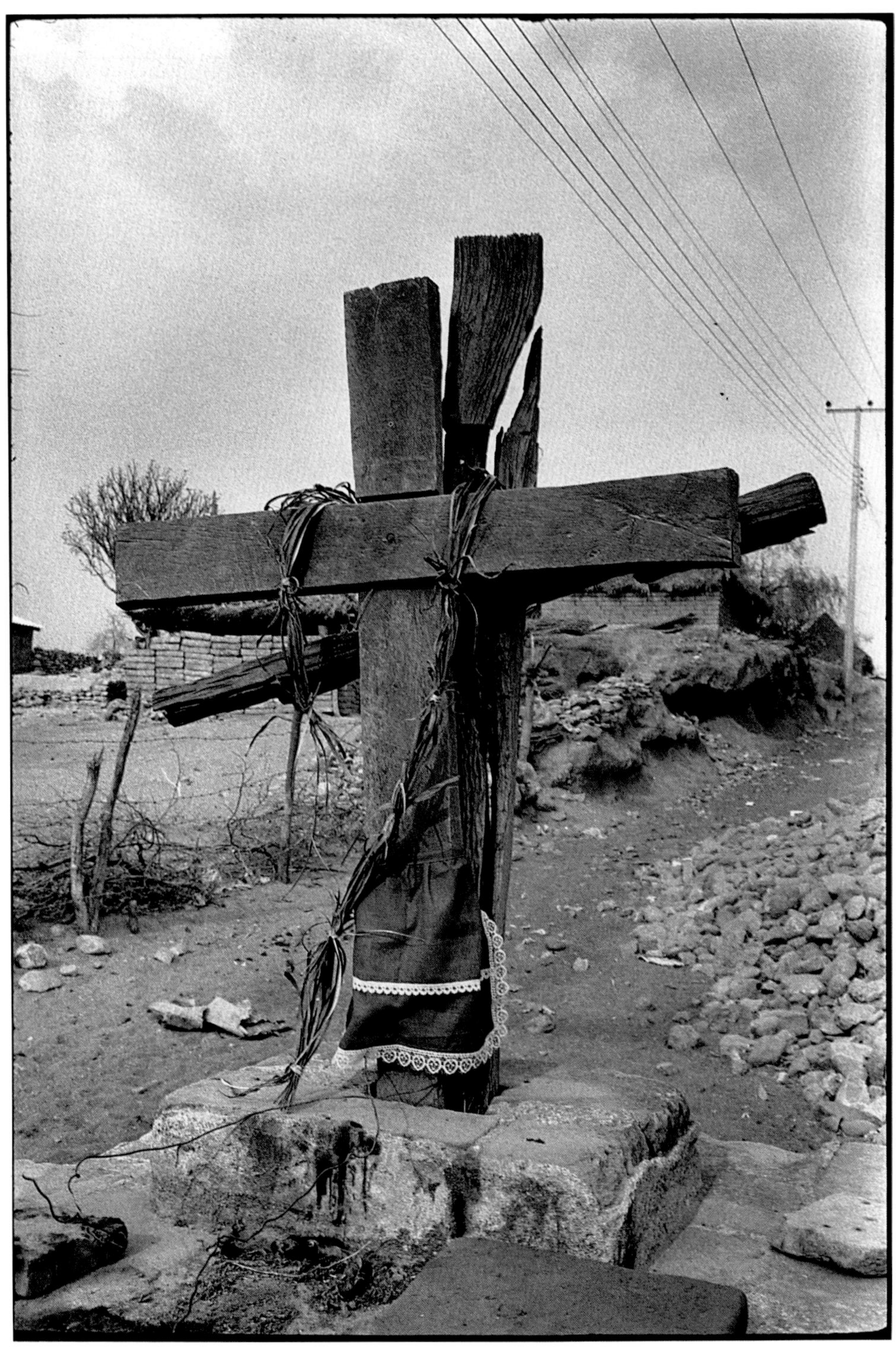

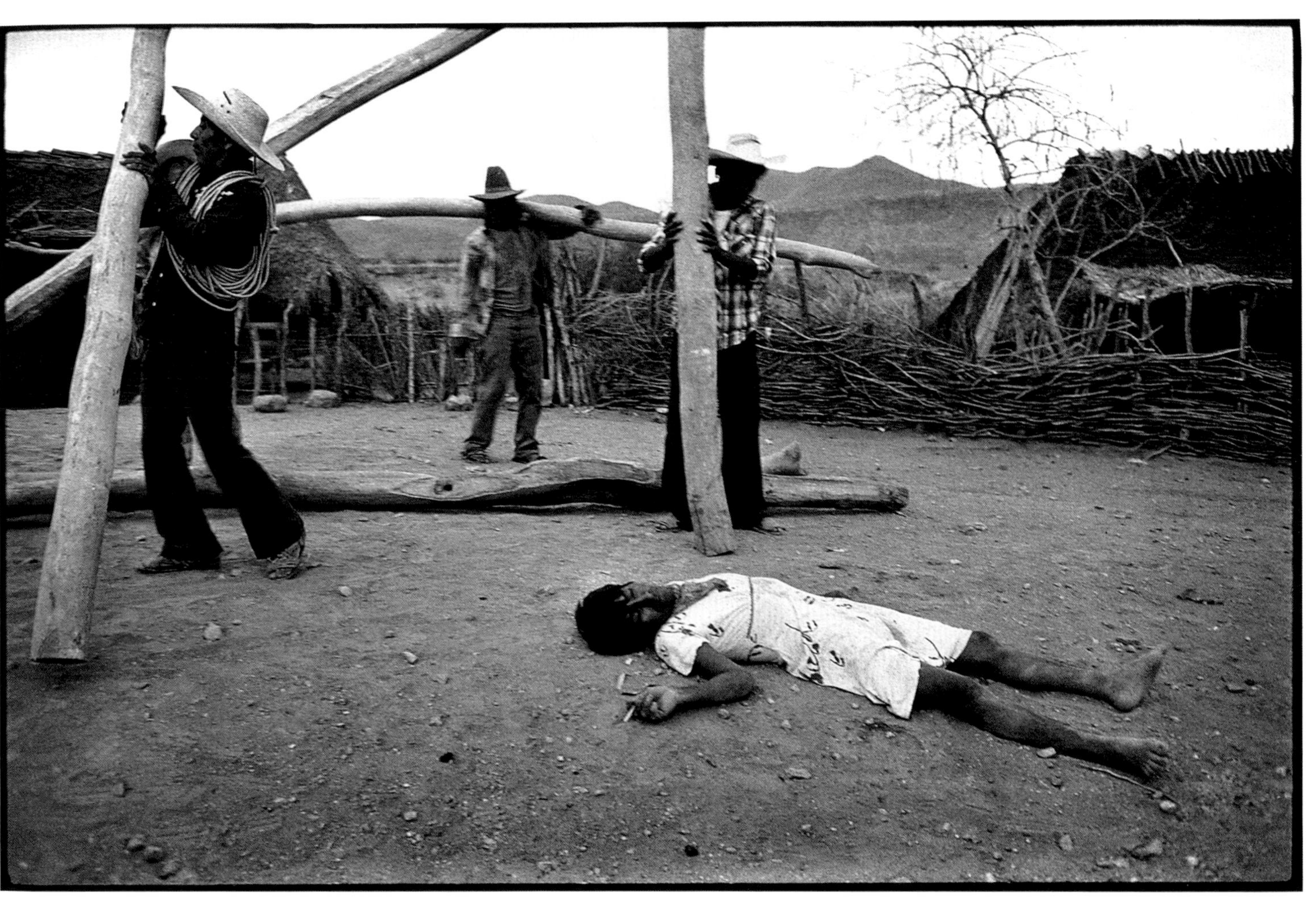

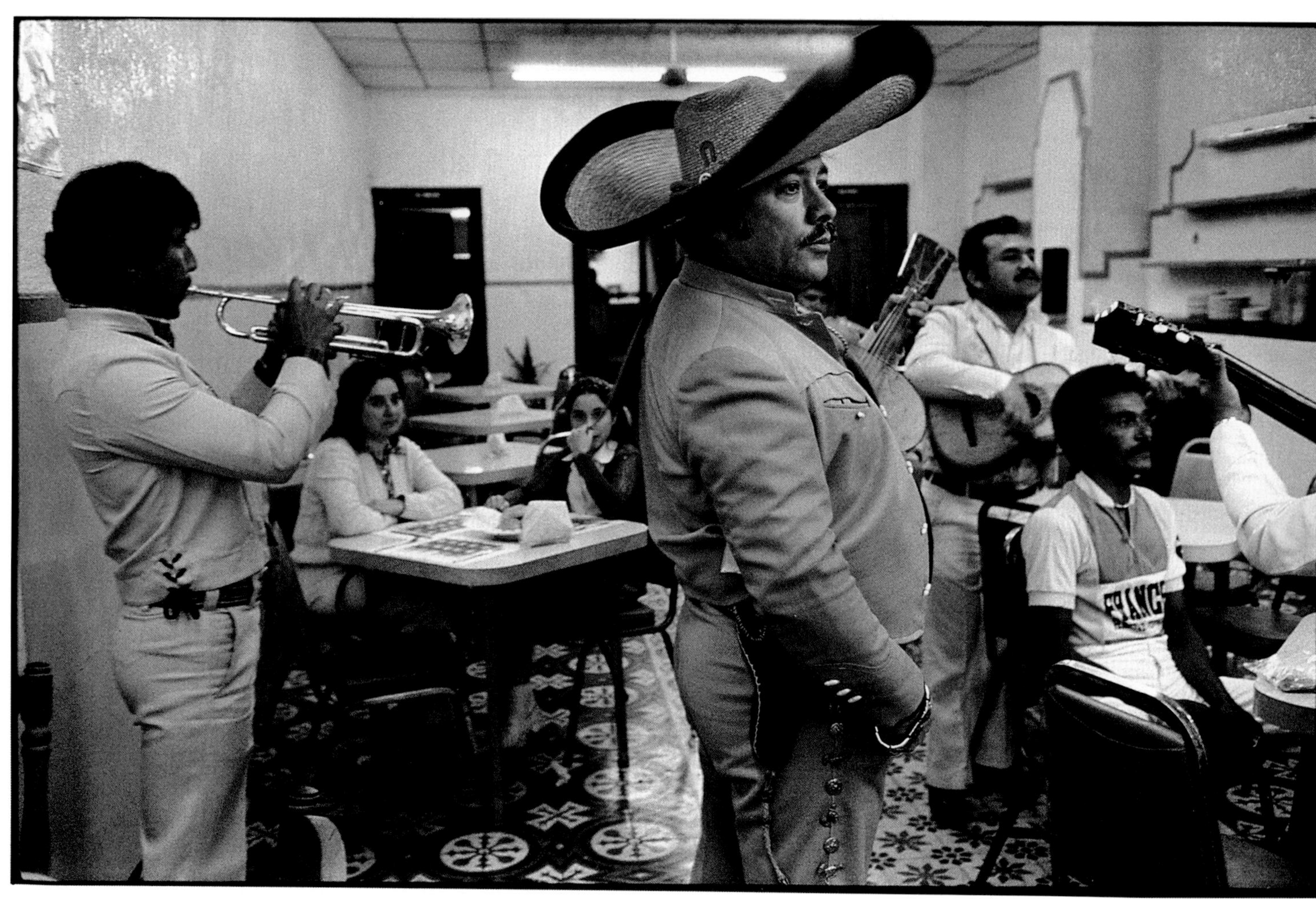

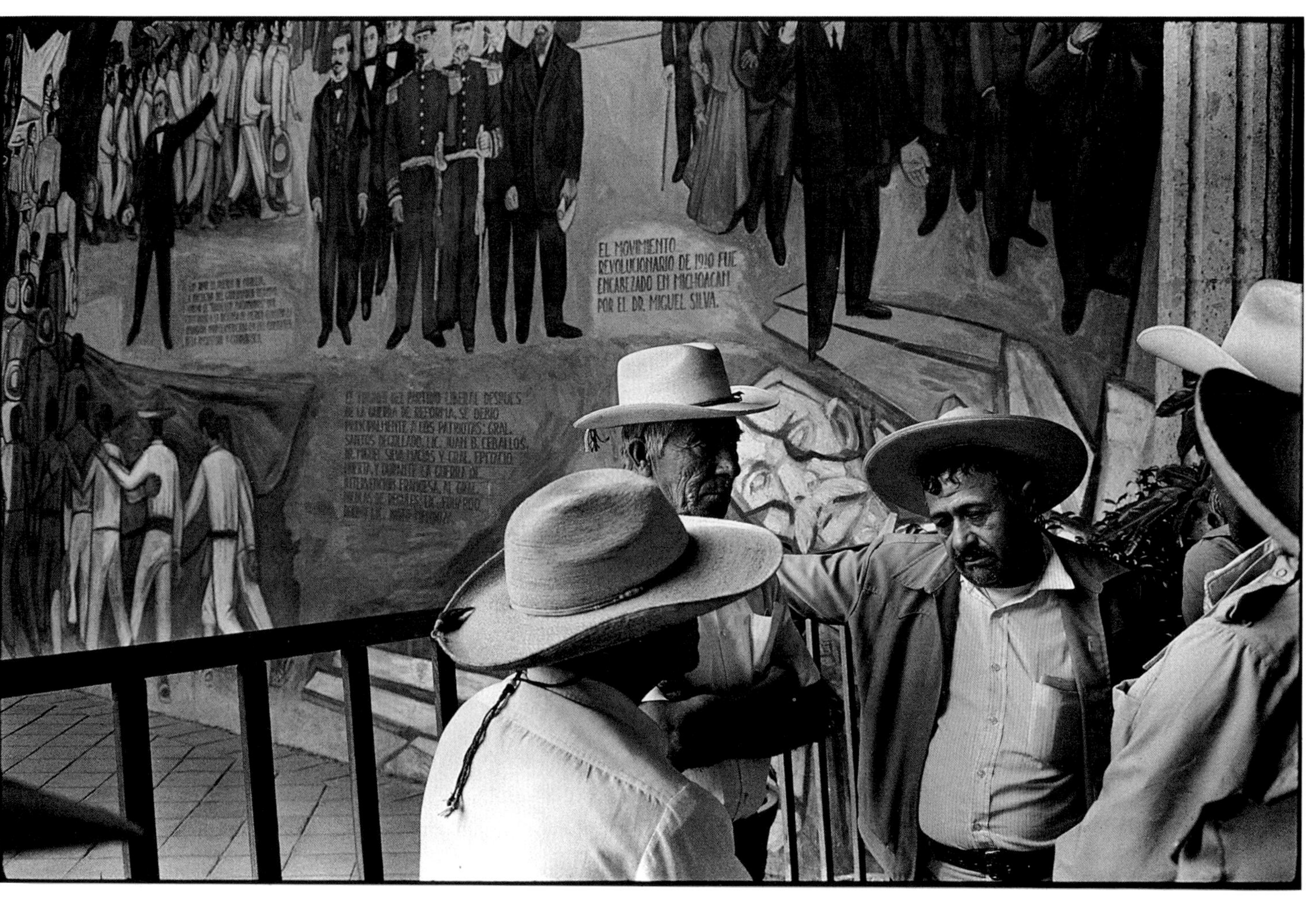
EL MOVIMIENTO
REVOLUCIONARIO DE 1910 FUE
ENCABEZADO EN MICHOACAN
POR EL DR. MIGUEL SILVA.

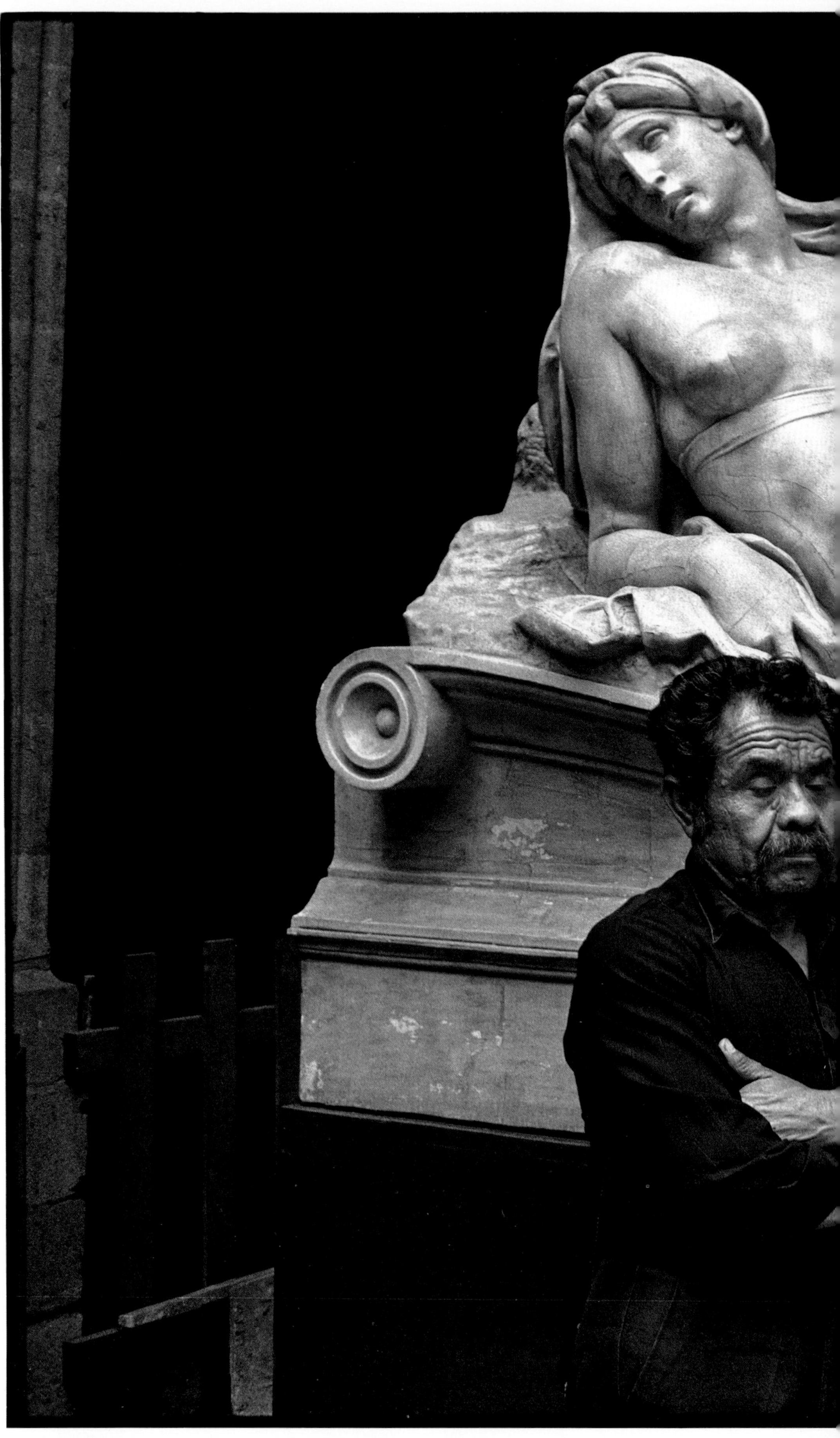

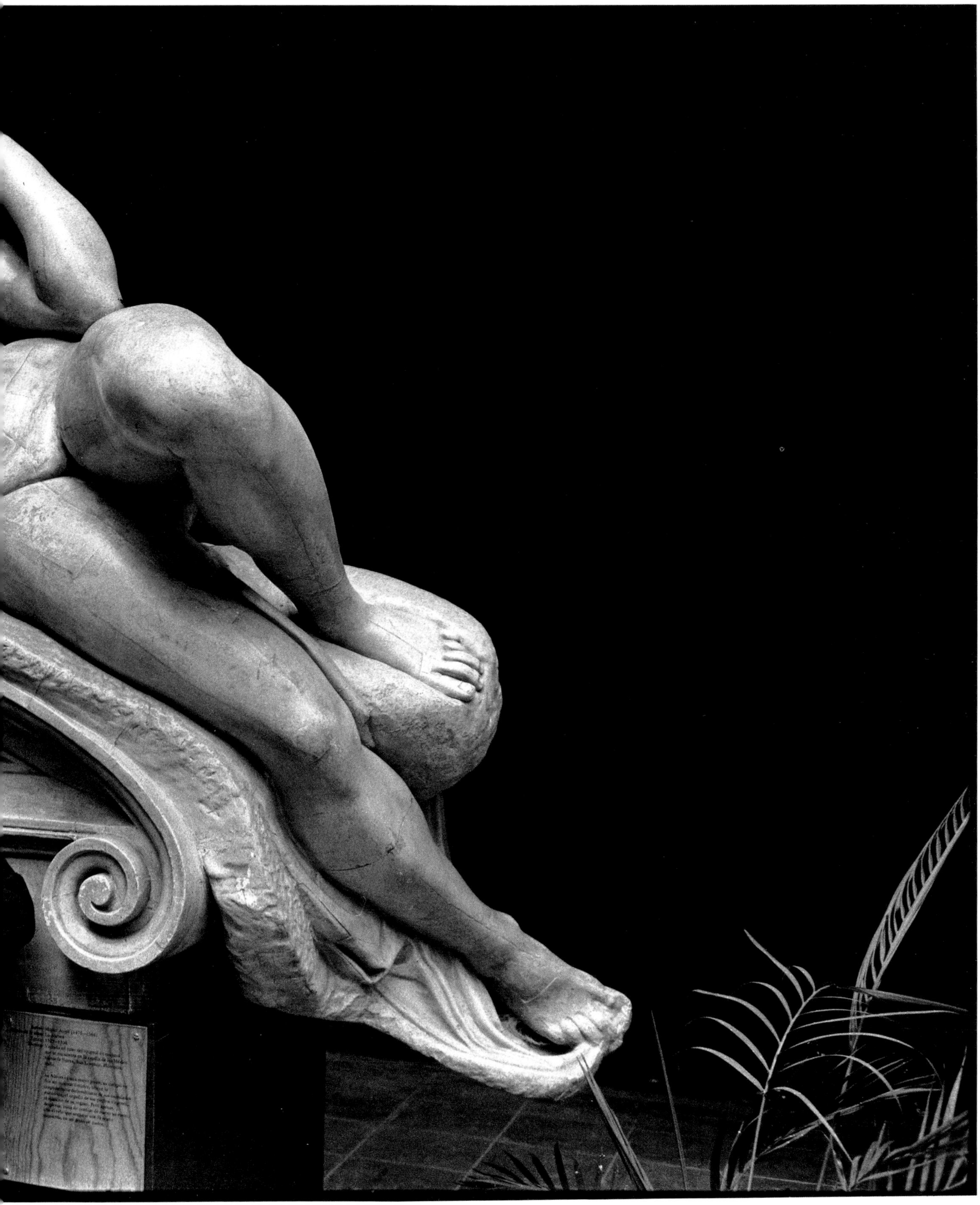

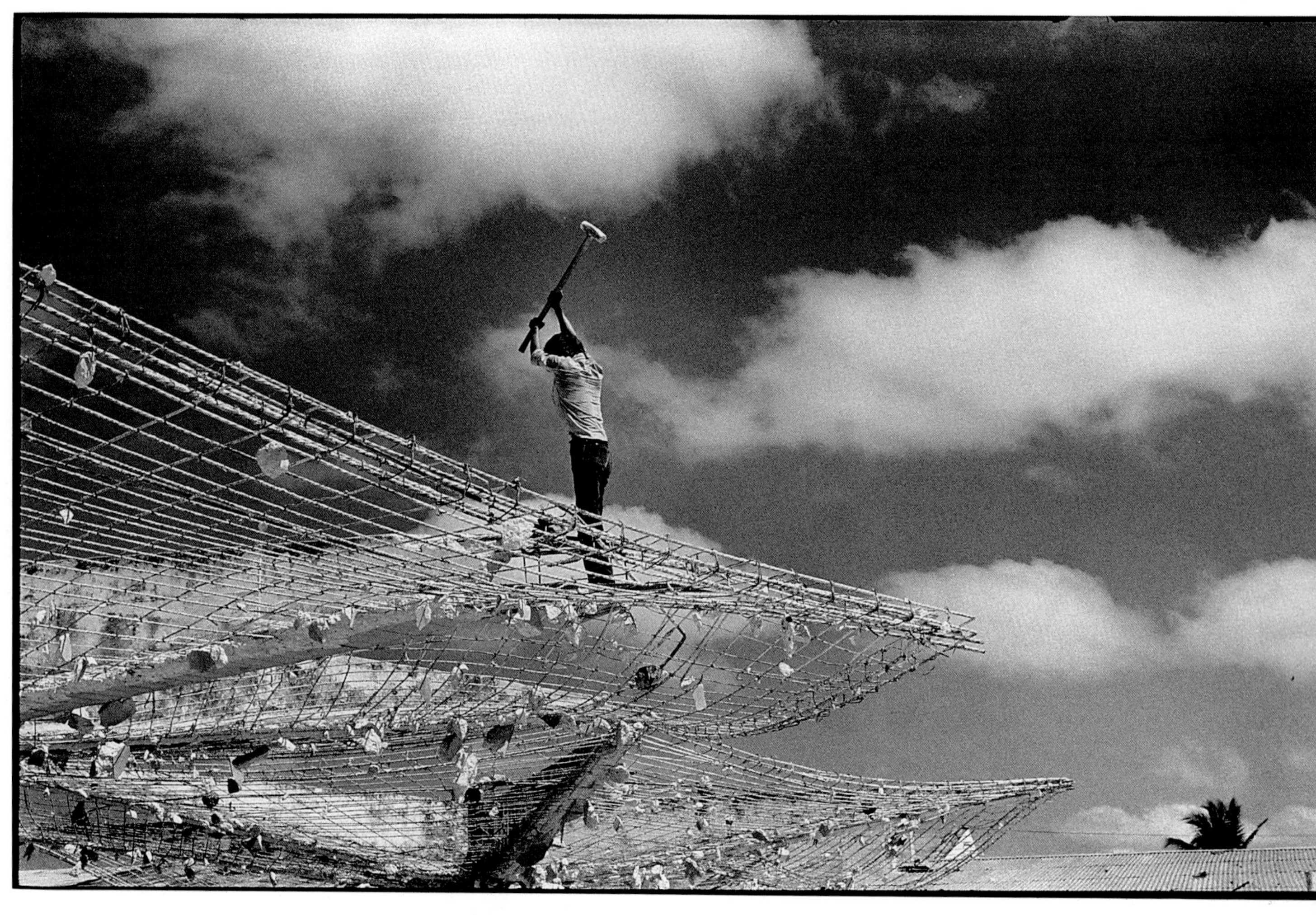

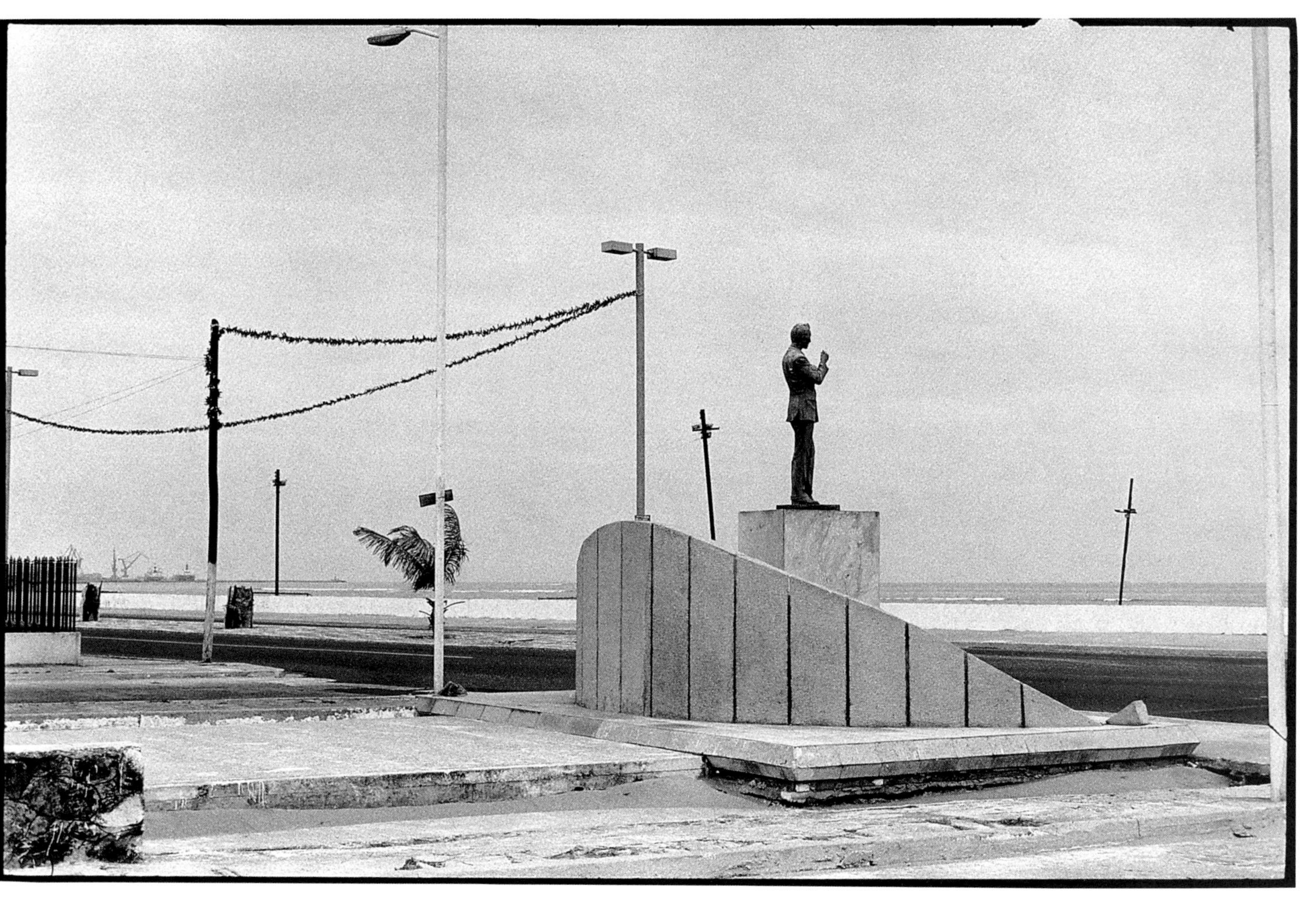

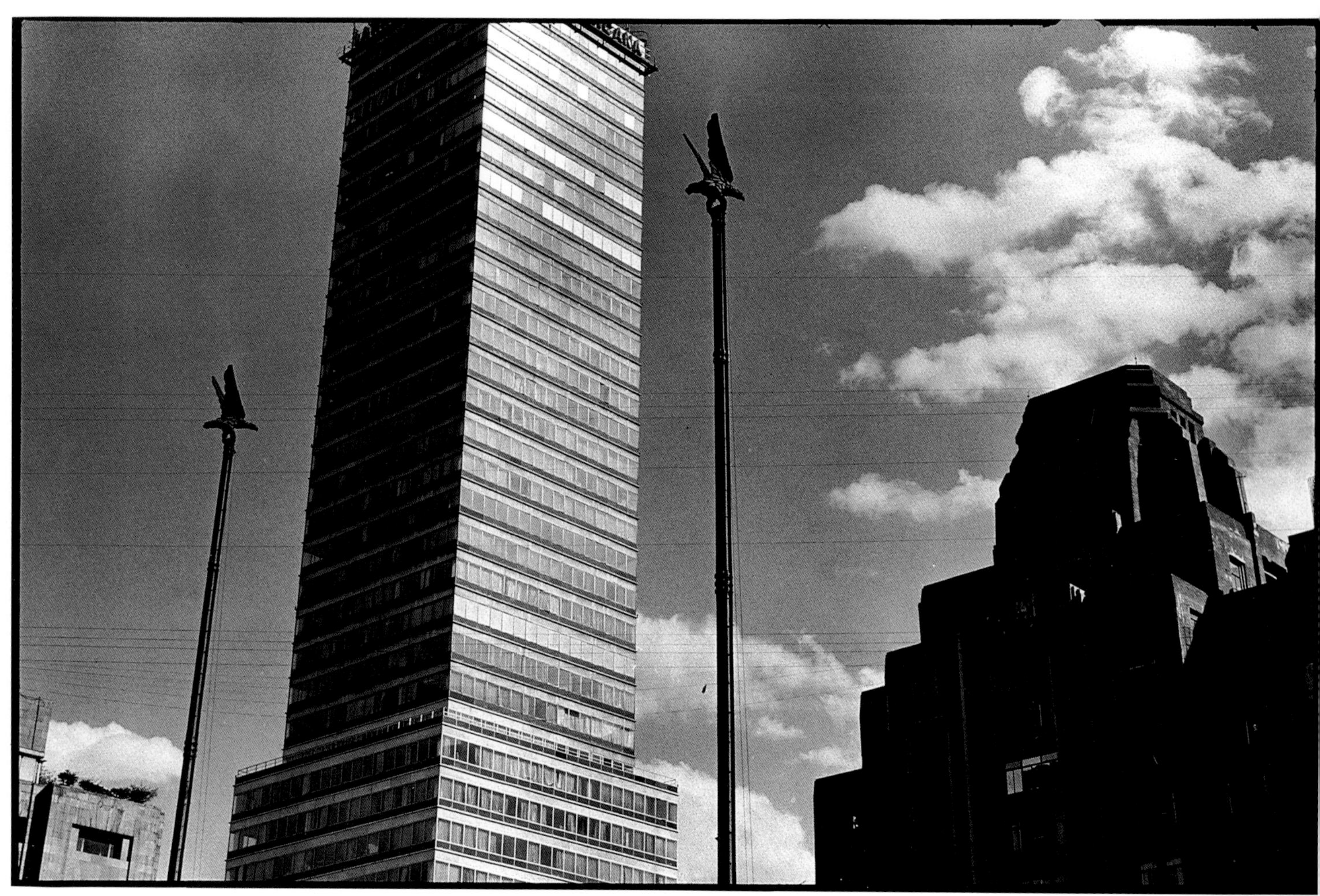

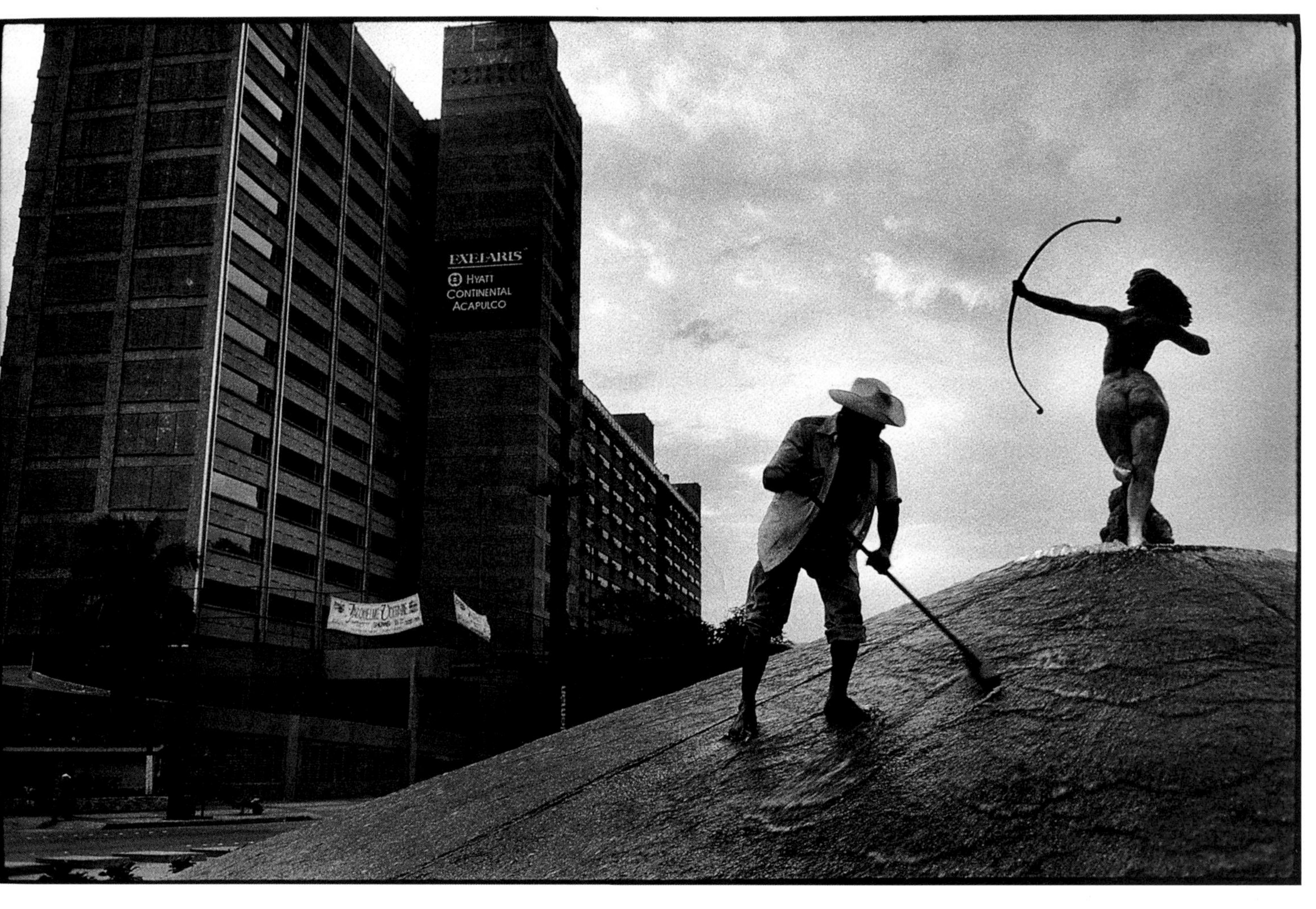
EXELARIS
HYATT
CONTINENTAL
ACAPULCO

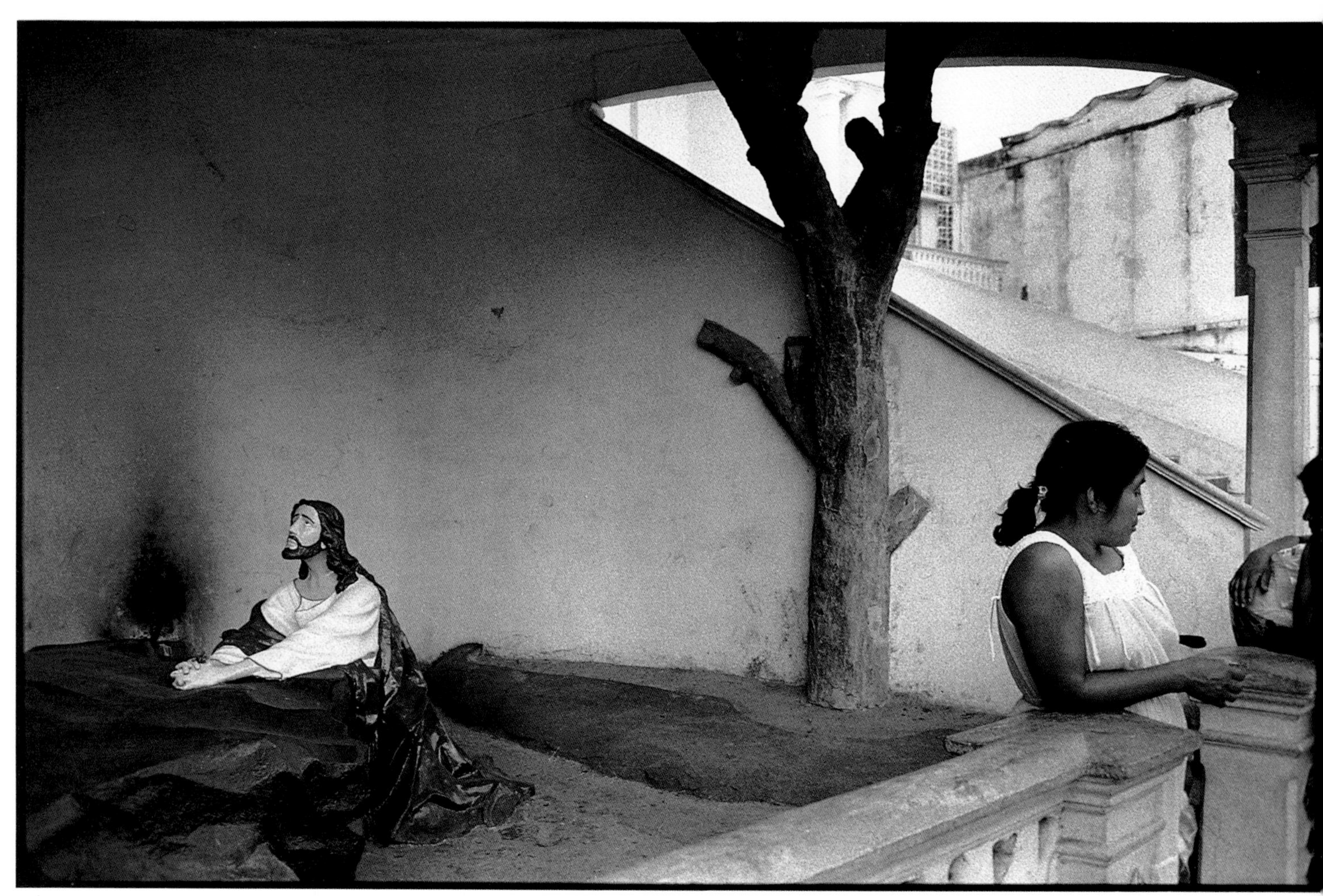

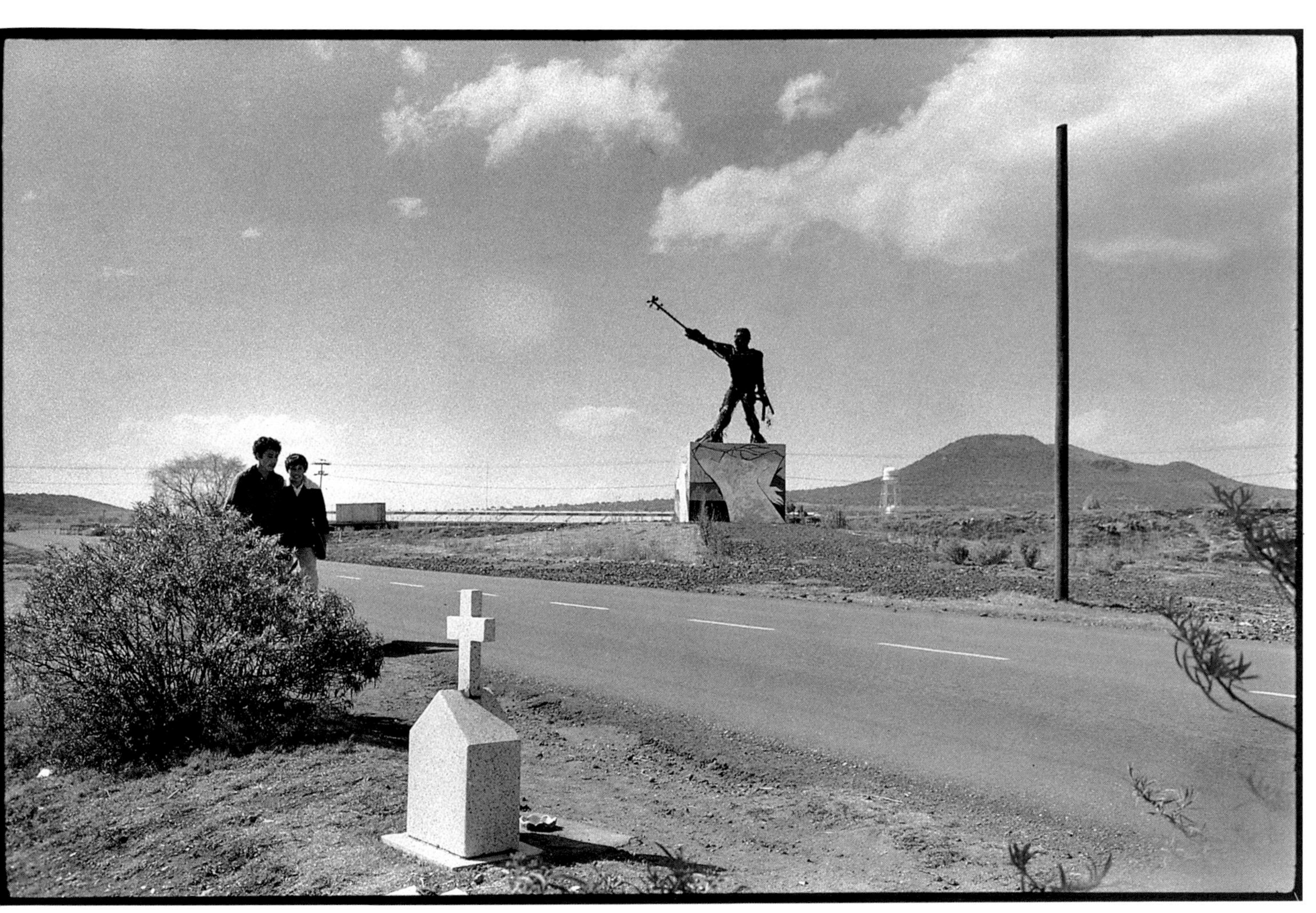

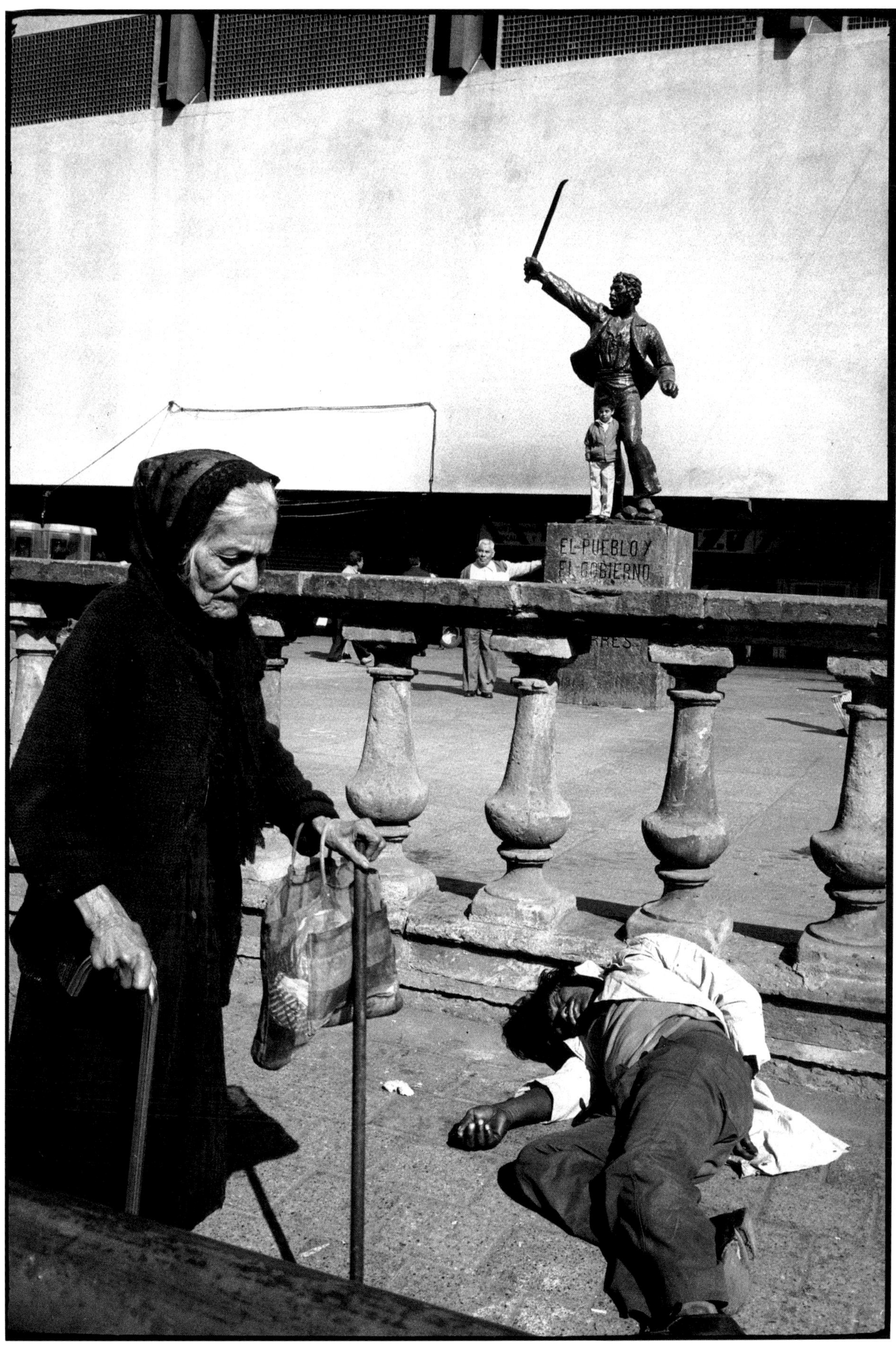
EL PUEBLO Y
EL GOBIERNO
RRES

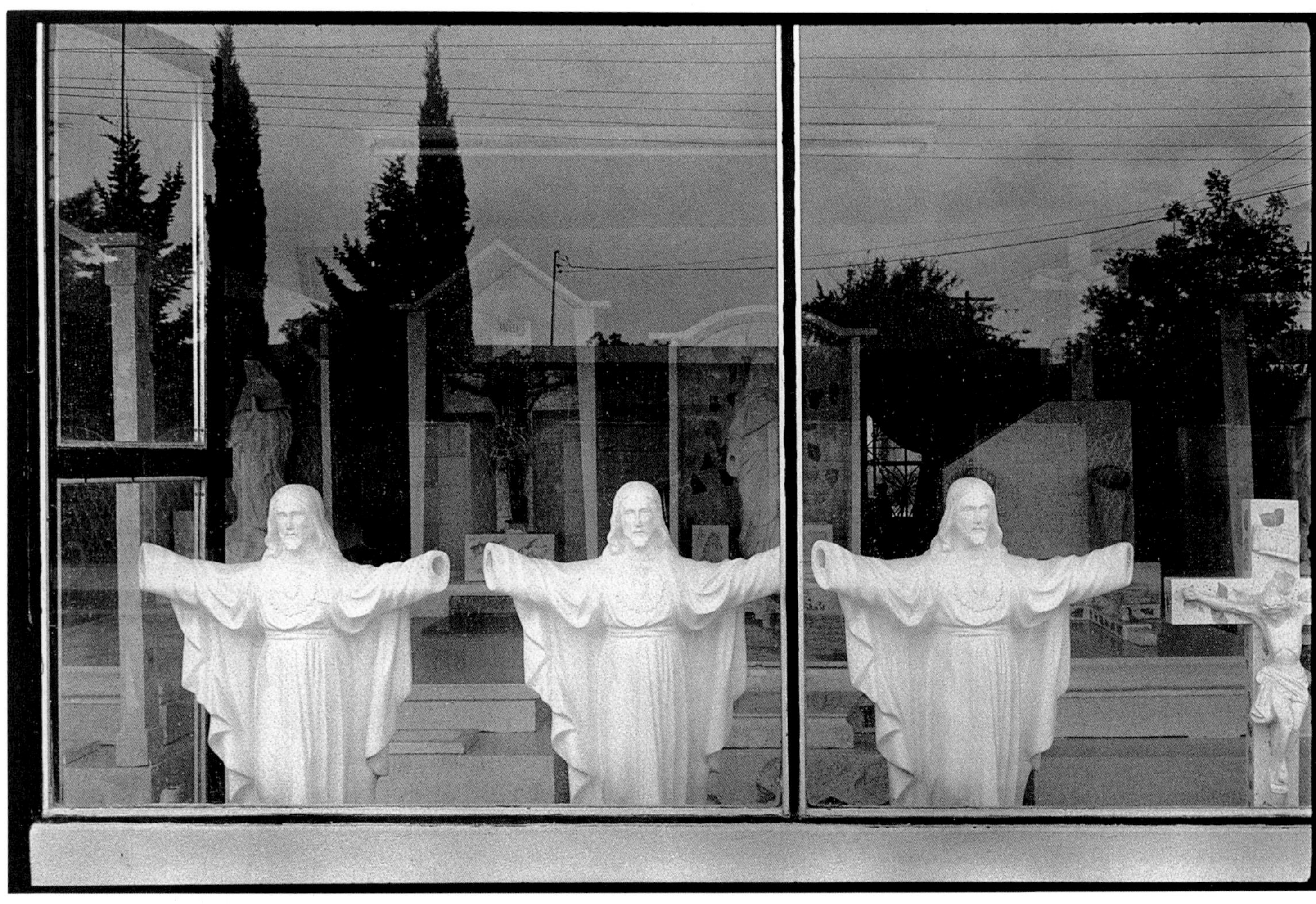

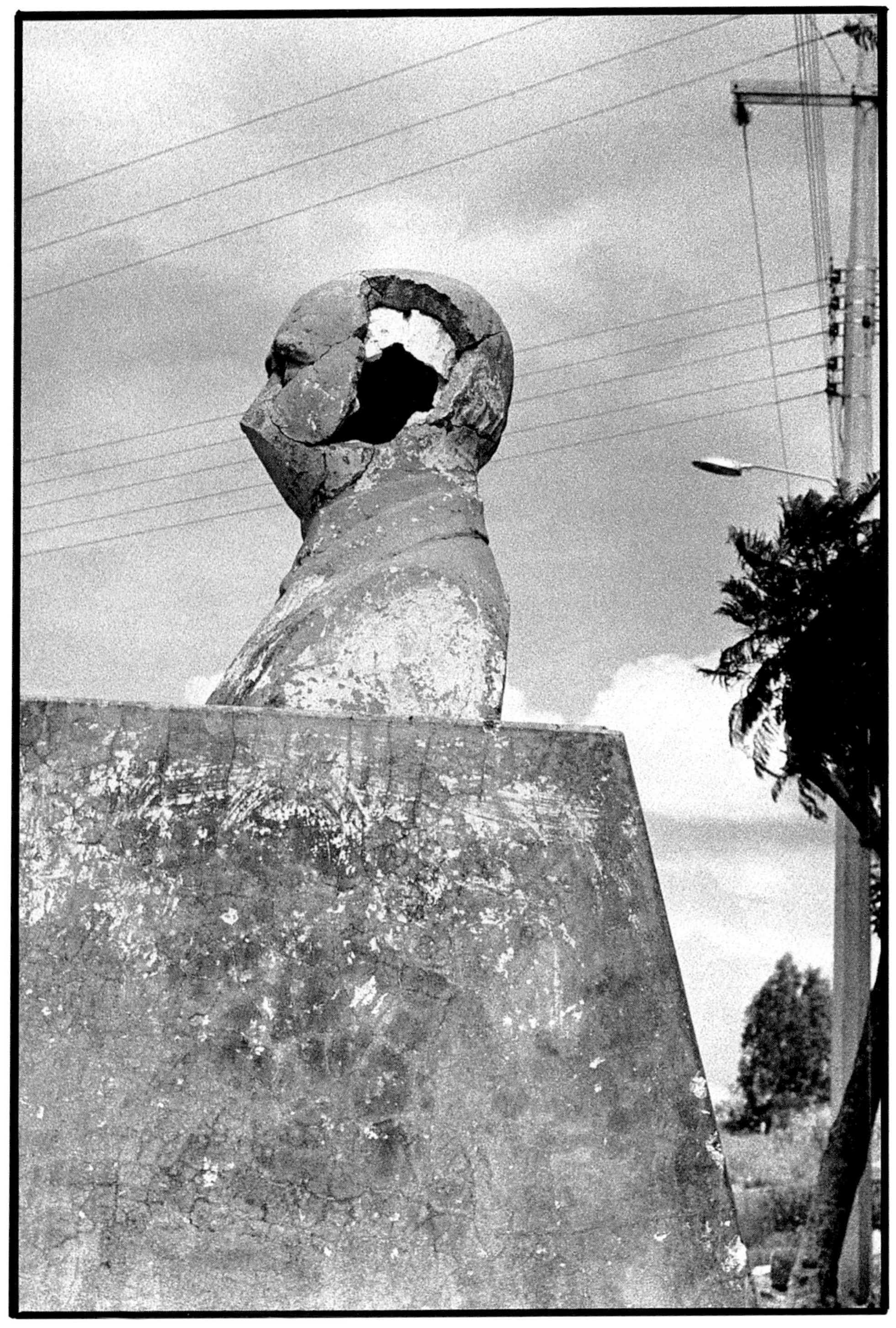

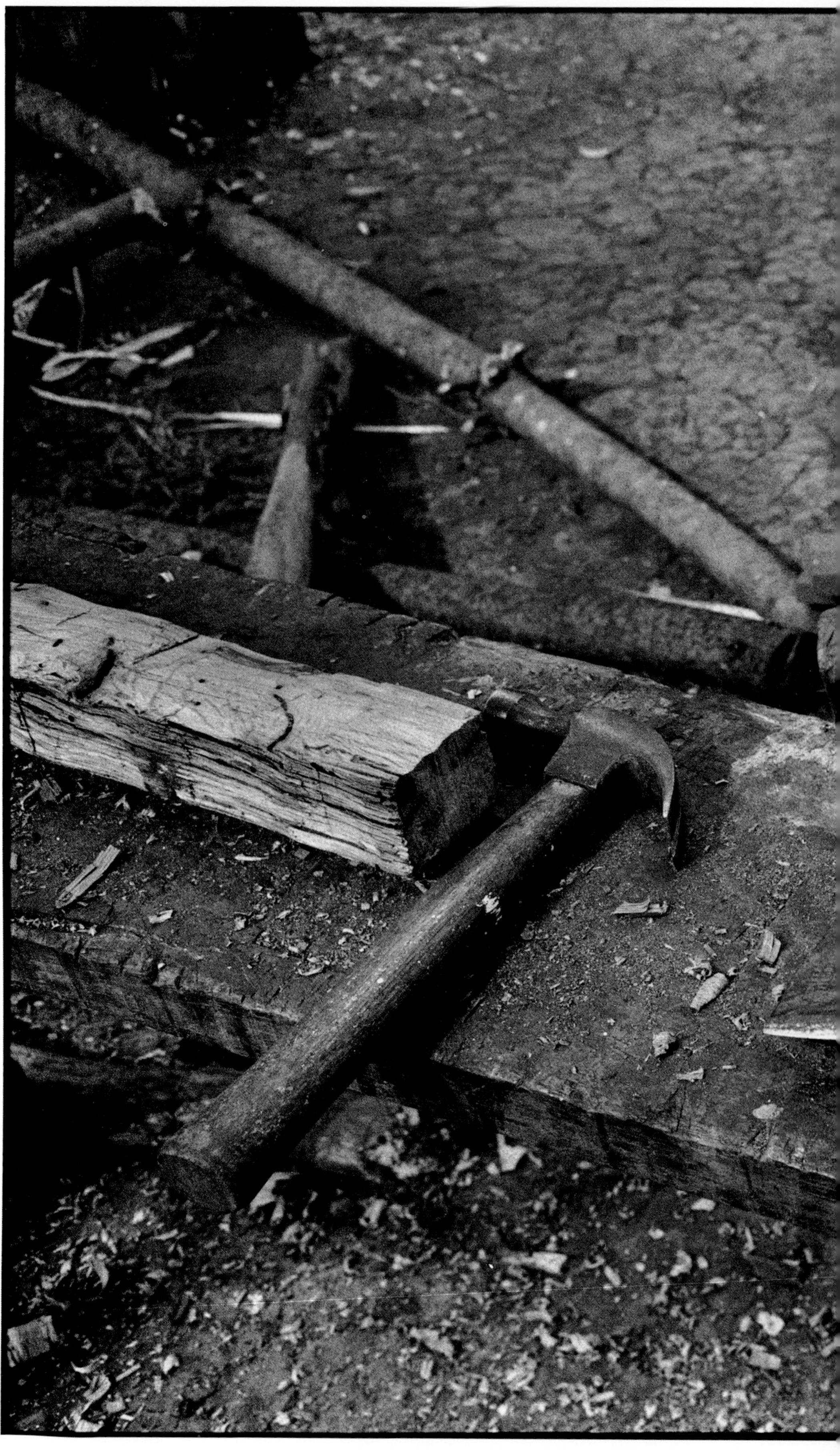

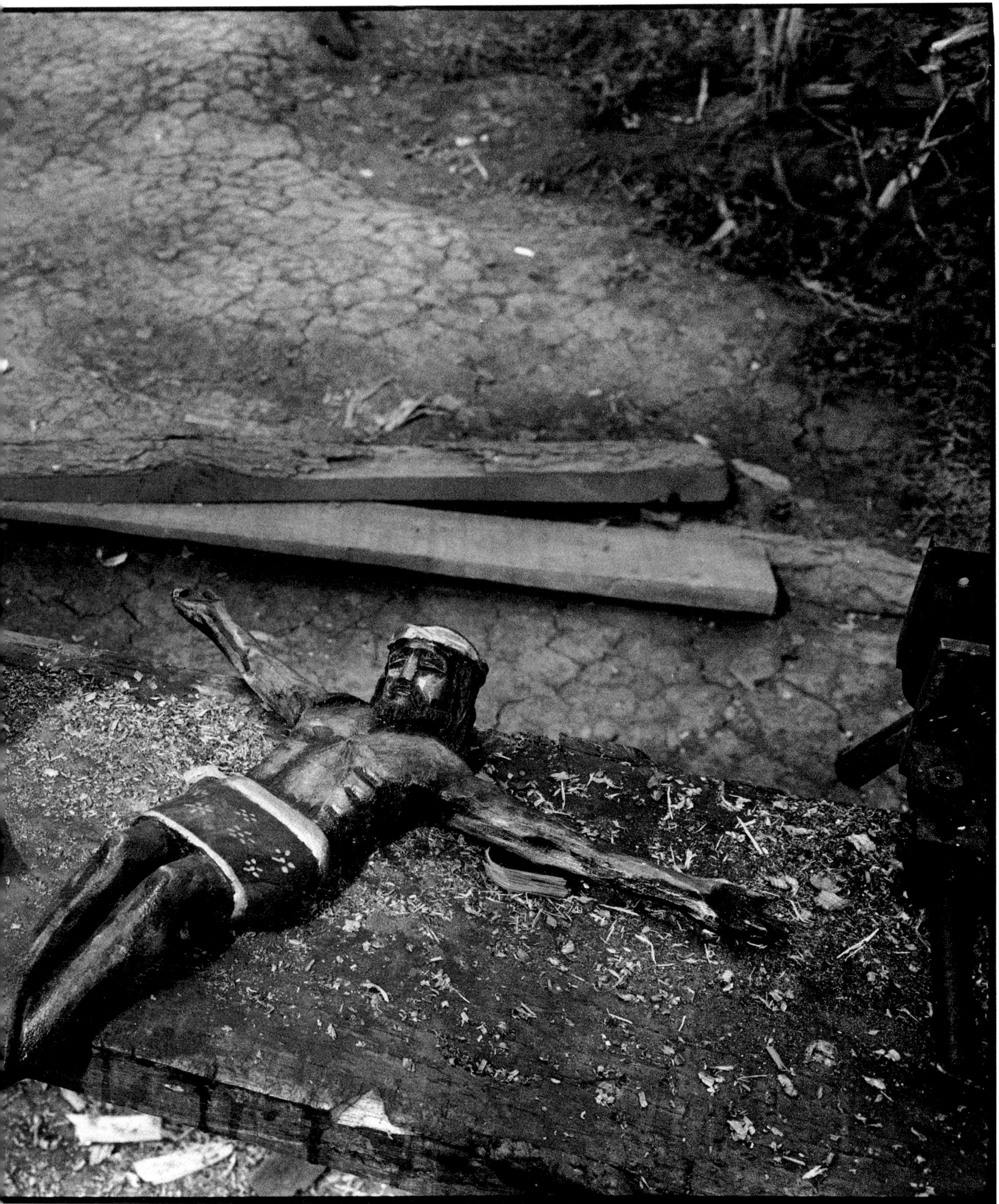

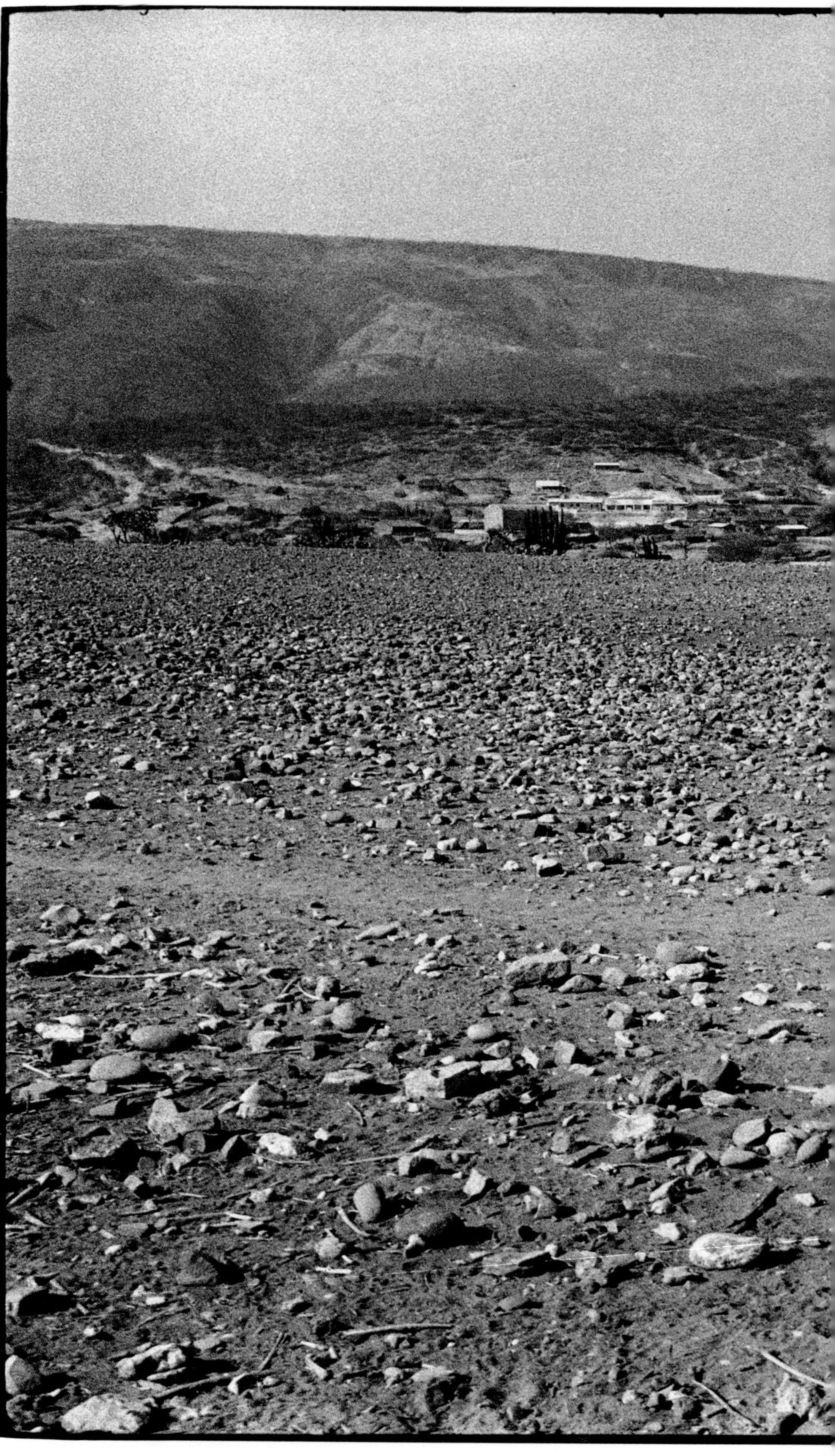

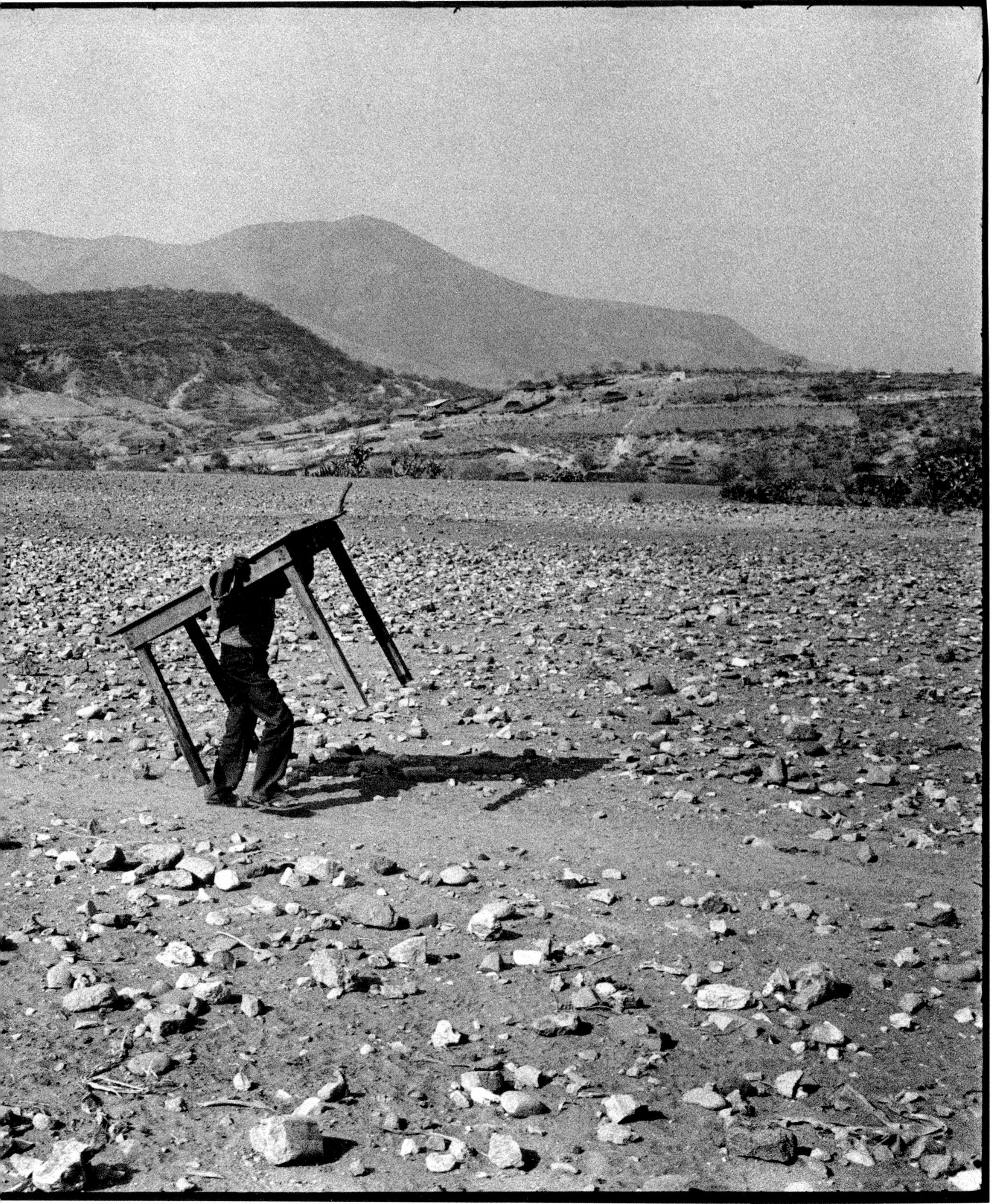

Return to Mexico

Abbas

Man's truth lies in what he hides.
—André Malraux

20 December
I spent the day with Tina. The opaque afternoon light on her tombstone, the already blurring poem by Pablo Neruda: "My sister, sleep, no, no, don't sleep . . .," the eucalyptus leaf slumbering on her name, the weeds all around, and the gloomy and mysterious space of the trees over the other graves . . . the *alcatraz* blossoms offered to the cement and to memory . . . the silence. . . . I wonder where Tina's soul is now. . . . I also wonder about Edward, and certain coincidences. . . .

I owed it to myself to lay flowers on Tina Modotti's grave in Mexico City: it's partly because of her that I've returned to Mexico after an absence that I hoped would be for only several weeks, but that lasted fourteen years. I was overcome with a longing for Mexico when I read Mildred Constantine's biography of Tina, *Una Vida Frágil*, a frail life. . . . I missed those streets in Coyoacan where we walked some forty-five years apart, I missed the intense cultural life she shared with Edward Weston during the nineteen twenties and the Mexican Revolution, and that I myself experienced in 1968, during the Olympic Games and the student revolution. . . .

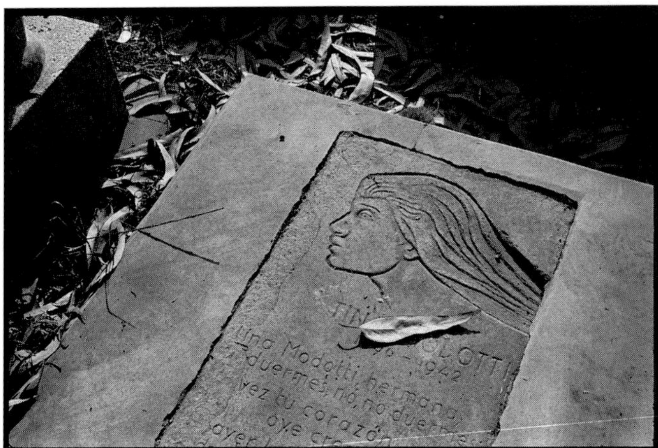

What a scream I must have been: a cynical reporter and hardened war correspondent, holding arums—Tina's *alcatrazes*—in one hand and the number of the graveyard lane in the other hand, walking through a Mexican afternoon, looking for the grave of a woman whom he was infatuated with, and who died before he was born. . . . *Pendejo romántico*, romantic whim! . . .

21 December
The best way to discover Mexico is to get lost. Take any bus at random, stop willy-nilly for encounters, events, or urban architecture, and spend the day trekking up and down the district. At last, a third-world city where I have complete freedom to photograph anything: no one urging me to "go look at the modern neighborhoods," no budding art director, no lens censor, no vision dictator.

Why this benevolence, this lack of personal aggressiveness? Because independence is no longer a sore point here? Because this country is accustomed to its tourists? . . . The tolerance of Indian culture and the every-man-for-himself attitude in the inner city?

Yet life is hard in this megalopolis of eighteen million people, with its oppressive rhythm, its yawning social gaps. One symptom of the illness that brought on the revolution in Teheran was precisely the aggressivity in the streets, the lack of courtesy among Iranians. All the cities in this rapidly developing Third World exhale that same violence: aggressive, even savage Lagos, aggressive Kinshasa, Algiers, Bangkok, Cairo, although the gentleness of Buddhism and the easygoing ways of the Nile may soften the hostility. The worst thing the Mexicans do is to turn away from my lens.

22 December
The journalist in me is conscious, and I am haunted by the question of what I want to do with these freely taken photos that have not been impelled by any global event. In Mexico City, I am not covering a war, a prerevolution, an earthquake, or a conference. But when I headed this way, I swore I'd find adventure. . . . And so?

*Translated from the French by Joachim Neugroschel.

23 December

Yesterday a completely unhurried trip to Juchitan in Graciela and Pedro's car [photographers Graciela Iturbide and Pedro Meyer], down the somber peaks surrounding Mexico City, toward the sea—transition from the scattered and thick-set vegetation to the profusion of the tropics. I was very moved when Graciela told me she had dreamt all night about the photos of Iran, Vietnam, and Ireland that I had shown her. She also said that I had touched a sensitive nerve the other evening when I asked Don Manuel (Alvarez Bravo) whether he had ever been tempted to add a social and political aspect to his photos. . . . It seems I caused him some distress, for he has actually begun wondering, at the age of eighty, after sixty years of photographing, whether he shouldn't have. . . .

In Juchitan a wall graffiti says, "Que muere la Coca-Cola"—Die, Coca-Cola.

28 December

It's no wonder some mornings are difficult, for at night I live my Iranian revolution, its violence and disappointments. The feelings I bottled up in order to function as a photographer are still exploding, three years later—time bombs in my dreams. . . . I feel lonely this morning, and I give in to my loneliness, whereas in my work—because of my voluntary professionalism—I keep all distractions at bay. In front of me, two empty benches enveloped in the cloudy gray of morning . . . Precisely what I feel . . . A photo . . .

The whole city of Minatitlan is dominated by the grand organs of its oil refinery. . . . When you say a city lives in the shadow of its factory, you're implying that the city's life is organized around this factory, that all its economic activity depends on it. Here, that's no figure of speech: the refinery literally dominates the city. . . . Happy the land where everything is visual.

But how should I shoot this factory town, capture the problems caused by the recent wealth brought by oil? It's too glib always seeking that image of slums against the background of a refinery flare. Economic development is more ambiguous than that. The sudden manna of petroleum doesn't just accentuate the social gaps. Here industrialization doesn't signify pollution and hellish rhythms; it means regular salaries, buying power, and social benefits—all the things that European workers dreamt of during the nineteenth century. The Mexican, just like the Iranian or the Nigerian, respects his factory, lives intimately with it. . . . (p. 59)

Normally, it's the inside of the plant that interests me, the relationship between the worker and the machine. This time, I'm not making any official contact, not requesting any authorization. The exterior suffices for me. The sky is on my side this morning; it's cloudy, uniform; it makes the scenes of life look heavy, crushing the perspective. The city's life seems embedded in the refinery's life. I work on the gray.

1 January

Ah, these Indians! I'm so frustrated. So sick of not being allowed to shoot the gloomy nave of the church of Chamula in the Chiapas country, the abrupt ray of light that illuminates an Indian kneeling between two rows of candles and the offering of three bottles of Pepsi. He passes a dead chicken across the candle flame, takes his son's pulse, and mutters secret incantations. Look but don't shoot? Play the tourist?

Nothing helps, not my letters of recommendation which are clustered with official stamps, not my arguments about the necessity of photographing their customs in order to preserve them. Forget it! The town chairman wouldn't hear of it. I respect these Indians, who refuse to be fair game for tourists. There are so many countries where tourism is leprosy. They have the right to their image, granted, but don't I have the right to the image?

6 January

Juan's memory haunts me in this tenacious mist of Sierra Mazateca. He drowned in 1970, perhaps a suicide. Was his death already written? One day, under the influence of mushrooms, Joaquin saw all his near and dear growing younger and younger until they disappeared into their births—all, except Juan.

I've brought along the photo that was salvaged from my 1969 reportage: Juan sitting in our hut, chewing his fingernails—a familiar gesture when he was mulling over his writing. He recedes behind the superimposition of the village of San Mateo: I inadvertently got a double exposure, and the film was saved during a raid because it was still inside my camera.

San Mateo no longer looks desolate and miserable: it seems prosperous. Electric power was installed in 1970. Dona Celia's ragamuffin son is now an engineer, and his daughter will soon be attending college. But I am told the village is jealous of her family, envying them for gaining a bigger profit from the mushroom bucks of hippies during the nineteen sixties. Dona Celia is scared. "They'll kill us the way they killed the shopkeeper who had two trucks." What tragedies lie hidden in such a little village.

9 January

In Huautla, on the facing peak, I follow a wedding procession, and I'm accepted as if I'd been invited. After mass, the bride and groom, in white, climb up to their hamlet, which perches high in the jungle. Three little girls clutch the bride's train, and they will soon be swallowed up by the somber

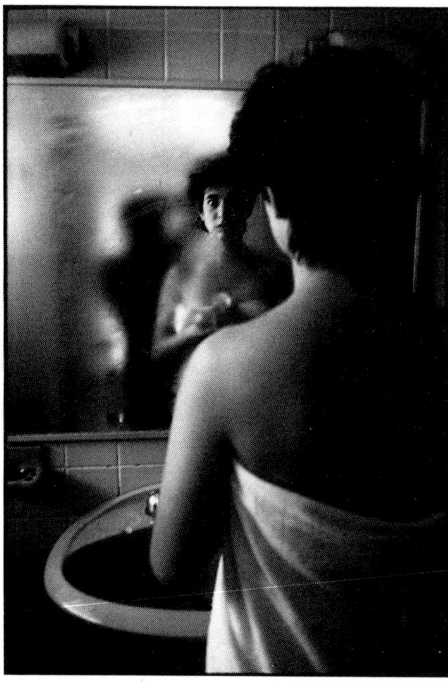

void of trees exploding in the oblique sunlight. A lovely image, of course, but is it relevant for the Mexico that I want to show? The beauty of photojournalism also consists in transcending the subject, catching images that live of their own accord, beyond their time and place. (p. 45)

12 January

At the exhibition opening, a friend remarked that the visitors were speaking only in whispers. Pictures of Iran, Vietnam, South Africa, Ireland, which I have gathered to exhibit, to exhibit myself. A woman weeps silently, another stammers to me about how moved she is. Could I hope for any better criticism?

15 January

Back to the poor outskirts of Mexico City. The townscape under construction has always fascinated me; the social tensions here are more powerful, and the contradictions of a society thrown off balance by industrialization are more blatant. In Santa Helena, where the communal land has been taken over by squatters, the people no longer demonstrate for electric power; they help themselves from the local pylons. (p. 62)

My photos of the city will always lack the noise, the nonstop cacophony of cars, radios, itinerant peddlers, the shouts of bus drivers hailing passengers, their tenacious beeping. I have never been able to compensate by showing the chaos of the city. What can I do? Even my shots of disorder are orderly. Yet the Iranian that I am ought to delight in the *sholooghi*—a Farsi word for any disorder: the turbulence of a disturbed man, the rowdyism of kids in the street, or a bloody popular uprising.

Each photo requires a multitude of immediate and simultaneous decisions: choosing the lens, speed, and aperture, picking the angle and the moment, snapping right off the bat or waiting for the action to unfold in the viewfinder, going for a long shot or a close-up, dwelling on the background or trying to make the people stand out. I like capturing up to five actions in one photo, coordinating them in a calm or choppy harmony, depending on the day's mood. (pp. 48–49)

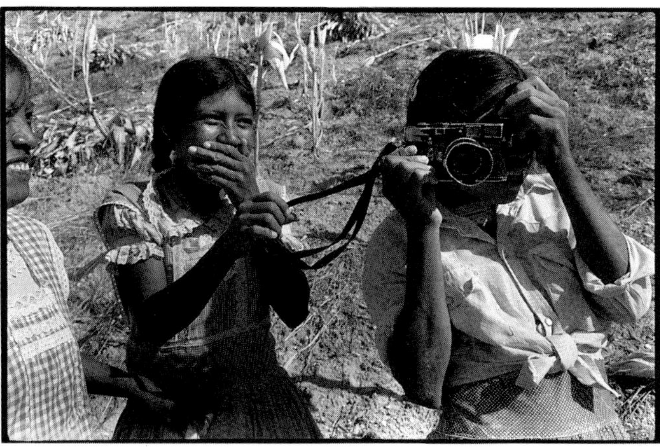

I have to see everything all the time and, even with my eye in the viewfinder, I have to be aware of anything happening outside the rectangle. After a good day's work, it's my nerves that are exhausted, not my muscles. For me, photographing is also a state of grace without which I would be incapable of marshaling the required muscular and nervous energy. On some nights, I feel as if I were returning from the front lines, even in a peaceful suburb of Mexico City.

23 January

Monterrey, the grand, haughty northern city, grows more interesting with every step I take, because of the juxtaposition of its Mexican and American cultures. In this city, I shoot against the light, for I glimpse nothing but urban violence. When I shoot against the light, the smallest lamppost turns menacing, each passerby becomes a dark shadow, each block of houses sneaky, each empty roadway a desert of basalt.

Many photographers have shot the inhumanity of the city as if it were as natural as the hostility of the jungle. I would like to show that this human solitude is not a product of chance, a whim of the gods, but the fruit of what man creates in his own image.

This is where I can provide the full social dimension of my work: it's not enough to convey the effects of Mexico's transition into a modern state; I also have to suggest the causes and present them in their historical perspective. This anarchic development of the inner city is not a random process; it is the child of an ideology, which is itself the heir to historical facts like colonization, the ornery coexistence with the powerful northern neighbor, the internal epic made up of violence, social tensions, explosions . . .

Photojournalism certainly has its limits, but isn't my goal to expand them?

Leaving Monterrey, I see that the sixteen clocks of the bus station each tell a different time. Is that the Machine's independence from Man or a reflection of Mexico's legendary disrespect for the dictatorship of time?

30 January

En route for Chihuahua . . . across a bare desert landscape, its dust, like that of the vast Asian plateaus, suddenly enveloping everything on the road. . . . And that wind, the desert flute playing through the panes . . . I love those stretches where the eyes are not under constant siege, where they can get lost in the immensity of the earth joining the sky, where dreams become possible. To travel in a bus, see the landscape roll by like a silent movie, and I absent, lost in my thoughts, sometimes feeling a total emptiness inside myself, gazing through the window but unconcerned about nature, people, or things, absorbing only the motion.

I like this availability of every moment when I travel. . . . Everyday life is suspended, forgotten in Paris, while I devote myself to the joyous priesthood of photography.

Who will someday sing the ballad of the Mexican bus driver? A great lover of *ranchera* music, which he ingenuously inflicts on all his passengers . . . A man who stops at noon, sometimes forgets to come back and has to be hunted down, who parks his bus at a crossroads, disappears, and then returns ten minutes later with three cases of Coca-Cola or a basket of tacos, who occasionally, after ten minutes of driving, makes all his passengers get out, refunds their money, and charges off in a different direction. In Mexico, you never know why the bus is stopping.

3 February

Waking up every morning with a new window, a new sky . . . The chopped-up time of traveling. I think of my schedule for tomorrow. . . . I no longer feel like going where my eyes happen to lead me. Time is starting to make its demands inside me. I have more and more days without photos. Yet I've risen early every day, eager to work. . . . No, I've lost my curiosity about faces and gestures. . . . The street no longer excites me. . . . After six weeks, my eye has gotten accustomed to everyday life and seeks only the exotic. . . . My star must be in an unfavorable constellation. . . .

What the hell am I doing here, just what the hell am I doing in this backwater dump of Cuauhtemoc?

5 February

Guadalajara. At the opera house, the governor delivers his annual State-of-the-State Address. The entire political class is present: businessmen, journalists, captains of industry, union bosses, executives. A conglomerate of sated VIPs. And outside, the signs and banners of poor people who have come to offer some rather dreary support. For a long time now, there has been nothing revolutionary about the PRI (Partido Revolutionario Institucional); but the fiction has to be maintained: a revolutionary party has to rely on the masses, so there are masses at even the most insignificant ceremony.

Next comes the luncheon, the back-patting, the *felicidades* and the displays of concern, the hearty thank-yous and the smiles of hope, the whispered requests and the exchanges of business cards, the slicked-back hair and the swaggering mustachios, the three-piece suits and the triumphant, well-to-do, and obsequious airs. A few old fogies, ex-governors, and ex-whatnots who are greatly sought after. The elegant eye-darting ladies in all colors of the rainbow. The ruling class and its great deeds (pp. 70–71).

Everything in Mexico is tragicomical: of the thousands of initial supporters, only a handful remains, a tiny claque when the governor leaves the luncheon. On the other hand, he can hear the shouts aimed at him: "Thief, murderer, drunkard, ally of the big landowners, heartless enemy of *la clase humilde* (the lower classes)."

Because the country is celebrating its constitution today, one opposition party after another stations itself two hundred yards from the luncheon to denounce the corruption, the confiscations of land, the killings of militant farmers, the election frauds, the police violence against demonstrators.

Is this a lesson in democracy for dictatorships? In any case, it's a closely watched democracy. There is a man jotting notes about everything: at first, I assume he's a journalist, but then I find him again at the luncheon, tranquilly sitting in the midst of the bodyguards. Upon finishing his meal, he returns to the demonstration and just as tranquilly resumes his jotting.

Shouts of "Zapata, wake up!"

7 February

An old man hauls me over the coals when I photograph a drunk sleeping blissfully under a statue of a revolutionary (p. 103). He reproaches me for giving Mexico a bad rep. He's not convinced when I tell him this picture won't be isolated, it'll have its place among the thousands of pictures I'm taking of his country.

I recall that nothing infuriated me more than the propensity of foreign photographers to include a woman in a *tchador*, a young, bearded militiaman, or a mullah—symbols of revolutionary Islam—in every photo snapped in Iran. And Westerners were astonished at my pictures of women in dresses, clean-shaven men, peaceful street scenes.

The symbolic photo is a digest (maximum information in the limited space of the print), creating a tenacious myth.

21 February

Every morning I watch a slaughter. . . . The vengeful violence of the ax smashing into the flayed skull that is already detached from the bull's body (p. 81), the slow and indifferent sadism of the *borracho*, drunkard, unable to find the jugular vein, exploring the pig's neck with his long pig-sticker . . . the human wailing of the animal that won't die

. . . the children around them, smiling, peering, and listening, unfazed. . . . I'm mesmerized by that daily, necessary, and innocent brutality. . . .

Yet there is harmony here between man and beast. . . . They coexist. . . . Why that useless sadism? . . . The liquor helping every Mexican to get out of himself? The impact of that torrid, barren, exalted nature? . . .

I spend three days in Oapan, that tiny hamlet in Guerrero. . . . The soil is sun baked, the tree roots monstrous, the bodies worn out from drudgery, the cacti ominously towering, the men deliberately getting drunk, lamentable stooges flopping in the dust. Violence is everywhere, in the earth, in the people.

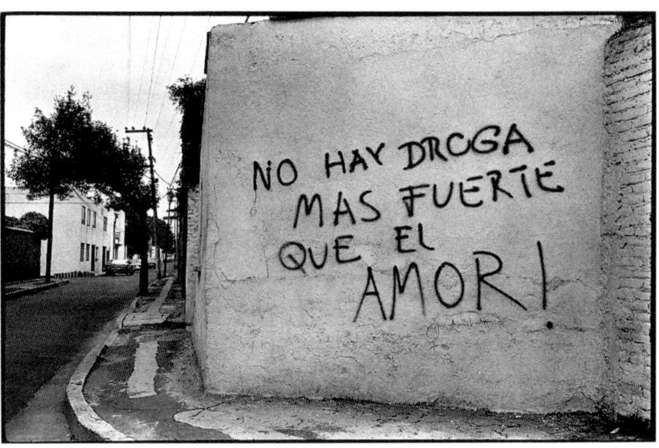

A small village, like so many in Mexico: it's had its electric power for four years now, its new school, its dispensary . . . "You understand, we always vote for the PRI—that way the government takes care of us. . . ."

The bus lumbers off on its sinuous route back. What a profession! Four days ago, I shook the white-gloved hand of Her Most Gracious Majesty Elizabeth II when she was on an official visit to Acapulco . . . and today this village at the edge of the world . . .

The next day

The village violence has seized hold of me. . . . In the returning bus, I suddenly realize that no photographer has ever truly dealt with the violence of everyday life. . . . The violence of war, the violence of the inner city, of disease, infirmity, yes! The violence of institutions, of society . . . the violence of men's indifferent madness, yes! Robert Capa, Weegee, Diane Arbus, Eugene Smith, Margaret Bourke-White have described those kinds of violence as effects. . . . But what photographer has cried out violence, cried out the violence that becomes visible only because it's inside each one of us? . . .

5 September

Abraham, my host in Oapan, has to spend three hours trudging up the mountain to sow his corn seeds in the middle of the gravelly marl. . . . Quite literally an uphill labor, and he can never be sure of a harvest if the rain fails to come, like last year. . . . "*Es muy triste la milpa*," the corn is very sad.

On the hill dominating Oapan, in the stone chapel, two old women perform a rather strange rite—pre-Columbian? The Virgin appeared to one of them in her sleep, and the old woman exhibits as proof the slipper that *la Virgen* left behind. A plastic slipper, familiar, ludicrous, pathetic . . . And then the Señor appeared, Christ, whose profile is engraved in the stone she now shows me. . . . Flowers everywhere in the gloomy den, the votive candles, the offerings of poor pesetas left by pilgrims climbing up from the village . . . A worship that seems to emerge from the innermost core of their collective psyche, from the Aztec night . . . The village is divided in regard to those cults. Some see the devil's hand. . . . A premonition of the tragedy that will strike one night? . . .

15 September

This is my third visit to Oapan . . . already? The villagers tolerate me: they allow me to shoot their fiestas, but not their funerals. An old woman explains it to me: "A photo is for the moments of joy, when we're having fun, not when we're sad!" The *borrachos* insist on being photographed, then they want to slash me with their machetes for having photographed them. . . . I have to improve my tactics, so that every villager is flattered at being photographed.

It's not easy getting accepted by these people. So far no one has told me about the village rivalries, the family vendettas. They must exist! People do not live together innocently for centuries. Among themselves, they speak only Nahuatl. I have to be very diplomatic, act open and firm. As usual, it will be a power struggle between the villages and me.

I've put her photo on the table, near the huge pile of cornmeal. She's smiling at me, from that Chilean lake all the way to the night of Oapan. . . . It's three A.M. The dreams of the pollola are waiting for me.

18 September

Today I shot the forms of the village—tree trunks, stones, cacti. But the 35mm film isn't ideal for that. It doesn't render all the finesse of the texture, the endless variation of tones between black and white. It's hard doing Weston with a Leica. Weston! One of the great influences on my work, along with Eugene Smith, Bill Brandt, Kertesz, and of course Robert Capa. Ultimately, I'm an orphan with many masters, but the child of none. After all, I'm not heir to several centuries of Western art; I don't have to reinvent the world every morning.

As I got out of the bus that February afternoon, it took me only one glance to realize that this would be *my* village, the one I'd been looking for since my first return to Mexico. This arid, ocher hamlet, where everything looked incomplete, where anything was possible. As if the gods had created it on the Third Day and then departed, neglecting to return and polish the people and the things . . . A village where I could experience the Mexican soul, its pre-Hispanic culture, its Aztec days . . .

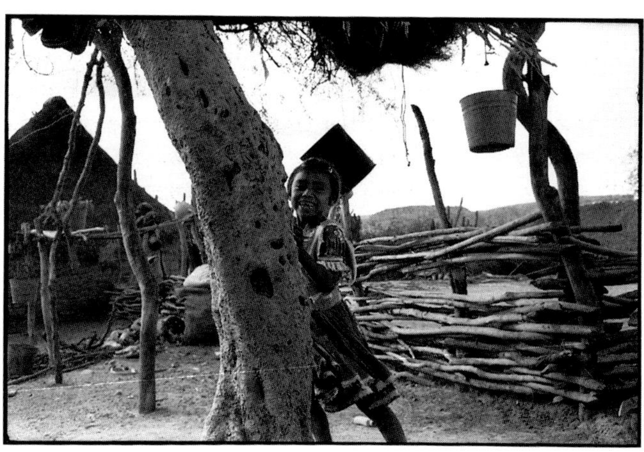

Why do I come back to Oapan so frequently? Am I seeking exoticism, am I trying to explore the shades of my new way of photographing? Because this village and its exteriors harmonize so violently with what my inner world has been ever since I embarked on this adventure, on these returns to Mexico? *Quien sabe?* Who knows?

People have often quoted my statement: "We photojournalists are not changing the world. All we can do is show why this world has to change, sometimes." Here, too, I can only show what is changing, can change, has to change. For I have no answers for the problem of economic change characteristic throughout the Third World . . .

Little has changed in Oapan since the time of the Aztecs, yet this hamlet is already suffering from an excess of technological inevitability! It's impossible to sleep with the *ranchera* music bawled by the loudspeaker belonging to the neighbor, who, with arrogant simplicity, has confiscated the sounds of the neighborhood. It always begins at five A.M., when the *campesinos* (peasants) set off for their fields. It continues in the evening, when the bodies exhausted from heat and drudgery yearn for nothing but rest, peace, impossible silence. How aggravating that permanent racket. And sometimes it resumes in the middle of the night when that boorish peasant, drunk on *cana* (sugarcane alcohol) plays the D.J., dedicating each song to one of the villagers! The loudspeaker has become the symbol of power: only the most prosperous farmers own them.

On the evening news, the U.S. president talks about the New Frontier of Space and exhorts the entire world to hurry toward it. Space research, seen from Oapan? What bitter irony!

21 September

Statues are very present inhabitants of Mexico. They are everywhere, on squares and opposite churches, in hotels and on shop roofs, at the edges of villages and outside factories. The Mexican streets are changing, modernity is stealthily creeping in. . . . The statues remain, eternal witnesses to the *locura Mexicana*, that joyful surrealistic madness. They have the knack of arousing my emotions, like a face, a movie, a symphony.

I've been shooting them since my first week in Mexico City, but today I crack up in front of two busts that turn their backs on each other, dragging a forgotten quarrel into eternity. I decide to make those statues the characters in my Mexican photo-novel. Will they escape me some day and lead their own lives?

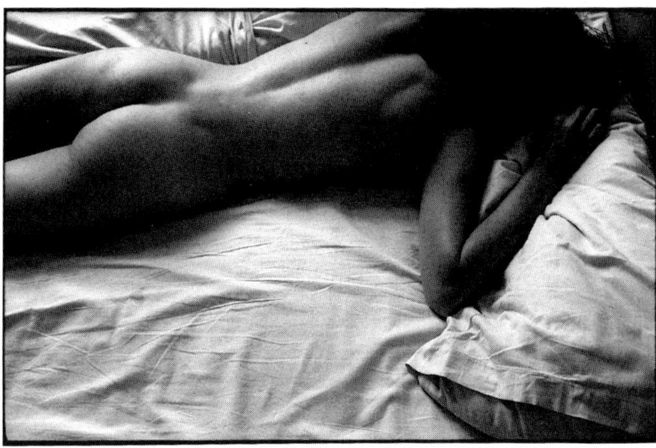

22 September

When I used the word "photo-novel" yesterday, was I being innocent? This is no essay that I am photographing—i.e., writing with light. I have nothing to prove or demonstrate, except myself. I've immersed myself in Mexico and I'm led by the rhythm of the country, possessed by its breathing—it isn't I who lead or possess. Isn't this how a novelist works? Statues have become characters here, as were the pre-Hispanic signs, religion and death, technology and the surrounding surrealism, the animals and the masks . . . the violence. . . . I'm not deliberately seeking the signs as in an essay, but I am alert to the traces. . . .

In my mind, I have established the three sections of my book. I insist on elliptical periods. . . . "The Soul," "Existence," "Eternity"—and I am surprised by my characters living their own life. I do not shoot my subjects only, but around them, too.

Who has written photography like a novel? Essays, autobiographical retrospectives, yes. Travel books with series of photos that sometimes converse with one another, yes. Collections of moods, feelings, meetings, yes. But a book in which imagination plays with reality?

15 October

My friends may be right: security in Mexico City leaves something to be desired. In an out-of-the-way nook at the university, the volcanic lava has congealed in a sea of black waves. A sculptor has surrounded this space with blocks of granite and titled the whole entity: *Espacio Cultural*. I'm here alone. Suddenly, two men point guns at me and say only one word: "*Dinero*" (money). This isn't a movie, the Colt bullets are visible and very real, and impatient.

I hand over my money but refuse to give up my Leicas. One of the *pistoleros* hits me while the other aims his gun at me, snapping, "I'm gonna kill this fucker!" Odd how time speeds up at such moments, just as I think faster. Logically, a barking dog doesn't bite, especially just for some cameras, but who knows? . . . What if they're desperadoes, fanatics? . . . *Carajo!* The photo I'm missing, the picture of my own mugging! Should I try it on the quiet? Won't I risk reminding them of the cameras, which they seem to have forgotten? Don't play the hero, the scene has taken only a few seconds, other visitors arrive, the *pistoleros* dash off.

The price of being powerless? For two days, I'll dream of nothing but vengeance, karate chops, emasculation.

17 December

Paris, work prints in front of me. In the Sierra de Puebla, I did a lot of fooling around with the depth of field to make the backgrounds cloudy.

Well, so much for that! Fuzzy images aren't for me. I want my photos to be the way I see: sharp. Even if I have to suffer from that excess of lucidity. I've also had it with pictures of sunlight piercing a mist, cast shadows, tender lyricism, which would be merely gratuitous with me. Those photos will never escape the contact sheet.

17 February

The grave hour of dawn, when the sun gently steals into my room in Mexico City—an auspicious time for reflecting, writing, before I'm overcome by the rage for action.

I've returned from the Yucatan after touring it for two weeks. I concentrated so hard on meandering without a plan, haphazardly, that sometimes I unintentionally found myself on the same road, in the same city.

A week of furious, solitary traveling . . . in order to forget? I've played so many scenarios in my head, some of them bitter and angry and some of them so understanding. . . . So much hate, and often love . . . I infiltrated deep into her mind and probed my own, reliving so many incidents of our brief but intense life together. I spoke so vividly with her voice, responded with the echo of my own. . . . I shared so many silences. . . .

A week of long tête-à-têtes with my notebook.

Have I described the wild bullfight, in which the bull is actually a huge, humped zebu? Have I talked about the toreador who had to whirl his cape at eye level, rising up on tiptoe to drive home the *estocada*, and I laughed so hard that I couldn't snap the picture? The ear that's presented to him is the size of a tortilla. This bullfight has nothing of the gold-and-carmine pomp and ceremonious violence of a Spanish *corrida*. It's merely a priming for butchery: once the zebu has been slaughtered, three butchers pounce on it, and, with their self-assured gestures, it takes them only six minutes to carve it up. And they say that the Mexican has a mañana attitude! The quarters of the afternoon's hero are quickly weighed and peddled to the wrangling crowd: "It's hot meat, it adds flavor to the *mundungo*," a specialty of the Yucatán.

Have I spoken about the Yucatán women, so stylish in their dresses with embroidered fringes, have I spoken about their voluptuous satin skin, their facial features—living testaments of the Maya days? . . . Have I spoken about the mysterious silence that imbues them, about their tranquil prayers? Is praying so simple?

Have I spoken about my torment, the agony of my aesthetic search, the emotions regaining their freedom, the approach of the spiritual? . . . I'm astonished by my reactions, awestruck at still being vulnerable (although reluctantly), at seeing that my inner citadels, which I've been building up so long and so patiently, can crumble so easily. . . . Is my photography about to change? . . .

The sun is flooding the room now, the paintings are awakening on the walls, the artists are becoming familiar, gazing at me, amused no doubt by my pain and my efforts. . . . A drawing by Diego Rivera, inherited by Pedro Diego, his grandson . . . A photo by Tina Modotti, a photo of Lupe Rivera by Graciela—in Mexico everything is interconnected. . . . Now Edward Weston comes in, his *Daybooks* are like messages from a big brother who went through the same experiences fifty years ago. . . . But what is time? I've just discovered these lines by his biographer, Ben Maddow:

> *It is one of the curious talents that a great artist has in common with an idiot: the ability to function in spite of emotional turmoil.**

Days of intense visions, emotions, thoughts. . . . That tumult inside me, and no girlfriend to share it with in the evenings. . . . Only this goddamn notebook. . . .

2 March

Tlacotalpan. I'm fed up with shooting the boats in the lagoon, the Cristo Maricon in the church, the shoes suspended on electric wires, the two piglets being nicely walked on leashes . . . I'm sick of those street scenes congealed in the hazy afternoon light. . . . How can I shoot these agreeable nothings in this sweet and manicured colonial city

**Edward Weston: 50 Years* (New York: Aperture, 1973).

if I'm seething with utter violence and frustration? Yes—professionalism or force of habit?—I've been photographing those shoes and piglets. But these are photos without any soul, I know it.

I'd rather be in Oapan, with its dense light, its giant cacti, its creeping roots, its desolation, and its undertone of magic. . . .

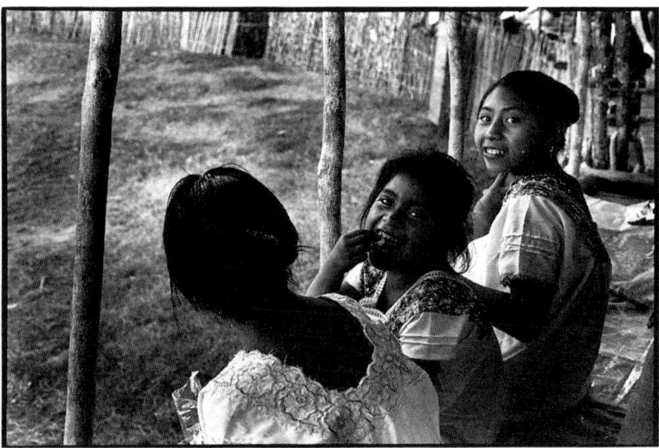

6 March

I've still got shivers running up and down my spine. A couple of minutes outside of Puente de Ixtla, a well-groomed, one-eyed accordionist climbs into the bus, sporting a small red scarf. . . . He's probably going to pour on the usual schmalzy love ditties. *Que non carajo!* He's going to bawl out the ballad of Zapata, the revolutionary who is still honored because he remained true to himself until the end, refusing the presidential chair that Pancho Villa offered him. Zapata, the revolutionary with the so simple and so terrible slogan: "*Tierra y Libertad.*" In Mexico, history is never very far off. It's alive. We are very near the place where Zapata was assassinated, where his myth was elevated by his martyrdom. I recall Casasola's photo of his corpse: he looked so much like the Che, the Christ who was crucified several decades later. . . .

10 March

All the ceremonies in Oapan, whether joyful or sorrowful, are accompanied by the *música*, the band, which reels through the narrow dusty lanes. . . .

Their dances are like their music: a rugged harmony, a sneaky grace . . . Dances made up of fits and starts, jumping and jolting . . . dances of possession, describing the endless battle against nature, the daily struggle against the spirits . . . and not a dance for taming nature as in Africa, for making the spirits feel at home, turning them into allies.

The men liquor up at every fiesta, the *borrachera* is an essential function here. Time is set apart for it as for eating, sleeping, working . . . and time is set apart for recovering from it. A little girl told me, "My papa is drunk," as if she were saying "My papa's away." In either case, he's gone. It's also the ultimate excuse—allowances are made because the *borracho* is not himself; he can kill with impunity, almost legitimately under the influence of alcohol. A number of villagers have started fights with me—and the next morning, they are very embarrassed and offer me a very simple, but effective, excuse: "I was *borracho*" (p. 88).

11 March

This morning, I got to understand how the pyramids were built. At dawn, the village is mobilized, a cohort of men and beasts, mules and donkeys, women and children, some balancing their buckets on shoulder poles, others holding a simple sack, they all head toward the river bank, looking for sand to cement the ground of the church. La Semana Santa, Holy Week, is around the corner, and thousands of pilgrims will be coming from the surrounding hamlets.

The rays of dawn are outlining this surefooted, hurrying throng of people carrying a heavy load. . . . A vision of the Aztecs who built the pyramids . . . A multitude of arms and legs, hands and feet, but the mind of a single head, a single soul directing, coordinating all these comings and goings.

I've organized my daily schedule now: rising with the sun, I walk through the village in the first rays, when the light is cold, moist, oblique, when people and animals emerge from the darkness and set out in quest of their first work, their first food. I often get my best shots during these earliest hours, as I do later on, in the afternoon, when the light is oblique again, but now dry and hot. . . .

Then again, on other days I go after the high, thick, ruthless light of noon, when the shadows are sharply etched, when everything is simply black and white, when the grays of dawn have blurred. Like my photo of the villager dragging the howling, recalcitrant piglet, shot during my first stay here (pp. 82–83).

I know that my photos of Mexico will be the most important work I've done since Iran: there, I was in a revolution—all I had to do was go outdoors at the right moment; here, nothing happens . . . I have to "see" everything. . . .

When people look at these photos later on, what will they see? Will they see nothing but Oapan? Will they glimpse me through these images? What will they know about the empty hours, the voids that sometimes? . . . The solitudes? Will they be aware only of fullnesses, which have left their frail, indelible traces on the silver film? What will they know about my turmoil, about the rage

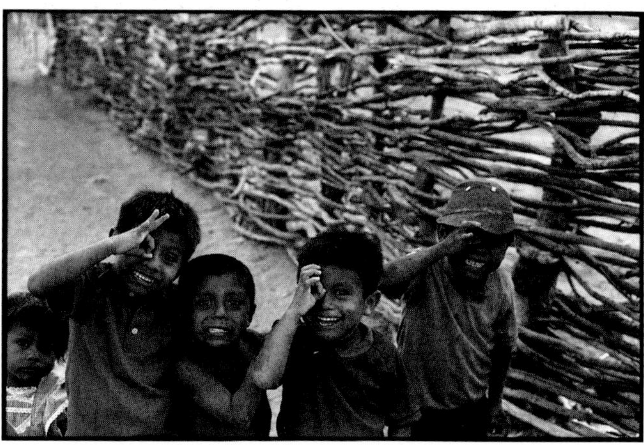

that sometimes grabs hold of me and that I cultivate? What will those future readers know about the thousand scenarios of revenge that I spool off in my mind? Is that the reason for this harmony between myself, my inner world, and this village, the outer world?

What am I doing in this miserable, uncomfortable village? . . . This dormant, dusty dump? . . . Do I feed my violence, my anger, my frustrations in order to create? . . .

I don't believe that my moods, my states of mind, my personality are of any interest to anyone else, apart from a close circle of friends. My forte as a photographer is my vision of the social and political—and sometimes psychological—instant, but not yet the spiritual.

Am I suffering from a huge ego now? Of course! Without this ego—the certainty that what I'm doing is important to the public—would I return so often to Mexico and to this godforsaken village? What else but this ego will enable me to endure the permanent financial precariousness of freelancing, the chronic emotional instability, the long and frequent absences from my near and dear?!

I see my solitude very clearly. I even nurture it, the way some people nurture friendships or their consciences. My solitude is the source of my creativity. Yet on certain evenings, my solitude is no longer a familiar companion—it becomes hateful, oppressive, final.

Without this ego, what photographer could endure the daily anguish of the defective film, the sneaky camera, the lost freight, the missed deadline, the lab technician who ruins everything while developing the film? . . . No creative person is prey to so many uncontrollable hazards. . . . We photographers are not free of this anguish until we hold the contact sheet in our hands.

Oh, well, that's enough! The sun has already vanished behind its hill. This is the frail and precious hour when the light is suspended, hesitant, between day and night. This is the hour when I take a dip in the Rio Balsas. I'm a photographer, I take photos . . . beyond that . . .

16 April

It's become a habit: each of my returns to Mexico begins and ends with a visit to Oapan. My arrival is a true rite: at Iguala's bus station, in the plain that anticipates the heat of the hills of Guerrero, I change into my Oapan outfit. This ceremony mobilizes my flesh and prepares my spirit for the rigors of the village, for the thousand adventures that lie in wait for me here. This earth is powerful, magical, sometimes cunning. You have to go forth as a warrior.

The Nahua Indians, who are waiting for this same bus, have placid bodies, tense eyes, transparent gazes. . . . Are they present? I can see their bodies, but what about their souls? What secret rite are they performing in order to prepare themselves for their return? Two hours from now, the bus will leave the tarred road and head into the sierra, and only then will the minds of these children of the Aztecs return to their bodies . . . an astonishing transformation. Their gazes will lose that wild emptiness, their eyes will no longer be watchful and uneasy whenever a mestizo approaches . . . They'll start talking and joking, their kids will start playing. . . . This arrival in Oapan is a true rite.

22 April

La Semana Santa is over. My hand isn't very steady as I write; for I've just run into Señor Six-Pack—my nickname for him, because every encounter costs me a case of beer. And since I had to carouse with him and his friends . . . I'm tempted to get roaring drunk for an entire week, so I can fall in with the mood of the villagers and "see" like them. But is it necessary? Am I not always intoxicated whenever I come to Oapan?

I've been walking its streets for several mornings now, my brain teeming with comparisons. I've already seen lots of reportages on rural communities, lots of beatific visions of villagers perceived as living in paradise by urbanites lacking a rustic nirvana, lots of photos that pretend to depict the dignity of the farmer but actually exalt and glorify country life, even though it's harsh and miserable. Here, I don't want my pictures to put minds at ease. I want them to unsettle people, to make them ask questions.

My vision of Oapan is total; the people are merely one of the components of this village. The trees are very present; they give birth to the people and feed on them. The animals—pigs, donkeys, hens and roosters, dogs—each have their own life; they cohabit with human beings. The stones are alive, like the soil, which is stricken, parched by this rainless season. The elements are also alive—the light, the wind, the water of the *rio*, the furnace of the noonday sun.

Yesterday, one of Abraham's nieces died—a baby girl, five months old. She still had no first name, because no birth certificate had been issued as yet. More of *Pedro Paramo?* I offered to photograph the tiny body lying in the coffin, surrounded by flowers, so that the family would at least have a memento. But the father refused. Grief is still private here, it's off limits to me.

I could have forced their hand, imposed myself. But was it necessary? Do I need pictures of corpses or funerals to convey the violent fragility of Oapan? Do I have to photograph the secret rituals of sorcery—as I originally attempted—in order to convey the magic of this village? Don't all my photos quiver with violence and magic? . . . Little girls running, vivacious shadows that will quickly vanish (p. 21).

I am working toward a book in which each image is not only important in itself but also contributes to the overall project, like every stone in a mosaic. That's what makes the layout so crucial: a linear book—whereas in Oapan everything is the opposite of linear? Time is chopped up, actions are suspended . . . Nothing has stirred in this village, nothing stirs during any of my visits, and yet everything has changed.

By now, I must know every square inch of this village, every household, every tree, every alley. And yet each stroll is an adventure, for I can see only things that are first perceived within me. I must have passed those two intertwined crosses dozens of times—why do they suddenly turn into a photo? Because of the light, the angle, or else the mood of the day, the scenario that dominates my mind at that instant? (p. 90).

Sometimes I don't shoot; I linger: I choose the frame in my viewfinder, including all the elements—walls, trees, pylons, spaces—that will provide the desired mood or character, and I wait patiently for the theater of life to surprise me with people, animals, shadows (pp. 24–25).

Yesterday a black dog bit me in the back, a little girl offered me a white dove, I gave it to Abraham's family. I left . . .

24 July
Paris airport. In a few hours, I'll be back in Mexico, but this time without exuberance. Doubt has infiltrated my mind, haunting me about the goal of this project. Are the eighty pictures I've promised myself worth all this grief? I'm fed up with crisscrossing Mexico unhampered. At times, freedom can be sterile. I'm fed up with shooting street corners, cast shadows, passersby. I'd love to cover an event in which I could show my true grit as a photojournalist.

6 August
At a ceramic workshop in Tonala, I notice some huge terra-cotta ears. And the potter tells me, "Well, you see, our town is going to be hosting a congress of deaf-mutes, so the authorities have ordered about a hundred ear-shaped ashtrays as gifts for the participants." And the two of us burst out laughing. Ay, México! Innocent surrealism or refined sadism?

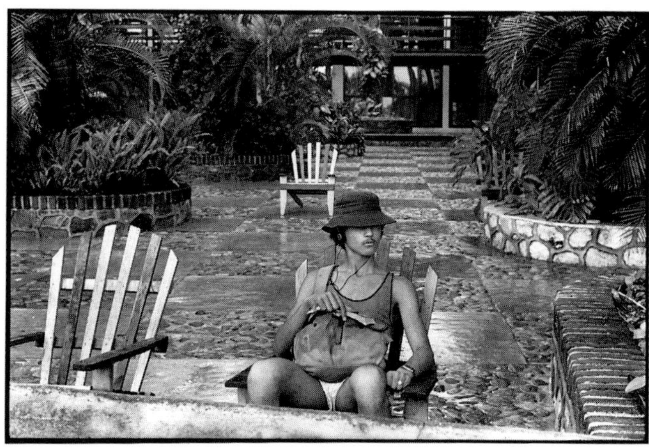

The qualms I felt in Paris have quickly dissipated, like a mist at dawn. I've worked on my first roll of film with my usual enthusiasm. And my Mexican friends react with the same enthusiasm when I show them my work prints: "You really understand us" is the best criticism they can offer me.

Sometimes I'm surprised by their élan and pleasure at the sight of certain photos that I myself find weak. I obviously lack their historical and cultural references. I wonder if a photographer who immerses himself in a country becomes a medium, instinctively and at times unwittingly capturing its strength.

When my Magnum colleagues criticize those same pictures, I learn more about their own personalities than about my photos. They see only with their own eyes, judge only by their own standards. None of them tries to see what I'm after.

10 August
My brother Bijane has just gone on his final journey, and we didn't say good-bye. I received the news here in San Cristobal. The last time I visited him, he was struggling courageously, talking about what he planned to do when he was cured. A friend of his had dreamed that Bijane was reciting these verses:

I cast my joy into the sky like a soaring bird.
The wing of misery flew away.
I can finally see the resplendent light.

Bijane said he took this as a sign of recovery. But the silence in his eyes told me that he knew. Were we too abashed to talk about this final voyage, lest we weaken his fighting spirit? You have to live your death. . . . Would he have liked to talk about it, let down the bold front he had to present to his children? It's hit me a lot harder than I would have thought—I, who have grazed death so often. But today, it's someone close to me who has died. Hamish, my son, was traveling with me. He is even more affected.

29 August
It's the Feast of Saint Augustine, the patron saint of Oapan, and it's not the *pachanga*, the joyous fiesta, that I've been looking forward to for a year now. These Indians will never stop surprising me: they seem to be making fun of everything. They scrupulously follow the routine of every ceremony—dances, prayers, processions, skits—but as if respecting the letter of tradition were more important than communing in the spirit of the tradition.

I've attended many festivities in Africa and Asia, times when the community was very different for a number of days, going inside itself in order to reach the sublime. Here the villagers seem to be striving for something ludicrous, the preposterous state of a permanent *borrachera*. Is this how the people of Oapan get beyond themselves, tearing down the walls of the internal solitude that imprisons them the rest of the time? Do they find the mystical and the sublime in drinking? *Quien sabe?*

They didn't give a damn about the photos of Oapan that I showed them for the first time. All they care about is recognizing themselves, seeing who does what. Of course, I suspected I wouldn't have any acerbic critiques—Oapan is not the site for the annual Magnum meeting. I knew that no village would go ape over my vision of their daily life. Still . . .

We have to assume that, in their eyes, it's enough for a photo mechanically to reflect reality. I offered an elderly lady a Polaroid of her proud face with its white mane. She puzzled over her portrait for a long time, then handed it back to me and asked me to do a full shot, head to toe. Does she feel that her body is mutilated in the flesh if it's cut off in the picture? Whenever I run into her, she'll be sure to remind me that I decapitated her.

The white dove I gave Abraham and his wife is still there, amorously cooing with its fellow doves. The family takes such good care of them that I thought they were mascots. But then all at once, my host asks me if I want to use them in a soup. . . . Three of the doves were eaten up by a nocturnal marauder—perhaps a cat. If it comes to that, we might as well eat them ourselves—these dear little *palomitas*.

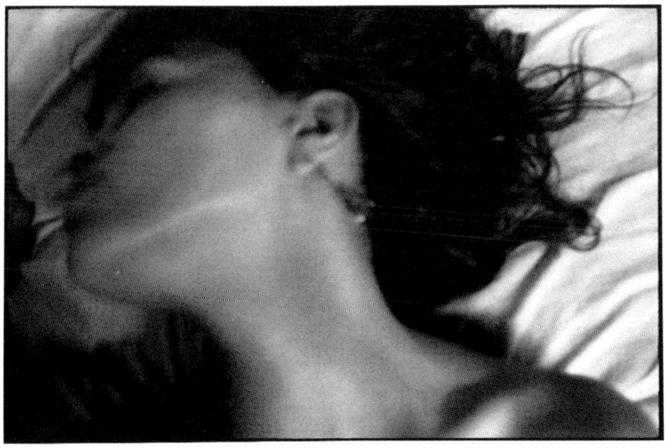

Sentence has been passed, and Petra, Abraham's wife, takes hold of each dove, one by one, fondles its body, caresses its throat, and then breaks its neck with a sharp twist! The feathers are then plucked, except from the heads. The doves lie there, comical and poignant with naked bodies and plumed heads. The soup will be good tonight (p. 89).

30 August

The fiesta is over. Three nights of being vehemently woken up by hyenalike shrieks from the crazy drunkards reeling through the village, dazed, disarticulate, spoiling for a fight, committing innocent violence. They give me the creeps—those howls that come from far away, from primordial barbarism. I feel so vulnerable in the night of Oapan. Before dropping off, I make sure that Abraham's machete isn't far away. . . . You never know. . . .

1 September

Don Alex's household is in the throes of a tragedy, and I walk in, I find little Lucia tearful and frightened, all alone in the big garden. I invite her to my room and, in order to put her mind at ease, I show her the photos of my twin boys who are the same age as Lucia. She peers hard and then asks: "Are they buried?" I realize that this little girl must have a bizarre background. She's an orphan who was taken in by her uncle, then sold—yes, sold. She starts browsing through the room, then plays with the two white *calaveras*, skulls, pushes them against her eyes. . . . *Carajo!* (pp. 86–87).

4 November

Today I learned to live with the dead, in great simplicity—a change from the obsessive worship of martyrs in Iranian Shiism. The sky is overcast, fortunately. How could I photograph the Day of the Dead under a desperately blue sky? In the morning, the municipal orchestra came and played some joyful ditties in this little graveyard of Chilico. In Mexico, everything is honored with music. Now, the people lapse into quiet meditation: the dead are here, and their families have come to spend the day with them, the way you visit friends. Food and *aguagardiente* (liquor), which the deceased liked, are offered to the guests. Bijane, my dead brother, is here, too (p. 31).

29 March

Flying to Mexico City. When I was first starting out fifteen years ago, I already saw that the Golden Age of photojournalism—with the great magazines of the nineteen fifties—was practically over. And yet, to cover any international event, all I had to do was hop a plane. The logistics of the Sipa or Gamma agencies came following after. What should I say now? More and more competent photographers and fewer and fewer interesting magazines mean that every departure has to be prepared down to the last iota. The economy has caught up with me, and I've got to have an assignment when I return to Mexico.

6 April

They're crazy—these Tarahumaras! It's midnight, and two men are locked in a bizarre duel on the church square. The Good Apostle is literally fighting with the wicked Pharisee. The whole mountain is humming with the dull, throbbing drum that the Tarahumaras play day and night. The Passion of Jesus of Palestine, transplanted here, will last for a week (pp. 28–29).

A group of five Mexican researchers is studying them with the jealous possessiveness that all anthropologists feel toward "their" Indians. I was warned that I had to photograph them respectfully. These Mexicans themselves photograph the Indians only from a distance, with long lenses. I do it with passion.

On Friday, the Pharisees—no doubt, in order to appear more evil—cover themselves with the white mud from the *rio*. When the mud dries, they look like zombies, the first inhabitants of the earth, suddenly emerging from its innards. I'm troubled by the magic of the spectacle and the oppressive mountain; I'm spellbound by the ceaseless drum. All at once, I'm possessed. Without my Leicas or the awareness that I have to take pictures, I'll strip to the waist, coat myself with mud, and be carried away by their frenetic dancing (pp. 16–17).

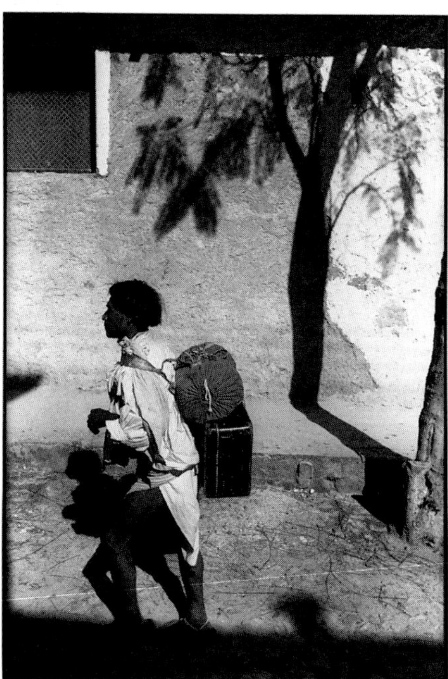

9 April

I thought I was playing the part of a Stanley, climbing on foot to see the Tarahumaras of Munerachi, with a guide carrying my satchel and my sleeping bag. What can you say about the Mexican TV crew rolling off to film another village, taking along tons of food donated by an American relief organization? Apparently this tribe is so disdainful of private property that they don't even see the necessity of working and accept charity without feeling humiliated. I leave disgusted.

The TV crew has presented them with two goats and a sheep; the people sacrifice the animals as if on a pagan altar and then stay up all night preparing them. In the morning, the men are still standing, waiting for alms. The meat banquet can't get started because the camera batteries are dead, and the van that went to recharge them in town hasn't come back as yet (pp. 18–19).

24 April

I photograph a rodeo, and if it weren't for the faces, you'd think you were in Texas. In their Gringo get-up, these Mexicans remind me of the Tarahumaras in their modern rags (pp. 66–67).

4 May

Oapan. The village is mad with heat. Men, beasts, trees, shacks, cacti—they're all motionless, suspended in a diaphanous haze. Everything seems to be floating, hallucinated. The dry season is ending, and every afternoon we are engulfed in a dust storm (pp. 14–15). I'll never be as hot as during this tenth return. . . . I know that this is the last time. You have to know when to stop a project, avoid staying past the moment when your presence becomes spiritless and your eye sterile.

When I arrived, I gave myself one week to obtain an image that's lacking from my fresco of Oapan: the intrusion of modernism into this primitive village. I've even drawn up a list: bus, TV, corn mills, electric calculators, and, of course, that wretched loudspeaker. I've often photographed them, but I have yet to produce their perfect and final image.

Why are my photos of modernity so anemic next to those of a tradition that is centuries old? Yet I've always believed that a factory can be as beautiful as a pyramid, the picture of a corn mill can be as powerful as that of a man dragging a piglet. During each visit, I've made a sustained and praiseworthy effort to photograph this twentieth century, which cohabits with the eighteenth. Am I influenced by the gazes of my friends, who always delight in the traditional and never in the modern because the latter is too familiar to them?

Since this is my final return, and I no longer have to treat the villagers with kid gloves, I've decided to brave the customary "*te voy a matar!*," "I'm-gonna-kill-you," and photograph a funeral. But no one's died this week.

I've learned that months ago, a malignant fever claimed a woman whose hands I had photographed—strong, supple hands kneading the tortilla dough on a stone slab which Indians have used for centuries. A premonition? She had asked me to do a portrait of her old mother. "This way, when she leaves, we'll have a memento." But the daughter left first. It depresses me to think that the only vestige of those hands is a photo made of silver salts (p. 23).

The power's been out for two days now—"*no hay luz*" (there's no light). The village is different at night. The moon adds an exalted dimension to people and things When I take a nocturnal stroll, I am awed by this life of which I had no inkling. The pigs, so independent in the daytime, are likewise creatures of the night. They wander alone through the dusty lanes—prehistoric silhouettes—to wallow in the river mud and seek some meager bit of food. The cacti, more somber and more ominous than during the day, stab the stars. All these fleeting shadows, these furtive and insidious blurs of the night in Oapan. Why have I never shot at night?

For two days now, there's been no bus service either. The bus probably broke down on the road. How fragile the modern world is here. So I have to try to hitch a ride on some passing truck—I have to get to Xalitla along this tarred road, where modernity is now a permanent fixture.

As I came here in the back of a dust-choked van, I suddenly thought of my father, who traveled the paths of a fierce Baluchistan some forty years ago. Was he innocent with his Faith? Did he suffer from the vanity of those who, armed with that Faith, want to change the world and humankind? He must have experienced the same emotions, fed on the same solitudes, found comfort in the same passionate desire to make his mark—a trace that was futile and ephemeral, but still and all *his* trace.

And what vanity do I suffer from? I have faith in people, not in the Supreme Being. All I've done is suspend the life of this village. But don't I secretly believe that my photos can change people and the world?

My last trip to Oapan? Strange how this place "grabbed" me when I first saw it that torrid afternoon almost three years ago. And when I left, I told myself that I had forgotten to snap some very simple photos: Abraham's patio and its empty spaces—spaces that, in several years . . . The small tree planted by the shopkeeper that would someday provide as much shade as the church tree . . . Overall views of the village . . . Very simple images . . . And in several years . . . Come back in twenty years? When Oapan will have changed . . . When I'll have changed . . . Until then . . .

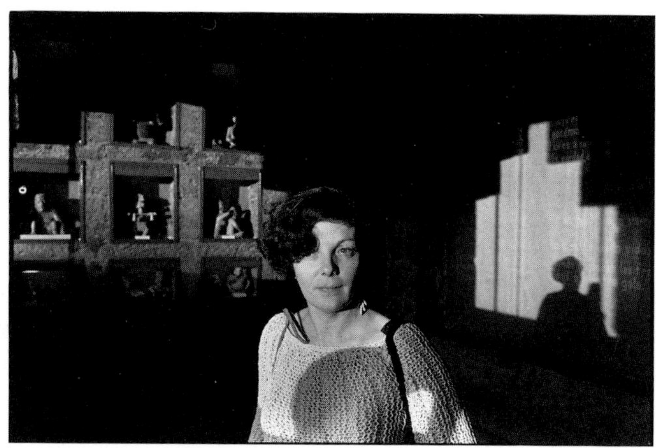

25 August

Casseneuil, France . . . I've seen my Oapan adventure three times: the first time by taking photos on location; then when reviewing the contact sheets and the work prints; and today by tapping my faithful journal in order to write a text for the book that's being published in Mexico. The Lot River, rich and peaceful, flows by in front of me. Everything is green here. . . . How far away Oapan is!

11 October

In color, Mexico City is a visual catastrophe! I never noticed the anarchy of all those primary hues clashing together, bouncing off one another. It took me two days to "see" in color, filter my gaze, because its natural tendency is to see in black and white.

31 October

This year, I've done reportages in Japan, Tunisia, the Bahamas, Miami, and Guyana, but it is only here, in Mexico, that I feel I'm fully living my photography.

My friend Graciela is astonished at my qualms about the word *artist*, for she glimpses lots of poetry in the violence of my images and, knowing me as she does, she thinks these photos describe me as well as the village.

Too many photographers hide behind that label of "artist," they are so fascinated with themselves, preoccupied solely with their own egos. A photojournalist's eyes have to look outside. His gaze is personal to him, of course, but he sees beyond himself, not inside himself, and in so doing, he is not a prisoner of reality—he transcends it. His feelings pass through form, and not vice versa.

The photographer suspends matter, time, movement. Why deprive him of the very dimension that makes him original: reality, and the limits it imposes.

Does Graciela realize it isn't humility that makes me think of myself as a photojournalist rather than an artist? It's arrogance.

3 November

This year, the Day of the Dead will not have the spirituality it had last year. As soon as I return to Paris I'll offer the magazines my color reportage, and they'll buy it, I have no doubts. I felt no passion, just my eagerness as a professional. Only the wind that day, on the road to Chalco, spoke to me about Persian genies.

28 March

This Passion in Ixtapalapa couldn't have sprouted in the crazy mind of the craziest movie director. At the crack of dawn, thousands of extras—Christs lugging heavy wooden crosses and wearing real crowns of thorns—take over the streets of this district in Mexico City. They form two lines flanking the long Calvary of Christ. The belly laughs of the wicked Romans, some of whose swords are machetes, the sincere weeping of the Virgin and Mary Magdalene. The actors, made up à la Hollywood, don't act. They live the Passion—a pagan festival condemned by the Church.

How recent Christianity must seem in the collective memory of these descendants of the Aztecs! I'll never forget that white-haired priest, a very straight, very tall, very worthy Hidalgo, whom the Chamulas had relegated to a corner of their vast church. The new faith could claim only a very tiny platform; the huge nave of the temple was reserved for practices that had nothing Catholic about them—sacrifices of chickens and offerings of Pepsi. Is history a perpetual renewal? Seventeen years ago, my first reportage for the international press was this very Passion of Ixtapalapa.

11 April

This must be the end of Mexico for me. Today, in Guadalajara, I caught myself looking for the photos I had shot three years ago: the two communions, the drunkard sleeping under the statue, the governor's luncheon. Finding nothing more to shoot, I preferred heading home rather than hunting for an image. . . . It's just dawned on me that this is the first time I've gone out to dinner without my cameras.

These returns to Mexico have been returns within myself. I now know that the journalist doesn't restrain the creator—he reveals him. Back in July, when I was co-opted as a member of Magnum (I became Ayatollah that day), my colleagues were worried that my Mexico was luring me away from photojournalism. Couldn't they see that I was actually getting closer, that I was seeking a new language? I still had to experience this adventure.

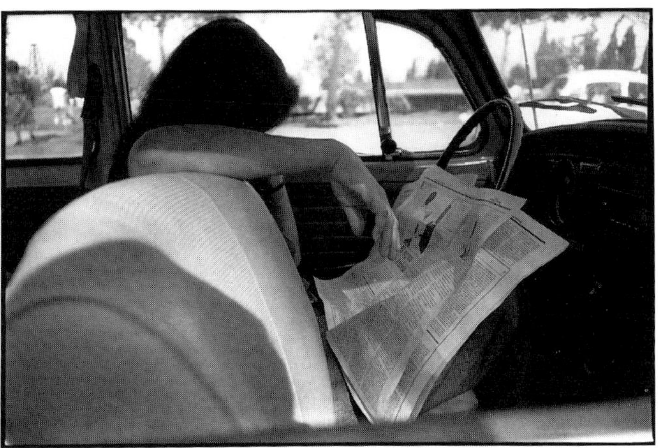

On the first day of my last return, I lost my bronze bracelet: I had received it in 1972 from the Meos of Vietnam, and I had been wearing it ever since. A mere coincidence, of course . . .

6 November

Paris. Graciela has sent me a notebook of amate-bark paper: on its pages she had meticulously copied the tale of Farid-al-Din Attar in black ink:

> *Simurgh, the King of the Birds, dropped a splendid feather at the center of China. The birds who decided to go in search of it experienced marvelous adventures, crossed seven valleys and seven seas, confronted a thousand dangers. Many perished, some deserted. Only thirty birds returned to the King's mountain. They gazed at it for a long time and then realized that they themselves were Simurgh, that Simurgh was in each of them and all of them.*

For several months now, I have been thinking about my next project: the resurgence of Islam in the world. Today . . .

Thank you:
To Dennis Stock for the kick,
To Martine Voyeux for the continuity,
To Fred Ritchin for the perspective,
To Isabel for certain rhythms,
To Agnès Sire for the words,
To Jim Mairs and Eve Picower for the book.